BACH
Through the Year

*The Church Music of Johann Sebastian Bach
and the Revised Common Lectionary*

John S. Setterlund

Lutheran University Press
Minneapolis, Minnesota

Bach Through the Year
The Church Music of Johann Sebastian Bach and the Revised Common Lectionary

By John S. Setterlund

ISBN: 978-1-932688-87-0

LCCN: 2013942916

Lutheran University Press, PO Box 390759, Minneapolis, MN 55439
www.lutheranupress.org
Manufactured in the United States of America

Preface

The church cantatas of J. S. Bach were designed, composed, and performed to enhance and interpret the message of the Bible to worshippers in the congregations which Bach served. The Lutheran church of 18th-century Germany appointed specific biblical texts to be read each Sunday and festival day of the year. This series of appointed readings, one from the New Testament letters and the other from one of the four gospels, was the lectionary. The lectionary readings determined the day's theme for the sermon, hymns, organ music, and the cantata.

The lectionary of Bach's day was an annual cycle, returning to the same readings for a given Sunday or festival each year. The one-year lectionary was retained by Lutherans in America and remained in use until the early 1970's, when, under the influence of the Second Vatican Council's *Ordo Lectionum Missae* (1969), a three-year system was adopted. This system, eventually emerging as the *Revised Common Lectionary* (1992), appoints two readings from the New Testament and one from the Hebrew Scriptures, to be read on each Sunday in a three-year cycle. The *Revised Common Lectionary* also reflects several minor changes in the liturgical year itself that have been made since the time of Bach.

Although Bach clearly indicated the occasion on which most of his cantatas were performed, the readings, and therefore the theme of the day do not necessarily coincide with the readings and themes of the modern church. For that reason *Bach through the Year* has reassigned the cantatas to the Sundays and festivals with whose current readings and themes they most closely correspond. In each commentary the relationship between a lectionary reading, usually the gospel, and the designated cantata is highlighted. Sometimes these relationships are explicit; other times they are more general. Since Bach composed several cantatas for most occasions, there are approximately as many to be distributed as there are Sundays in the modern three-year lectionary. The three years of the lectionary are designated by A, B, and C. Where no year-designation is given, the day or occasion is intended for annual observance.

In addition to the church cantatas themselves, Bach's motets, passions, and oratorios are included in this work. Each composition is identified by its *BWV* number: *Bach Werke Verzeichnis* is a thematic, systematic index of the musical compositions of Johann Sebastian Bach, compiled by Wolfgang Schmieder (Breitkopf & Härtel, Leipzig, 1950, 1961, 1998). Following the numbers of the 1850 Bach Gesellschaft edition of the cantatas, Schmieder's catalogue remains the standard enumeration of Bach's works, although no systematic rationale for the *BWV* numbers themselves has yet been discovered.

This book is an expansion and revision of my *A Bach Lectionary* (2005), supplying commentaries for all the alternates, and presenting them in the chronological order of the church's liturgical year. Cantatas are provided for numerous minor festivals and occasions, reflecting the calendar of *Evangelical Lutheran Worship* (Augsburg Fortress, 2006). Indices and two appendices are also included.

Libretto texts have been incorporated into the commentaries and are indicated by double-quotation marks. English translations of the libretti are often awkward, as the available collections—by Z. Philip Ambrose, W. Murray Young, Richard D. P. Jones, Alison Dobson-Ottmes et al., Stewart Spencer et al., and Richard Stokes—are less than ideal for use in the church. Translations of scripture passages are borrowed from the New Revised Standard Version of the Bible (1989); hymn titles, from *Evangelical Lutheran Worship* and *Lutheran Service Book* (Concordia, 2006).

J.S.S.

Urbana, Illinois

June 2010

Contents

BACH
Through the Year

*The Church Music of Johann Sebastian Bach
and the Revised Common Lectionary*

First Sunday of Advent
November 27 – December 3

Year A   Matthew 24:36-44

BWV 62   *Nun komm, der Heiden Heiland*

"Come now, Savior of the Gentiles, known as the virgin's child. … The highest ruler appears to the world; here the treasures of heaven are disclosed." In their concern about the end of the world and return of Christ, the disciples ought to remember the great flood, which both doomed the world and also preserved Noah, his family, and an arkful of creatures. Whatever surprises lie ahead, Christians should be eager and ready for God's next act of salvation in Christ: "Fight, conquer, strong hero! Be mighty for us in the flesh. Be active in making strong the capability of us weaklings." The cantata, one of two with this opening line (see *BWV* 61), presents the hymn *Savior of the Nations, Come* in the first and last movements.

> *Alternate: BWV* 127   *Herr Jesu Christ, wahr' Mensch und Gott*
> "Lord Jesus Christ, true man and God … be gracious to me a sinner." Amid the uncertainties and fear about the last days, people should be prepared and alert: "When in the last days everything takes fright … enough that faith then knows that Jesus stands by me." Jesus will appear as the Son of Man, coming to redeem his people: "When one day the trumpets sound and when the structure of the world, alongside that of the firmament, collapses, dashed to pieces, then remember me, my God, for good."

Year B   Mark 13:24-37

BWV 61   *Nun komm, der Heiden Heiland*

"Come now, Savior of the Gentiles, recognized as the virgin's child." Amid the apocalyptic signs accompanying the end of the world, Christians should be neither surprised nor dismayed, but awake and alert to what God is doing. The Savior will return, the same Jesus born to Mary, and will accomplish the work of salvation already begun: "You come and bring your light to shine with full blessing." The cantata, one of two with this first line (see *BWV* 62), sings the hymn of welcome, *Savior of the Nations, Come*: "Open up, my whole heart, Jesus comes and enters in. … I await you with great longing."

> *Alternate: BWV* 70   *Wachet! betet! betet! wachet!*
> "Watch and pray." Amid apocalyptic signs which will mark the return of the Son of Man, Jesus points his followers to the fig tree. Its growth is certain, although no one knows the exact day of fruition. Therefore constant vigilance

3

[70] is summoned: "Be prepared at all times, till the Lord of glory brings this world to an end. ... The Savior summons you, when all else crumbles, before his exalted presence; therefore be not afraid. ... Awaken, souls, from your complacency. ... The spirit is willing, but the flesh is weak. ... Christ's word must remain unshaken."

Year C   Luke 21:25-36

BWV 70   *Wachet! betet! betet! wachet!*

"Watch, pray, pray, watch. Be prepared at all times till the Lord of glory brings this world to an end." Before the end of the world there will be great and terrible signs, but Christians should see them as signs of redemption: "Awaken, souls, from your complacency, and believe: This is the final hour. ... Heaven and earth may perish, but Christ's word must remain unshaken." Nevertheless, they should watch and pray, so that they might be prepared for that day. The cantata vividly points out the ridicule that the faithful may receive from their neighbors, as well as the apocalyptic terrors that might arise. Jesus, the risen Christ and the coming judge, will, however, bring them safely to heaven: "Lift up your heads and be comforted ... and serve God eternally."

Alternate: BWV 61   *Nun komm, der Heiden Heiland*

Astrological signs, floods, and wars will precede the final reign of God on the earth. Believers are to remain alert and strong, to receive the Son of Man: "Come now, Savior of the Gentiles. ... Come to your church, and grant a blessed new year." The Savior's promises remain, to bring blessings and salvation to the entire world: "Behold, I stand at the door and knock. If anyone hears my voice and opens the door, I will come in. ... I become his dwelling. Oh, how blessed shall I be!"

ANDREW, APOSTLE
November 30

John 1:35-42

BWV 9   *Es ist das Heil uns kommen her*

"Salvation has come to us." At the direction of John the Baptist, the disciples turn their attention to Jesus, "the Son of the Highest." Through the miracle of faith, Andrew announces to Peter, 'We have found the Messiah': "Whoever now trusts him, whoever builds on his passion shall not be lost. ... Lord, rather than at good deeds, you look at the heart's strength of faith: only faith is acceptable to you. ... We look forward with hope to the time that God's goodness has promised us, but of which out of wise counsel he has concealed the hour from us."

Year A   Matthew 3:1-12

BWV 90   Es reißet euch ein schrecklich Ende

"A terrifying end sweeps you away, you sinful despisers!" The baptism of John the Baptist in preparation for the coming of Christ is accompanied by stern words of repentance and judgment: "The Highest's goodness is new from day to day. ... Is your heart not moved, so that God's goodness leads you to true repentance?" Similar words of apocalyptic warnings are heard in this cantata and throughout the New Testament, disclosing the rift between God's kindness and goodness and the blasphemy and mischief of too many people. It is the hope of Christians that they and others will never stray: "Yet God's eye looks upon us as the elect. ... Lead us with your right hand ... so that we are with you forever."

Alternate: BWV 30   Freue dich, erlöste Schar

"Rejoice, O redeemed host!" Both parts of the cantata support John's proclamation of the reign of God: "Your prosperity now has a truly sure foundation on which to shower you with blessing. ... The herald comes and announces the king. ... Prepare the way of the Lord." Matthew underscores the urgent call to repentance and reform: "I will now hate and abandon all that is offensive to you, my God." That acceptable day can no longer be far off or delayed.

Year B   Mark 1:1-8

BWV 30, part 1   Freue dich, erlöste Schar

"Rejoice, O ransomed throng!" Mark, along with all the gospels, places the appearances of John the Baptist at the beginning of Jesus' public ministry. In contrast to the ominous challenge of John, the cantata emphasizes the joys unleashed on earth with the coming of the heavenly kingdom, a release from burdens of the law and oppression: "Your prosperity has found a sure and solid means of showering you with well-being." The bass aria's "faithful servant" is John, as are the alto recitative's "herald" and the chorale's "voice": "His faithful servant has been born ... to prepare the way of the Lord. The herald comes and announces the king." A stanza of the hymn *Comfort, Comfort Now My People* concludes the section: "A voice makes itself heard far and wide in the wilderness. ... Make for God a smooth path."

Alternate: BWV 132   Bereitet die Wege, bereitet die Bahn

As the final prophetic herald, John announces the good news of the coming of God's Messiah: "Prepare the ways, prepare the path. ... The Messiah draws nigh." In fulfillment of ancient promises, John calls the people to prepare themselves to receive him: "My heart, prepare even today the way of faith to the Lord. ... Although my mouth and lips have called you Lord and Father, my heart has turned away from you. ... Awaken us through your grace."

Year C   Luke 3:1-6

BWV 132   *Bereitet die Wege, bereitet die Bahn*
"Prepare the ways, prepare the path. ... The Messiah draws near." The coming of John the Baptist reminds all Israel of the prophecies of Isaiah 40: "Remove the hills and the mountains that stand in the way." The cantata picks up that powerful message, to summon the people to repentance and preparation for the coming Messiah: "Consult the commandments. They will tell you who you are." Those baptized into Christ are made clean by his continuing grace: "Help me, that with steadfast fidelity I may ever renew through faith the covenant of grace."

> *Alternate: BWV* 62   *Nun komm, der Heiden Heiland*
> John the Baptist appears as a prophetic voice in the desert, calling people to prepare the Lord's way: "Come now, Savior of the Gentiles. ... Marvel, O people, at this great mystery: the great Ruler appears in the world. ... The hero of Judah appears, to run his course with gladness and to redeem us fallen ones."

THIRD SUNDAY OF ADVENT
December 11-17

Year A   Matthew 11:2-11

BWV 186   *Ärgre dich, o Seele, nicht*
"Do not be offended, O soul, that the Most High Light, God's brightness and image, disguises himself in a servant's form." The arrest of John the Baptist presents a crisis for his disciples and for the followers of Jesus. The time seems urgent, and they seek assurance. As Jesus points his followers to the events of healing and hope, so the cantata turns its attention to Jesus himself as God's real presence: "My Savior lets himself be known in his deeds of grace. ... The Lord will embrace the poor with grace both here and there." Christians should not worry about grandiose miracles, as Christ acts in the commonplace and among the humble, in the best way at the best time: "He gives them of his highest mercy the highest treasure, the word of life."

> *Alternate: BWV* 152 *Tritt auf die Glaubensbahn*
> In answer to the questions of John the Baptist, Jesus points to his own works of healing and teaching. John's faith and that of all disciples are what grant true greatness in the kingdom of heaven: "Walk on the path of faith. ... Blessed is a chosen Christian who lays the foundation of his faith on this cornerstone, for thereby he finds salvation and redemption."

Year B   John 1:6-8, 19-28

BWV 30, part 2   *Freue dich, erlöste Schar. … So bist du denn, mein Heil*
"Rejoice, O ransomed throng. … And so, my Savior, you intend faithfully to uphold the covenant you made with our ancestors, and to rule over us with grace." The prologue to the fourth gospel ties the ministry of John the Baptist intimately to the incarnation of the divine Word: "As often as day dawns … so long shall I live … for your glory alone." The cantata rejoices in the new-found freedom, light, and hope which have arrived through the witness of John and the birth of the Savior: "The splendor of your joy, of your contentment shall endure for evermore."

> *Alternate: BWV 167   Ihr Menschen, rühmet Gottes Liebe*
> Though a secondary witness to the Messiah, John is a powerful forerunner, preparing people to receive one even greater: "O mortals, extol God's love … that he, at the appointed hour, has given us the horn of salvation, the path to life in Jesus, his Son." From his conception, John was a miracle of God: "At first it was John who came, who had to prepare the path and the way for the Savior. … Zechariah, struck dumb, with pure voice praises God for his wondrous deed."

Year C   Luke 3:7-18

BWV 136   *Erforsche mich, Gott, und erfahre mein Herz*
"Search me, O God, and know my heart." Despite his flaming rhetoric, John the Baptist makes no grandiose claims for himself. Rather he defers to the coming Messiah, whose rule will be far greater. The cantata recognizes the sinful human condition to which John speaks, calling on God in words from Psalm 139: "Test me and know my thoughts." The convicted sinner can only turn to the coming Christ for redemption: "Who can hope for good fruit, while this curse pierces the soul, which now brings forth thorns of sin? … The day will dawn which will terrify you, O hypocrites, and be unendurable. … For the fury of its zeal will destroy what hypocrisy and cunning have invented."

> *Alternate: BWV 168   Tue Rechnung! Donnerwort*
> John, speaking in the strongest terms, calls the people to repent and reform their lives before the coming of the Messiah: "Give an account of yourself, thunderous words. … Soul, go forth. Ah, you must return to God his possessions, body and life. … Exalted hands have entrusted them to me, that I might manage and administer faithfully. … Because you know that you are a steward, be concerned and ever mindful. … Burst the bonds of mammon, O heart. Hands, scatter good abroad. … Strengthen me with your Spirit's joy."

FOURTH SUNDAY OF ADVENT
December 18-24

Year A   Matthew 1:18-25

BWV 36   *Schwingt freudig euch empor*

The first account of Jesus' birth is seen as a joyful fulfillment of ancient hopes for a savior. Songs of praise soar to God, who not only lives in highest heaven but now has come near: "Soar joyfully up to the lofty stars, you tongues which are now cheerful in Zion." Familiar hymns, *Savior of the Nations, Come* and *O Morning Star, How Fair and Bright*, appear in the cantata: "Come, Savior of the Gentiles, known as the virgin's child. ... Welcome, dear treasure! Love and faith make room for you in my pure heart."

> *Alternate: BWV 40   Dazu ist erschienen der Sohn Gottes*
> Joseph receives divine instruction on accepting Mary and her child, with focus on his name, 'Jesus, for he will save his people from their sins': "For this the Son of God has appeared: that he may destroy the work of the devil." This fulfills the prophecy of 'Emmanuel': "The Word became flesh and dwells in the world. ... It pleased his majesty to become a little human child."

Year B   Luke 1:26-38

BWV 1   *Wie schön leuchtet der Morgenstern*

"How beautifully gleams the morning star, full of the Lord's mercy and truth!" The angel Gabriel appears to the Virgin Mary and announces that she will become the mother of the long-awaited Savior. That message is summarized in the first recitative, with an emphasis on the general happiness that this promise brings to humanity: "True Son of God and Mary, King of the elect, how sweet to us is this Word of life ... which Gabriel there in Bethlehem [*sic*] had promised." In the movements that follow are signs of the specific rapture that accompanies conception: "A joyous ray has come to me from God; a perfect treasure, the Savior's body and blood, is there for our delight." The first and last stanzas of title hymn *O Morning Star, How Fair and Bright!* open and close the cantata, and the other stanzas are paraphrased, all expressing the excitement and delight in the incarnate nearness of Mary's divine son. References to the expected Jesus as the bread of heaven and to the Savior's body and blood focus the church's vision on the eucharist as a foretaste of the great banquet in heaven.

> *Alternate: BWV 147 Herz und Mund und Tat und Leben*
> "Heart and mouth and deed and life must give witness to Christ ... that he is both God and Savior." Mary's humble acceptance of Gabriel's announcement, that she will bear the Son of God, is a model of faithfulness that creates both courage and joy: "Mary makes known her innermost feelings through thanks and praise. ... Stubbornness can blind the mighty, till God's arm hurls them from their seat; but this arm exalts ... the suffering people whom he shall save. ... Prepare now, O Jesus, the way."

Year C   Luke 1:39-55

BWV 243   *Magnificat anima mea*
When the pregnant Virgin Mary is congratulated by her relative Elizabeth, she responds with a great song of praise: "My soul proclaims your greatness, O God. ... You have done great things for me, and holy is your name. ... You have come to the aid of your servant Israel, to remember the promise of mercy ... to Abraham and his children forever." This setting of the Latin *Magnificat* incorporates four additional movements, especially appropriate for Christmas.

> *Alternate: BWV* 10   *Meine Seele erhebt den Herren*
> "My soul magnifies the Lord." The cantata, composed for the Visitation (May 31), may be sung in Advent, when the same gospel is read. In this season, ancient promises are recalled with eager anticipation: "The Almighty's goodness and faithfulness are new every morning. ... That which God has spoken and promised to the ancients, is fulfilled in his words and deeds."

NATIVITY OF OUR LORD
Proper *i* – CHRISTMAS EVE
December 24

Year A   Luke 2:1-14

BWV 110   *Unser Mund sei voll Lachens*
"May our mouths be full of laughter ... for the Lord has done great things for us." At the appointed time Mary and Joseph travel to Bethlehem and there give birth to Jesus. Angels announce the event to nearby shepherds: "He becomes man, and just for this: that we may be heaven's children." The cantata does not narrate the story, although it quotes the angels' song of praise: "Glory be to God on high and peace on earth and good will towards mankind!" Rather, the believer is called to turn from sin and all evil and be filled with joyous praise of God.

> *Alternate: BWV* 248, part 1   *Jauchzet, frohlocket, auf, preiset die Tage*
> "Shout for joy, exult, rise up, praise the day, extol what the Highest has done today!" In fulfillment of ancient prophecies and in compliance with the imperial edict, Mary and Joseph travel to Bethlehem, where the Christ Child is born: "The comfort and salvation of the earth shall at last be born." The cantata rejoices over this wondrous event, emphasizing the miracle of the heavenly Son coming to earth and entering the lives of believers: "How should I receive you? ... Jesus, place your lamp by me. ... He who preserves the whole world and created its splendor and adornment must sleep in a hard crib."

Year B   Luke 2:1-14

BWV 121   *Christum wir sollen loben schon*

"To Christ we should sing praises, the Son of Mary." Joseph and Mary, obeying the emperor's decree, arrive in Bethlehem just in time for Mary to give birth to Jesus: "God would through flesh achieve salvation of the flesh. ... God chooses a pure body as temple of his honor, to turn his wondrous form to humankind." Nearby shepherds see a vision of angels and hear the news of the birth of one called Messiah and Savior: "My heart would leave this world to hasten with fervor to your crib." This cantata praises the newborn Christ and God in heaven for granting such a gift to humankind: "God, who was so boundless, took on servile form and poverty."

Alternate: BWV 91   *Gelobet seist du, Jesu Christ*

Mary and Joseph travel to Bethlehem and there give birth to Jesus, and heavenly angels announce the event. Christians join the angels in rejoicing for the birth of the Messiah: "May you be praised, O Jesus Christ, since you were born a man. ... Make yourself ready to receive the Creator. The great Son of God comes to you as a guest ... to show his great love."

Year C   Luke 2:1-14

BWV 248   Christmas Oratorio, part 1:
               Jauchzet, frohlocket, auf, preiset die Tage

"Shout for joy, exult, rise up, praise the day, extol what the Highest has done today!" In fulfillment of ancient prophecies and in compliance with the imperial edict, Mary and Joseph travel to Bethlehem, where the Christ Child is born: "The comfort and salvation of the earth shall at last be born." The cantata rejoices over this wondrous event, emphasizing the miracle of the heavenly Son coming to earth and entering the lives of believers: "How should I receive you? ... Jesus, place your lamp by me. ... He who preserves the whole world and created its splendor and adornment must sleep in a hard crib."

Alternate: BWV 151   *Süßer Trost, mein Jesus kommt*

The birth of Jesus promises salvation to faithful parents, wondering shepherds, and all who wait upon the Lord's promises: "Sweet comfort, my Jesus comes, Jesus now is born." In this humble event, God's greatest gift is given to the world: "God has sent his dearest Son. ... In Jesus' meekness I can find comfort, in his poverty riches. ... Today he opens wide again the door to beautiful paradise."

NATIVITY OF OUR LORD
Proper *ii* – CHRISTMAS DAWN
December 25

Year A   Luke 2:8-20

BWV 91   *Gelobet seist du, Jesu Christ*

"May you be praised, O Jesus Christ, since you were born a man." Angels bring to Bethlehem shepherds the glad tidings of the savior's birth, and they go to worship him. The cantata invites its hearers to share the mystery and excitement felt by those shepherds that first Christmas, marveling that the eternal, infinite God would become a mortal: "Make yourselves ready to receive the Creator. The great Son of God comes to you as a guest … to show his great love." This can only be explained by the greatness of God's love for the human race.

> *Alternate:* BWV 248, part 2 *Und es waren Hirten*
> "And there were shepherds in the same region … and the angel said to them … today the Savior is born to you … Christ the Lord." When the shepherds hear the angels' message, they hurry to Bethlehem to see the newborn child, and they worship him. The cantata begins with a sinfonia, evoking a pastoral setting and recalling God's pastoral image. The ultimate praise is sung by the angels: "Glory to God on high and peace on earth."

Year B   Luke 2:8-20

BWV 151   *Süßer Trost, mein Jesus kommt*

"Sweet comfort, my Jesus comes, Jesus now is born." When the shepherds of Bethlehem hear the news of the Savior's birth, they hurry to see him. Their great joy and excitement are reflected in the cantata, especially the knowledge that God has descended to earth in Christ. His meekness has won blessings for the people in this life and for eternity: "The pain shall now cease, which for so long has oppressed you. God has sent his dearest Son. … He leaves the throne of heaven and would deliver all the world from its chains of poverty and servitude. … O precious Son of God, you have opened heaven wide for me."

> *Alternate:* BWV 133 *Ich freue mich in dir*
> Hearing the chorus of heavenly angels, the shepherds go to Bethlehem and find the Christ child in a lowly manger. They are amazed and tell others the great things they have seen and heard: "I rejoice in you and bid you welcome, my dear little Jesus. … He has become a little child, and my sweet Jesus is his name."

Year C   Luke 2:8-20

BWV 248   Christmas Oratorio, part 2: *Und es waren Hirten*
"And there were shepherds in the same region…and the angel said to them … today the Savior is born … Christ the Lord." When the shepherds hear the angels' message, they hurry to Bethlehem to see the newborn child, and they worship him. The cantata begins with a sinfonia, evoking a pastoral setting and recalling God's pastoral image. The ultimate praise is sung by the angels: "Glory to God on high and peace on earth."

Alternate: BWV 121   Christum wir sollen loben schon
Hearing the angels' message, the shepherds hurry to Bethlehem to see the Christ child for themselves: "To Christ we should sing praises." They go forth telling others and praising and glorifying God for all they have heard and seen: "Seek not to understand, but merely wonder: God would through flesh achieve salvation of the flesh. … Let us join the choir of angels in singing our thanks and praise."

NATIVITY OF OUR LORD
Proper *iii* – CHRISTMAS DAY
December 25

Year A   John 1:1-14

BWV 133   *Ich freue mich in dir*
The miracle of God's becoming flesh and blood and living among humanity is the fountainhead of salvation. The humbling of God has exalted humanity, and for this the cantata rejoices: "I rejoice in you and bid you welcome, my dear little Jesus. … A holy body encloses the incomprehensible being of the Most High." The curse of Adam's mortality is canceled by the birth of Jesus, and all people are united to God through him.

Alternate: BWV 248, part 3   Herrscher des Himmels, erhöre das Lallen
"Ruler of heaven, hear our babble; let our faint songs please you." The prologue to the fourth gospel raises Jesus' glory to the highest degree and exults in the incarnation of God within human society. The cantata traces the path of the shepherds to the Word-made-flesh, whom they worship: "And they came in haste and found … the child lying in the crib." Their joy and excitement are proclaimed to people of all times and places.

Year B   John 1:1-14

BWV 63   *Christen, ätzen diesen Tag*
"Christian, engrave this day in metal and marble." The fourth gospel's account of the birth of Jesus climaxes with the Word's becoming flesh to dwell among us. "Come and

hasten with me to the manger." The cantata reminds the church of the surpassing glory of this event, greater even than the many ancient acts of salvation: "O wondrous day on which the Savior of the world ... reveals himself completely. ... The Godhead itself deigns to take on human shape and on earth to be born in a stable." Fulfilling all God's promises, the birth of the Messiah offers every blessing and evokes heavenly worship from all people.

Alternate: BWV 110 Unser Mund sei voll Lachens
"Let our mouth be full of laughter." The miracle of the Word of God which has become flesh means God truly is among mortals: "The Lord has done great things for us... He becomes man, and just for this: that we may be heaven's children." Divine glory now shines on the earth: "Glory be to God on high and peace on earth and good will towards mankind."

Year C   John 1:1-14

BWV 248   Christmas Oratorio, part 3:
            Herrscher des Himmels, erhöre das Lallen

"Ruler of heaven, hear our babble; let our faint songs please you." The prologue to the fourth gospel raises Jesus' glory to the highest degree and exults in the incarnation of God within human society. The cantata traces the path of the shepherds to the Word-made-flesh, whom they worship: "And they came in haste and found ... the child lying in the crib." Their joy and excitement are proclaimed to people of all times and places.

Alternate: BWV 63 Christen, ätzen diesen Tag
"Christian, engrave this day in metal and marble." The fourth gospel's account of the birth of Jesus climaxes with the Word's becoming flesh to dwell among us. "Come and hasten with me to the manger." The cantata reminds the church of the surpassing glory of this event, greater even than the many ancient acts of salvation: "O wondrous day on which the Savior of the world...reveals himself completely. ... The Godhead itself deigns to take on human shape and on earth to be born in a stable." Fulfilling all God's promises, the birth of the Messiah offers every blessing and evokes heavenly worship from all people.

STEPHEN, DEACON AND MARTYR
December 26

Acts 6:8 – 7:2a, 51-60

BWV 57   *Selig ist der Mann*

"Blessed is the man who endures temptation; for after he is tested, he will receive the crown [*stephanon*] of life." Because of his insistent call to attentiveness and obedience to God's words, the newly-appointed deacon Stephen is stoned to death: "Then compose

[57] yourself … cease to weep; the sun will shine brightly again, which now shows you clouds of woe." He becomes the first martyr for the Christian faith, witnessing to Christ even in his dying words: "Ah, Jesus, the heavens open for me, as they were for Stephen." The cantata, quoting James 1, praises the righteous who would suffer to resist evil, and entrusts everything to Jesus: "My heart is already prepared to climb up to you."

Alternate: BWV 46   Schauet doch und sehet, ob irgendein Schmerz sei
The martyrdom of Stephen recalls the persecution of the prophets as well as the passion and death of Jesus: "Behold and see if there be any sorrow like my sorrow, which has been inflicted on me." The pains of all who suffer, and the evils that cause them, invoke the mercy and love of God: "Yet do not imagine, O sinner, that Jerusalem alone, above all other places, was full of sins. … Yet Jesus would be, even in chastisement, shield and support of the devout."

JOHN, APOSTLE AND EVANGELIST
December 27

John 21:20-25

BWV 64   *Sehet, welch eine Liebe hat uns den Vater erzeiget*
After the resurrection Jesus defends the right of the beloved disciple to continue with the rest. Traditionally this disciple is identified with John, the son of Zebedee, and is the presumed author of the fourth gospel and the three epistles of John. The cantata opens with a quote from 1 John 3, expressing the wonder of the love shown in the incarnation of God's Son and the eternal blessings granted to all followers of Christ: "See what love the Father has show to us, in that we are called God's children. … What do I ask of the world and all its treasures, when I can have joy only in you, my Jesus? … Heaven remains certain for me, and I possess it already through faith."

Alternate: BWV 133   Ich freue mich in dir
The author of the fourth gospel, rejoices for the incarnation of the divine Word in the birth of Jesus: "I rejoice in you and bid you welcome, my dear little Jesus. … A holy body encloses the incomprehensible being of the Most High. … God himself lodges with us." Jesus' commendation of his beloved disciple gives courage and peace to all believers: "Death's fear and pain are not considered by my comforted heart."

THE HOLY INNOCENTS, MARTYRS
December 28

Matthew 2:13-18

BWV 58   *Ach Gott, wie manches Herzeleid*

"Ah God, how much heartbreak do I encounter at this time!" King Herod's fear of the newborn king drives him to kill the children of Bethlehem, although Jesus and his parents escape to safety in Egypt: "And though the furious Herod passes a sentence of ignominious death upon our Savior, an angel comes in the night who lets Joseph dream that he should flee from the murderer and go to Egypt." No greater tragedy can befall parents than the death of their child. This grim event foretells the future suffering of Jesus, and it both warns and encourages all Christians, as the cantata shows: "God's hand shows me another land ... here is anguish, there glory!"

> *Alternate: BWV 153   Schau, lieber Gott, wie meine Feind*
> The little children of Bethlehem are massacred by jealous King Herod in his attempt to destroy a rival king: "See, dear God, how my enemies ... are so cunning and so mighty that they easily subdue me. ... Storm then, storm, you whirlwind of tribulation!" Baby Jesus, however, is spared as his parents take him to safety in Egypt: "Disturb my repose, you enemies. For God says to me comfortingly: I am your refuge and deliverer. ... Jesus, when still of tender years had to undergo far greater woe, when the tyrant Herod threatened him with the utmost danger of death. ... He had hardly come on earth before he had to become a fugitive."

FIRST SUNDAY OF CHRISTMAS
December 26-31

Year A   Matthew 2:13-23

BWV 153   *Schau, lieber Gott, wie meine Feind*

"See, dear God, how my enemies ... are so cunning and so mighty. ... And these, through rage and ferocity ... want to put an end to me completely." The cantata reminds Christians that they need not be afraid when dangers and hard times come their way, according to the words of Isaiah 41: "Fear not, I am with you. ... I will help you with the right hand of my righteousness." The opposition of King Herod to the birth of Jesus is ominous, and the holy family flees to Egypt for safety from Herod's purge: "Jesus, when still of tender years, had to undergo far greater woe, when the tyrant Herod threatened him with the utmost danger of death with his murderous fists! He had hardly come on earth before he had to become a fugitive."

> *Alternate: BWV 58   Ach Gott, wie manches Herzeleid*
> "Oh God, what deep affliction befalls me at this time!" By providentially escaping to Egypt, Joseph protects the infant Jesus and his mother from the tragic massacre in Bethlehem: "And though the furious Herod passes a sentence

[58] of ignominious death upon our Savior, an angel comes in the night, who lets Joseph dream that he should flee from the murderer and go to Egypt." Afterward they relocate to Nazareth: "God's hand shows me another land … here is anguish, there glory!"

Year B   Luke 2:22-40

BWV 83   *Erfreute Zeit im neuen Bunde*
"Glad time of the new covenant, when our faith holds Jesus." At the age of forty days, Jesus is presented in the temple and received with great joy by the aged Simeon and Anna. This new presentation of God's salvation brings light and hope to all Christians. Simeon's prayer of valediction is quoted in part in the cantata: "Lord, now let your servant depart in peace. … Death is an end to this time and trouble. … It can joyfully make the utterance: 'For my eyes have seen your Savior, whom you have prepared before all peoples.' … You shall certainly recognize his bright light in death itself."

> *Alternate: BWV 125   Mit Fried und Freud ich fahr dahin*
> In seeing and holding the newborn Christ, Simeon gives thanks and is filled with joy and peace: "In peace and joy I now depart … consoled in heart and mind." The promises now fulfilled bring salvation and hope to the entire world: "A mysterious light fills the whole world. … Every faithful soul shall be summoned to God's realm of grace."

Year C   Luke 2:41-52

BWV 154   *Mein liebster Jesus ist verloren*
"Beloved Jesus, my desire, tell me where I may find you." In the singular scriptural account of Jesus in his older-childhood years, he strays from his family to discuss religious matters with the elders in the temple: "How is it that you sought me? Did you not know that I must be about my Father's business?" The cantata focuses on the panic and grief felt by Mary and Joseph when they thought him lost. The Christian is assured that Jesus, who is doing the work of his heavenly Father, is protection and comfort for whatever distress life may bring: "If you curse worldly trifles and enter this dwelling alone, you can fare well both here and there. … My God, open for me the gates of such grace and goodness."

> *Alternate: BWV 32   Liebster Jesu, mein Verlangen*
> "Beloved Jesus, my desire, tell me where I might find you." Twelve-year-old Jesus calms the anxieties of his parents, who supposed him lost: "How is it that you sought me? Did you not know that I must be about my Father's business?" God's house and God's Word remain the refuge of all who seek peace and love: "If you curse worldly trifles and enter this dwelling alone, you can fare well both here and there. … Open for me the gates of such grace and goodness."

January 1

Year A   Luke 2:15-21

BWV 28   *Gottlob! Nun geht das Jahr zu Ende*

"Praise God! Now the year comes to an end. The new one already draws near." Rather than the circumcision and naming of Jesus on the eighth day after his birth, the cantata focuses on the turning of the calendar year. Its quote from Jeremiah reminds the Christian of God's promised blessings, those already enjoyed and those anticipated in the new year: "God says, 'I will rejoice in doing good to them'." Trusting in God's unfailing love, it is possible to look ahead with hope and joy: "Now praise the Lord, my soul, whatever is in me, praise his name. ... All such goodness of yours we praise, Father on heaven's throne, as you show us through Christ, your Son."

> *Alternate: BWV* 248, part 4: *Fallt mit Danken, fallt mit Loben*
>
> "With thanks and praise prostrate yourselves before the merciful throne of God on high!" A week after his birth Jesus is circumcised and named according to the law: "God's Son would become Savior and Redeemer of the earth. ... His name was called 'Jesus'." The cantata features the many salutary facets of the name 'Jesus', as it offers to the world consolation and salvation: "My Jesus is my delight, my Jesus comforts heart and breast. Jesus, my dearest life, my soul's bridegroom." As Savior of the world, the fate of Jesus is tinged with pain. "Your name inscribed within me has driven away the fear of death. Your name alone shall be in my heart."

Year B   Luke 2:15-21

BWV 190   *Singet dem Herrn ein neues Lied*

"Sing a new song to the Lord. ... Lord God, we give you praise, that with this new year you give us new happiness and blessing. ... For your paternal faith is boundless; it is renewed each morning with us." The birth and naming of Jesus usher in a new era of salvation: "This only I ask of the Lord ... that Jesus my joy ... might embrace me as a lamb of his pasture this year also with his protection." The cantata, with verses from Psalms 149 and 150 (see also *BWV* 225), sings praises most of all for the gift of God's own Son: "Jesus, grant me that with the new year his anointed one too may flourish." This Jesus forms the basis and focus of the Christian's life, and in him it is possible to pray for peace and prosperity: "Let us complete this year in praise of your name."

> *Alternate: BWV* 171   *Gott, wie dein Name, so ist auch dein Ruhm*
>
> "Your name, O God, like your praise, reaches to the ends of the earth." The new-born Messiah is circumcised and named 'Jesus', as the Savior announced by the angels: "The sweet name of Jesus is my peace." On the eighth day of Christmas, the name of Jesus ushers in a new calendar year: "Jesus shall be my first word in the new year." In this holy name believers offer their prayers to God: "Savior of the world, reject us no longer, and protect us throughout this year."

Year C Luke 2:15-21

BWV 248/4 Christmas Oratorio, part 4
Fallt mit Danken, fallt mit Loben

"With thanks and praise prostrate yourselves before the merciful throne of God on high!" A week after his birth Jesus is circumcised and named according to the law: "God's Son would become Savior and Redeemer of the earth. ... His name was called 'Jesus'." The cantata features the many salutary facets of the name 'Jesus', as it offers to the world consolation and salvation: "My Jesus is my delight, my Jesus comforts heart and breast. Jesus, my dearest life, my soul's bridegroom." As Savior of the world, the fate of Jesus is tinged with pain. "Your name inscribed within me has driven away the fear of death. Your name alone shall be in my heart."

> *Alternate:* BWV 143 *Lobe den Herrn, meine Seele*
> The name 'Jesus' proclaims the new-born boy as Savior of the world, and is the name at which every knee bends and in which shines the glory of God: "Praise the Lord, O my soul. ... Prince of peace, Lord Jesus Christ, true man and true God ... in your name alone we cry to the Father. ... Remain our refuge in the future, that this year bring us good fortune. ... O Jesus, guide your flock into the coming new year."

SECOND SUNDAY OF CHRISTMAS
January 2-5

Year A John 1:1-18

BWV 41 *Jesu, nun sei gepreiset*

The good news of the birth of Jesus is summarized in the prologue to the fourth gospel. "Jesus, now be praised at this new year ... the new gladsome time that hovers full of grace and eternal salvation." The cantata expresses thanks for past blessings and seeks God's presence and blessings in the new day that has dawned with the coming of Christ: "Allow our soul still your saving Word. ... Yours alone is the honor, yours alone is the renown. ... This is sung today without jest by the host faithful to Christ, wishing with mouth and heart a blessed new year."

> *Alternate:* BWV 173 *Erhöhtes Fleisch und Blut*
> That the Word of God inhabits the earth as flesh and blood remains the first great miracle of Christianity: "Exalted flesh and blood which God takes upon himself, for which already here on earth he ordains a heavenly salvation, to become a child of the Most High!" The divine love shown in the incarnation overcomes the darkness of evil: "God has so loved the world ... that he gives us his Son, to partake of the gifts of grace that flow like rich streams." So, all humanity can worship Jesus as the Son of God: "Sing gratefully, for his manifested light inclines to his children and appears mightily to them."

Year B   John 1:1-18

BWV 122   *Das neugeborne Kindlein*

"The newborn infant child, the dearly-beloved little Jesus, brings once more a new year to the chosen Christian throng." The prolog to the fourth gospel portrays the incarnation of the divine Word as the culmination of cosmic history. The cantata connects the birth of Jesus to the new year, symbolic of a new age for the world. All creation can join the angels in rejoicing, for God has opened the gates to heaven: "The angels ... now throng the air in a lofty choir to rejoice at your salvation. ... The infant Jesus is with us. God is with us and shall protect us. This is the day the Lord himself has made, who brought his Son into this world."

Alternate: BWV 40   *Dazu ist erschienen der Sohn Gottes*
"For this purpose the Son of God was manifested." The monumental prologue to the fourth gospel reveals the glory of God in the newborn Christ: "The Word was made flesh and dwells in the world. ... God is with us now in our need. ... Jesus, who can save, will gather his chickens under his wing." The cantata, sung at the beginning of a new calendar, invokes a blessing for the year: "Give to all the Christian throng peace and a blessed year."

Year C   John 1:1-18

BWV 171   *Gott, wie dein Name, so ist auch dein Ruhm*

"Your name, O God, like your praise, reaches to the ends of the earth." The cosmic scale of the incarnation of God's Word is shown in the prologue to the fourth gospel. As the cantata opens, Psalm 48 reflects the universal majesty of one whose name is Jesus. "O sweet name of Jesus, in you is my repose, you are my solace here on earth ... you are my light and my life, my honor and my faith. ... Jesus shall be my first word in the new year." This same Jesus is present for every believer, on the lips of all who pray for God's peace: "Jesus shall also be my final word. ... Give peace to all around, give to all the land your pure and joy-inspiring Word."

Alternate: BWV 190 *Singet dem Herrn ein neues Lied*
"Sing to the Lord a new song!" The Word is God, and now dwells as a mortal among mortals: "Let everything that has breath praise the Lord!" He is Jesus, and he brings the blessings of heaven to earth: "Jesus, my joy ... may his kindly Spirit, which shows me the way to life, govern and lead me on an even course." For this alone Jesus is worthy of worship, love, and obedience: "Jesus shall be my beginning; Jesus is my light of joy."

EPIPHANY OF OUR LORD
January 6

Year A   Matthew 2:1-12

BWV 65   *Sie werden aus Saba alle kommen*

"They will all come out of Sheba, bearing gold and incense, and proclaiming the Lord's praise." Worship of the Christ child by the magi reveals the universal scope of God's salvation: "What Isaiah had there foreseen has happened in Bethlehem. Here the wise men appear at Jesus' crib and would praise him as their king. ... You, O prince of life become the light of the Gentiles and their redeemer." The opening quote from Isaiah 60 grounds this event in the promises of ancient scripture, repeated by the hymn *A Child Is Born in Bethlehem*. Like the Magi, Christians are called to offer their gifts and worship to Christ: "Do not disdain, you light of my soul, my heart, which I bring you in humility."

> *Alternate: BWV* 248, parts 5 & 6 *Ehre sei dir, Gott, gesungen ... Wenn die stolzen Feinde*
> "Glory be sung to you, O God!" The arrival of the Magi brings the Gentile world into the sphere of God's salvation: "Behold, there came wise men from the east to Jerusalem, saying 'Where is he that is born king of the Jews? ... We have seen his star in the east and have come to worship him.' ... Blessed are you who have seen this light. It is come for your salvation." The divine light of Christ reveals the shadows of evil: it raises the hostility of King Herod. "Lord, if proud enemies rage, grant that we, in steadfast faith, may look to your might and help. ... 'Go and search diligently for the young child ... that I may come and worship him also'." When some worship, others plot to destroy. Such irony is sounded in the final chorus, where the 'Passion Chorale' is sung in a particularly triumphant setting.

Year B   Matthew 2:1-12

BWV 16   *Herr Gott, dich loben wir*

"Lord God, we give you praise ... the first offering of our hearts." With the Magi, the church joins in adoration of the newborn Christ. "Protect, as in the past, your precious Word ... that your kingdom might increase and Satan's wicked guile be destroyed." The cantata praises God, who through this baby has given the world a new day, a new year, and a new age: "Beloved Jesus, you alone shall be our souls' wealth. ... Grant us a peaceful year, to protect us from all sorrow and gently to sustain us."

> *Alternate: BWV* 65 *Sie werden aus Saba alle kommen*
> "They will all come out of Sheba, bearing gold and incense, and proclaiming the Lord's praise." Worship of the Christ child by the Magi reveals the universal scope of God's salvation: "What Isaiah had there foreseen has happened in Bethlehem. Here the wise men appear at Jesus' crib and would praise him as their king. ... You, O prince of life become the light of the Gentiles and their redeemer." The opening quote from Isaiah 60 grounds this event in the promises of ancient scripture, repeated by the hymn *A Child Is Born in Bethlehem*. Like the Magi, Christians are called to offer their gifts and worship to Christ: "Do not disdain, you light of my soul, my heart, which I bring you in humility."

Year C Matthew 2:1-12

BWV 248 Christmas Oratorio, parts 5 and 6:
Ehre sei dir, Gott, gesungen … Wenn die stolzen Feinde

"Glory be sung to you, O God!" The arrival of the Magi brings the Gentile world into the sphere of God's salvation: "Behold, there came wise men from the east to Jerusalem, saying 'Where is he that is born king of the Jews? … We have seen his star in the east and have come to worship him.' … Blessed are you who have seen this light. It is come for your salvation." The divine light of Christ reveals the shadows of evil: it raises the hostility of King Herod. "Lord, if proud enemies rage, grant that we, in steadfast faith, may look to your might and help. … 'Go and search diligently for the young child … that I may come and worship him also'." When some worship, others plot to destroy. Such irony is sounded in the final chorus, where the 'Passion Chorale' is sung in a particularly triumphant setting.

> *Alternate: BWV 16 Herr Gott, dich loben wir*
>
> "Lord God, we give you praise… the first offering of our hearts." With the Magi, the church joins in adoration of the newborn Christ. "Protect, as in the past, your precious Word … that your kingdom might increase and Satan's wicked guile be destroyed." The cantata praises God, who through this baby has given the world a new day, a new year, and a new age: "Beloved Jesus, you alone shall be our souls' wealth. … Grant us a peaceful year, to protect us from all sorrow and gently to sustain us."

SUNDAY 1
BAPTISM OF OUR LORD
January 7-13

Year A Matthew 3:13-17

BWV 7 *Christ unser Herr zum Jordan kam*

"Christ our Lord came to the Jordan … was baptized by St. John to fulfill his work and duty." Based on Luther's baptismal hymn, the cantata accompanies Matthew's version of Jesus' baptism, one of the few events narrated by all four Gospels, one that clearly inaugurates Jesus' public ministry. In this account John the Baptist questions the propriety of his baptizing Jesus, whether it should not be the other way around. The cantata tells how Jesus fulfills all righteousness in the mission of his life and death and how through holy baptism all people are drawn into righteousness and eternal life: "What God himself calls baptism … God's Word and God's Spirit baptize and cleanse sinners. … He said, 'This is my beloved Son'. … We should believe without doubt that it was the Trinity itself who prepared baptism for us."

Alternate: BWV 37 Wer da gläubet und getauft wird
Despite John's objections, Jesus submits to baptism 'to fulfill all righteousness':
"Faith is the pledge of the love that Jesus has for his own people." The cantata
celebrates the salvation of all who are baptized: "Forever shall my heart praise
him. ... Faith alone ensures that before God we are justified and saved."

Year B   Mark 1:4-11

BWV 37   *Wer da gläubet und getauft wird*

"Whoever believes and is baptized will be saved." That Jesus is inaugurated into his
ministry at John's baptism is attested by all the gospels. John's own words foretell that
ministry: 'One greater. ... repentance and forgiveness. ... Holy Spirit. ... Son of God.'
Into the same ministry Christians are baptized: "Lord God ... you have loved me in the
world's eyes eternally in your own Son." The cantata's title quotes Mark 16:16, assuring
all believers of salvation, which is echoed throughout: "Baptism is the seal of mercy that
brings us God's blessing. ... Bestow belief on me in your Son Jesus Christ."

Alternate: BWV 123 Liebster Immanuel, Herzog der Frommen
As John announces one more powerful, who 'will baptize you with the Holy
Spirit,' Jesus appears and is baptized by him: "Dearest Immanuel, Lord of the
righteous ... come quickly." Heavenly power descends on Jesus, by which he
will save the world: "When I utter the name of Jesus ... my heart, even in the
peril of pain, is transported through the power of Jesus. Even the cross's cruel
journey and the bitter nourishment of tears do not frighten me. ... Even death
itself has no power. ... Jesus, you are mine and I am yours. ... My whole life
shall be given up to you."

Year C   Luke 3:15-17, 21-22

BWV 123   *Liebster Immanuel, Herzog der Frommen*

"Dearest Immanuel, prince of the righteous, savior of my soul, come quickly. ... Just as
the dew refreshes the arid land, so my heart, even in peril and pain, is transported
through the power of Jesus." Key to Jesus' baptism by John is the heavenly voice,
designating Jesus as God's Son. In the cantata the name of Jesus is linked to Immanuel,
meaning God-with-us, and to Savior: "Jesus sends me from heaven salvation and light.
... My whole life shall be given up to you." The presence of God's Son transforms life
for every believer, like dew to the arid land, sunlight parting the storm clouds, joy
overcoming sadness.

Alternate: BWV 7 Christ unser Herr zum Jordan kam
"Christ our Lord came to the Jordan ... was baptized by St. John." The people
come to John in search of a Messiah, but he defers to Jesus as the one who will
prepare them for judgment: "God himself calls baptism. ... God's Word and
God's Spirit baptize and purify the sinner. ... He said, 'This is my beloved Son,
in whom I am well pleased.' ... The Holy Trinity itself gave baptism to us."

Sunday 2
January 14-20

Year A   John 1:29-42

BWV 9   *Es ist das Heil uns kommen her*

"Salvation has come to us from grace and pure goodness." After the baptism of Jesus, John the Baptist twice proclaims him to be the Lamb of God who takes away the sins of the world. John's disciples soon turn to follow Jesus: "Faith looks to Jesus Christ. … The law had to be fulfilled; therefore came the salvation of the earth, the Son of the Highest." The cantata, based on the hymn *Salvation unto Us Has Come*, describes the wondrous salvation that has arrived on earth in Christ, and is impressed on the baptized: "This may be called our comfort: that in the gospel we again become glad and joyful."

> *Alternate:* BWV 23 *Du wahrer Gott und Davids Sohn*
> John the Baptist announces Jesus as 'the Lamb of God' and 'the Son of God'. John's disciples greet Jesus as 'Rabbi' and soon know that they have encountered David's great son, 'the Messiah': "True God and son of David … have mercy on me! … Do not pass by. You, the salvation of all mankind, have indeed appeared to serve the sick and not the healthy. … Christ, Lamb of God, you who bear the sins of the world, give us your peace."

Year B   John 1:43-51

BWV 79   *Gott der Herr ist Sonn und Schild*

"The Lord God is a sun and shield. … No good thing will he withhold from those who walk uprightly." After Philip meets Jesus, he introduces him to Nathaniel, 'truly an Israelite in whom there is no deceit'. The cantata quotes Psalm 84, giving thanks for past and present blessings: "Our thankful souls therefore praise his goodness, which he fosters for his little band." Jesus is the fulfillment of the law and prophets. Even greater is the assurance of his eternal blessings: "We know the proper path to blessedness, for, Jesus, you have shown it to us through your word. … Let your word shine on us brightly."

> *Alternate:* BWV 145 *Auf, mein Herz, des Herren Tag* †
> From the onset of his ministry, Jesus calls people to faith and through faith to eternal life: "Rise up, my heart. … If you acknowledge Jesus with your mouth, that he is Lord, and believe in your heart that God raised him from the dead, then you shall be blessed." Those who trust and follow him will receive the blessings of heaven: "I live, my heart, to your delight; my life raises your life on high. … Your savior is alive; let this be a firm foundation for your belief."

---

† = *So du mit deinem Munde bekennest* = *Ich lebe, mein Herze, zu deinem Ergötzen*

Year C   John 2:1-11

BWV 155   *Mein Gott, wie lang, ach lange*

"My God, how long, oh how long? ... No end do I see to pain and sorrow." When the wine runs short at the wedding in Cana, Jesus' mother asks for his help: "The wine of joy is lacking. My confidence has all but gone." He answers that the time is inappropriate: "Jesus knows the right hour to gladden you with his help." Mary's confusion and frustration, voiced in the opening lines, are elaborated in the cantata. It is the same impatient reaction many have in critical times or everyday life. Now, as then, people may confidently turn to Jesus for aid in due time: "He will bring wine of joy and comfort. ... Be more certain of his word."

> *Alternate:* BWV 13 *Meine Seufzer, meine Tränen*
> Although written to accompany the day's gospel, the cantata bears little of the cheerfulness of a wedding at Cana, the changing of water into wine, or resultant belief in Jesus: "My cup of woe is filled to the brim with tears." Jesus' reply to his mother's query is echoed: "The hour can be seen approaching from afar", as are the generous supply of wine: "God can with ease turn bitterness into joyful wine", and the disciples' faith: "Whoever looks toward heaven and seeks solace there, a beam of joy can with ease appear in his grieving heart."

CONFESSION OF PETER
January 18

Matthew 16:13-19

BWV 92   *Ich hab in Gottes Herz und Sinn*

"I have surrendered to God's heart and mind." Peter, who recently sank like a rock into the sea because of his doubt, here proclaims his confidence in Jesus, who had saved him from drowning: "Even if he should cast me straight into the sea ... he would only be training me, to see whether I will think of Jonah, or whether, with Peter, I will direct my mind toward him." Because of his faith, Peter is called 'Rock' (*Petros*), the firm foundation (*petra*) of the church: "He will make me strong in faith, he will watch over my soul and accustom my spirit, which always wavers and yields. ... If I keep firm and am found to be rock-firm in faith, then his hand ... knows how to exalt me again. ... Let Satan rage, storm, and crash: the powerful God will make us invincible."

Year A   Matthew 4:12-23

BWV 230   *Lobet den Herrn, alle Heiden*

Jesus' ministry begins in his home territory, bringing light and healing to 'Galilee of the Gentiles'. His fame spreads far and wide: "Praise the Lord, all nations, and honor him, all peoples, for his mercy and truth watch over us eternally. Alleluia." The motet summarizes this fame in the two verses of Psalm 117, proclaiming the global scope of God's love.

> *Alternate: BWV 41 Jesu, nun sei gepreiset*
> "O Jesus, now be praised … for your goodness shown to us." In fulfillment of Isaiah's prophecies, Jesus brings hope to people in spiritual darkness: "Your hand, your blessing alone must be the A and O, beginning and end. … Provided that you have granted a noble peace for our body and station, then allow our soul still your saving word."

Year B   Mark 1:14-20

BWV 168   *Tue Rechnung! Donnerwort*

"Give an account of yourself, thunderous words." Jesus calls twelve disciples to accompany him in his ministry, the first of whom are the fishermen, Peter, Andrew, James, and John. His words to them, 'Follow me', are the call to all people to have faith in Jesus: "Soul, go forth. Ah, you must return to God his possessions, body and life. … Exalted hands have entrusted them to me, that I might manage and administer faithfully." The cantata underscores the ultimate importance of living in love and commitment to the mission of Jesus: "Because you know that you are a steward, be concerned and ever mindful. … Burst the bonds of mammon, O heart. Hands, scatter good abroad." Only through him come forgiveness and salvation: "Strengthen me with your Spirit's joy."

> *Alternate: BWV 94 Was frag ich nach der Welt*
> "Why inquire after the world and all its treasures, when I can only rejoice in you, my Jesus?" Jesus calls fishermen as his first disciples. Without apparent hesitation they leave their families, friends, and occupation to follow him: "The world seeks glory and fame among the high and mighty. … I shall choose my Jesus … and practice faith and penitence, that I become rich and blessed." Commitment to Jesus Christ is the essence of discipleship: "Jesus is my life, my treasure, my property, to whom I am devoted."

Year C   Luke 4:14-21

BWV 143   *Lobe den Herrn, meine Seele*

"Praise the Lord, O my soul." In Nazareth Jesus reads from Isaiah 61, interpreting his own mission in its light. With several quotations from Psalm 146, the cantata (see also *BWV* 69 and *BWV* 69a) praises Christ as the prince of peace, a helper of the needy, and bringer of a year of grace: "O Prince of Peace, Lord Jesus Christ … you are a strong helper in need. … Remain our refuge in the future. … Let us henceforth hear your godly word sound even longer in peace."

> *Alternate: BWV 136 Erforsche mich, Gott, und erfahre mein Herz*
> Jesus' reading of Isaiah 61 in his hometown synagogue is initially received with enthusiasm by the people of Nazareth. Soon, however he uncovers the hidden intentions of their hearts: "Search me, O God, and know my heart. … The children of darkness are often wont to dissemble as angels of light. … The day shall come that will pass sentence on what is hidden. … Whoever is cleansed by the blood of Jesus … has in Christ, no less, righteousness and strength."

CONVERSION OF PAUL
January 25

Luke 21:10-19

BWV 183   *Sie werden euch in den Bann tun*

Saint Paul, once the persecutor of Christians, suffers rejection and abuse throughout his missionary work, and is finally martyred: "They will place you under a ban, but the time will come when whoever kills you will think he does God a service thereby." Like him and all the apostles, there is no need for faithful disciples to fear or despair, since God promises to grant endurance: "My entire being shall be dedicated to you. … Highest Comforter, Holy Spirit … help my infirmity with your intercession … till he has helped who alone can help."

SUNDAY 4
January 28 – February 3

Year A   Matthew 5:1-12

BWV 107   *Was willst du dich betrüben*

"Why would you grieve, O my dear soul? Devote yourself to him who is called Emmanuel!" Jesus begins his Sermon on the Mount with the beatitudes, a series of blessings. These revolutionize popular ideals of success, and describe earthly participation in God's heavenly kingdom: "God forsakes no one who trusts in him.

… You may stake your life on him with fearless courage." In the seven stanzas of the title hymn, the cantata exhorts the Christian to be cheerful, strong, and faithful against all evils and even the devil, for ultimate blessedness comes from God: "Though from hell Satan himself would confront you … what God wills, that is done."

Alternate: BWV 78 Jesu, der du meine Seele
The 'poor' of Jesus' beatitudes are those who know their need of God: "Jesus, by whom my soul … from the devil's dark cave … has been forcibly torn out … be even now, O God, my refuge." The blessedness of the heavenly kingdom comes through Jesus and is assured to all in need: "You faithfully seek the sick and straying. … Jesus stands at my side so that I am heartened and victorious. … If Christians believe in you, no enemy in all eternity will steal them out of your hands."

Year B   Mark 1:21-28

BWV 78   *Jesu, der du meine Seele*

"Jesus, you have wrested my soul … from oppressive anguish most forcefully." The healing hand of God is shown as Jesus drives out unclean spirits, to the amazement of onlookers: "Be even now, O God, my refuge. … You seek to help the ailing and erring." The cantata praises the power of God over grief, error, sin, and death: "The blood which eases my guilt makes my heart feel light again and sets me free. … Your word offers me hope." The sacrificial death of Jesus has made victory possible for all his followers: "If Christians believe in you, no foe shall ever steal them out of your hands."

Alternate: BWV 69a Lobe den Herrn, meine Seele
As Jesus begins his ministry in Galilee, he teaches and heals the sick. In amazement the people recognize powerful blessings from God: "Bless the Lord, my soul, and do not forget his benefits … for all my life God has done so much for me that I cannot thank him in all eternity." The fame of Jesus spreads throughout the region, and people come seeking health and comfort: "My redeemer and preserver … stand by me in affliction and suffering."

Year C   Luke 4:21-30

BWV 181   *Leichtgesinnte Flattergeister*

"Scatter-brained, fickle spirits deprive themselves of the word's strength." Jesus' career in his hometown comes to a quick end, when he follows his synagogue reading from Isaiah 61 by identifying himself with the prophet. The people of Nazareth are not happy to be compared to the faithless of ancient Israel, and their earlier flattery becomes condemnation, rage, and violence: "Hearts of rock which spitefully resist will forfeit their own salvation. … The noble seed will lie unfruitful, if we do not live according to the Spirit." The cantata offers a severe critique of those who are insincere, fickle, or hardhearted. They pose a danger to any who are sincere and obedient: "Give us, O Lord, in every season our heart's repose, your holy word."

Alternate: BWV 167 Ihr Menschen, rühmet Gottes Liebe
"Mortals, extol God's love." The people of Nazareth become angry when Jesus, a hometown boy, speaks to them in prophetic terms. He is driven out of town, and takes his ministry elsewhere. "Jesus himself appeared to gladden us poor creatures and the lost sinners with grace and love." Faith and hope are needed to appreciate the blessings he brings: "May God increase in us what he pledges us in mercy, that we may firmly trust in him."

PRESENTATION OF OUR LORD
February 2

Luke 2:22-40

BWV A159   *Ich lasse dich nicht*
"I will not leave you before you bless me, my Jesus." Forty days after his birth, Jesus is presented in the temple, as is the custom for the oldest son. There he and his parents are met by Simeon and Anna, who prophesy about him. The title line from Genesis 32 (see also *BWV* 157) describes the tenacious faithfulness of Anna and Simeon, content now and at peace, having been assured of God's presence in the Christ child: "I thank you, Christ, Son of God, that you fill me with this knowledge by your divine word; grant me constancy as well, for the salvation of my soul. Praise, honor, and glory to you for all the good you have done me."

Alternate: BWV 82 Ich habe genug
"It is enough." The aged Simeon greets the newborn Jesus and his parents in the temple and recognizes the child as 'the consolation of Israel ... the Lord's Messiah ... your salvation': "I have taken the savior, the hope of the devout, into my longing arms." Fulfilled and satisfied, Simeon is willing and ready to depart this life in peace: "Like Simeon, I already see the joy of that life beyond. ... Here it is misery that I must attend, but there I shall behold sweet peace, silent repose."

SUNDAY 5
February 4-10

Year A   Matthew 5:13-20

BWV 39   *Brich dem Hungrigen dein Brot*
"Break your bread with the hungry." The teachings of Jesus bring to life words of the ancient prophets. Quoted in the cantata is Isaiah 58, a search for honest worship and true righteousness: "Then your light shall break forth like the dawn ... and the glory of the Lord shall take you to his home." Believers in every age know that they are to reflect God's special concern for the poor and hungry: "To become like one's creator

still on earth, though only as a pale imitation, is a foretaste of eternal bliss. ... Do not forget to do good, for God is well pleased with such offerings."

Alternate: BWV 9 *Es ist das Heil uns kommen her*
"Salvation has come to us." In his great Sermon on the Mount, Jesus exhorts his followers to witness to God's grace and holiness by lives that are exemplary and beyond reproach. The cantata emphasizes that faith in God is the basis of human righteousness: "Good deeds no longer help us: they cannot protect us. ... God gave us a law, yet we are too weak to be able to keep it. ... Lord, rather than at good deeds, you look at the heart's strength of faith. ... Let his word be more secure for you."

Year B   Mark 1:29-39

BWV 69a   Lobe den Herrn, meine Seele
"Bless the Lord, my soul, and do not forget his benefits." As Jesus travels through the land, healing the sick and proclaiming the good news of God, many are moved to praise God for the great things they see and hear: "For all my life he has done so much for me. ... My voice is weak and my tongue is silent in lauding and praising you." The cantata, one of three with the opening line of Psalm 103 (see *BWV* 69 and *BWV* 143), offers thanksgiving from all who have been healed, comforted, or otherwise blessed. It also prays for God's continuing protection and guidance: "Stand by me in affliction and suffering. ... Though I be cast onto the rough road by affliction, death, and misery, God shall hold me ... in his arms." A stanza of the hymn *What God Ordains Is Good Indeed* concludes the cantata.

Alternate: BWV 8 *Liebster Gott, wann werd ich sterben*
From the beginning of his ministry, Jesus heals many who are sick, including Peter's mother-in-law: "Dearest God, when shall I die?" Human frailties and mortality are seen as assaults of evil powers and the results of sin, which can only be overcome by divine mercy and power: "Daily my body bows nearer the earth, and there its place of rest must be. ... Where will my loved ones in their sadness be scattered and banished? ... From God's abundant store the greatest blessing shall be mine."

Year C   Luke 5:1-11

BWV 88   Siehe, ich will viel Fischer aussenden
After a miraculous catch of fish at Jesus' direction, the disciples are commissioned to be catching people for the kingdom of God: "I am now sending for many fishermen, says the Lord, and they shall catch them." The cantata recalls the words of Jeremiah 16, which warned of God's purge of all idolaters, a stark warning to anyone who turns away from God: "God is always eager that we be on the right path, sheltered by the light of his grace." Jesus' words to Simon Peter and the others, however, intend that believers should be urgent in their dedication to gathering people into the community of faith: "Do not be afraid; from now on you will be catching people. ... If God himself calls, then his blessing must fall abundantly on all that we do."

Alternate: BWV 45 Es ist dir gesagt, Mensch, was gut ist
Jesus calls fishermen to come and begin catching people. Amazed and inspired, they follow, leaving their former lives to proclaim righteousness and godliness to all: "He has told you, O mortal, what is good; and what does the Lord require of you? ... Fear, humility, and love, as a test of the obedience which I practice. ... Whoever acknowledges God from the depths of his heart, God will acknowledge also. ... That he might see his work accomplished through me."

Sunday 6
February 11-17

Year A   Matthew 5:21-37

BWV 33   Allein zu dir, Herr Jesu Christ
"In you alone, Lord Jesus Christ, my earthly hope is placed." Jesus' interpretations of the commandments on killing, adultery, and swearing warn the crowds and convince his disciples of their own guiltiness in every case: "My God and judge, if you would question me from the law, then I could not answer. ... Cast me not away from your presence, though I still daily transgress your commandment; even the smallest one is too hard for me to keep." Overcoming human failure to keep the law is the purpose of the gospel, to bring people to Christ and find in him comfort, righteousness, and hope for eternal life with God: "Grant that out of pure impulse I love my neighbor as myself."

Alternate: BWV 170 Vergnügte Ruh, beliebte Seelenlust
In his Sermon on the Mount Jesus deepens the message of the commandments, touching not only prohibitions and actions, but also intentions and relationships: "Contented rest, beloved pleasure of the soul: you cannot be found in hell's sins, but rather in heavenly concord." Love and respect reflect faith in God and guide daily living: "Nothing but virtue's gifts shall have their dwelling in my heart. ... Righteous God, how far man is alienated from you. ... I quite tremble and feel a thousand pains when they merely rejoice in vengeance and hatred. ... I too should love my enemy like my best friend. ... My heart flees from anger and resentment."

Year B   Mark 1:40-45

BWV 72   Alles nur nach Gottes Willen
"All things according to God's will, in pleasure as in sadness, in good times as in evil." The leper who comes to Jesus for healing is relying entirely on 'if you will': "Blest Christian, who always immerses his will in God's will, whatever may befall, in health and sickness. ... Lord, if you will, I shall grow well again and pure." He trusts completely, and Jesus responds with pity: "Your savior says 'I will' ... when affliction and suffering frighten you." The cantata proclaims the trustworthiness of God, made know to all in the death and resurrection of Jesus. Christians are invited to follow according to God's perfect will, the way of the cross.

Alternate: BWV 111 Was mein Gott will, das g'scheh allzeit
A beggar appeals to Jesus' mercy and is healed: "May God's will always be
done. ... He helps us in need, this righteous God." Despite a stern warning, he
cannot resist spreading the good news abroad: "Happy is he who chooses this
protection in trusting faith. ... Help, guide, and defend, O God my Lord, to the
honor of your name."

Year C   Luke 6:17-26

BWV 20   O Ewigkeit, du Donnerwort

Luke's version of the beatitudes includes woes or warnings to the rich: "O eternity,
word of thunder! ... I do not know which way I should turn." The cantata, one of two
with this opening line (see *BWV* 60), concentrates on the horrors of damnation,
exhibiting the Christian's own fear of punishment and also the everlasting condemnation of others: "The Lord is just in all his works. ... Our time is short, death is swift.
... Flee from Satan's slavery and free yourself from sin." Commitment to Christ
remains the only hope: "Forsake, O mortal, the pleasure of this world. ... Consider ...
while the tree of life still flourishes for you, what best serves your peace."

Alternate: BWV 107 Was willst du dich betrüben
In Luke's version of Jesus' sermon we hear both beatitudes and woes: "Why
are you so distressed, my dear soul?" God-with-us demonstrates the way of
blessedness and life: "Devote yourself to love him who is called Emmanuel. ...
With him you shall achieve that which serves and helps you. ... I shall only
strive for that which he approves. ... With purest mercy you avert want and
harm."

SUNDAY 7
February 18-24

Year A   Matthew 5:38-48

BWV 138   Warum betrübst du dich, mein Herz

"Why are you distressed, my heart ... over mere temporal matters?" The most difficult
challenges of the Sermon on the Mount are policies of non-retaliation and loving one's
enemies. These illustrate the perfection God seeks in believers: "If God would neither
leave nor forsake me, then I can compose myself in patience and tranquility." In the
cantata such troubling lessons accuse, and are answered by the comforting assurance of
God's presence and fatherly support: "My faith lets him rule." Shame and sadness are
transformed by God's mercy into gladness and hope.

Alternate: BWV 77 *Du sollt Gott, deinen Herren, lieben*
In his Sermon on the Mount Jesus goes beyond the traditional commandments, by advocating love to the stranger and even one's enemies: "Grant me besides, my God, the heart of a Samaritan, that I may also love my neighbor and in his pain be distressed over him." This means striving for God-like selflessness: "Grant that I may hate self-love."

Year B   Mark 2:1-12

BWV 48   *Ich elender Mensch, wer wird mich erlösen*

"O wretched man that I am, who shall deliver me from the body of this death?" As he enables the paralytic man to walk, Jesus relates the physical healing directly to the forgiveness of sins: "The poison born of sin rages in my breast and veins. My world becomes a house of infirmity and death." Recalling St. Paul's frustrations from his own sinfulness, the cantata quotes him, Romans 7. It is a typical expression of a person caught in the paralysis of guilt. Through the mercy of God, in Christ the lame walk and the guilty are forgiven: "Spare the soul and make it pure. … The power of Jesus is made known to us. Those who are weak in spirit, he can make their body sound, their soul strong. … My body and soul shall be healed."

Alternate: BWV 38 *Aus tiefer Not schrei ich zu dir*
"In deepest need I call to you, Lord God." The paralyzed man, helped by his friends, desperately seeks Jesus for healing, and in the process he receives both health and forgiveness: "In Jesus' mercy alone can there be comfort and forgiveness for us. … Though my despair, like chains, fetters one misfortune to the next, yet shall my savior free me suddenly from it all."

Year C   Luke 6:27-38

BWV 24   *Ein ungefärbt Gemüte*

"An unstained mind … makes us beloved of God and mortals." This portion of Jesus' teaching demands radical love to all neighbors: "A Christian's deeds and actions … should rest on the same foundation. … If our heart strives for goodness, it must be governed by God's own Spirit." That means behavior in keeping with the 'golden rule', which is quoted in the cantata: "Do not make your neighbor an enemy. … Make yourself the image you would like your neighbor to be." Hypocrisy and all sorts of destructive behavior must be overcome by faithfulness, sincerity, and truth.

Alternate: BWV 138 *Warum betrübst du dich, mein Herz*
Jesus' insistence that his followers love enemies as well as friends not only reveals the great love of God, but convicts sinners of their never-ending need for mercy and forgiveness: "Why are you troubled, my heart? … Who shall deliver me from the body of this evil and wicked world? … Put trust in your Lord and God. … He cannot and will not forsake you. … I put my trust in God, my faith lets him govern. … Now I can live as though in heaven."

MARTIN LUTHER, RENEWER OF THE CHURCH
February 18

John 15:1-11

BWV 82 *Ich habe genug*

"I have enough. ... My faith has pressed Jesus to my heart." With words of consolation and encouragement Jesus bids farewell to his disciples, assuring them of God's never-ending love: "My consolation is this alone: that Jesus might be mine, and I his own." This assurance gave Luther both confidence for his reform efforts and also, like ancient Simeon, peace, as he faced death in 1546: "When will that 'now' come, when I shall depart in peace? ... With joy I anticipate my death."

SUNDAY 8
February 25-29

Year A Matthew 6:24-34

BWV 187 *Es wartet alles auf dich*

"These wait all upon you, that you may give them their food in due season." In comforting words from his Sermon on the Mount, Jesus assures the disciples that they need not be anxious about the future: "When you open your hand, they are filled with good things... Therefore you should not worry or say, 'What shall we eat? What shall we drink?'" Whatever comes, it is in God's care. The cantata's opening lines, recalling Psalm 104, are joined by verses from the gospel, together showing the expansiveness both of the created world and also of God's careful attention to everyone's needs: "For your heavenly Father knows that you have need of all these things."

> *Alternate:* BWV 51 *Jauchzet Gott in allen Landen*
> "Shout to God for joy." Jesus' lessons in godly devotion and trust are examples
> of faith that brings forth confident hope. For this, humankind can raise hymns
> of gratitude and praise: "We praise what he has done for us. ... A grateful spirit
> in return shall show through its devout life, that we are called your children."

Year B Mark 2:13-22

BWV 103 *Ihr werdet weinen und heulen*

"You shall weep and lament, but the world shall rejoice." When criticized for his association with sinners, Jesus contrasts their spiritual needs, which he has come to serve, to the needs of the self-righteous. He draws similar contrasts between the penitence of the unforgiven with the joy of those who know the reality of salvation: "And you shall be sorrowful, but your sorrow shall be turned into joy. ... No physician but you can be found ... who shall heal the wounds of my transgressions." The cantata describes an ironic reversal, quoting John 16, when the faithful suffer temporarily at the hands of the world. Even then, they know a new day is coming and theirs will be the final joy: "I shall make ready for your coming, I have trust in your promise."

Altenate: BWV 135 *Ach Herr, mich armen Sünder*

"O Lord, do not punish a poor sinner. … Kindly forgive my sins and show mercy." Jesus is more interested in meeting and befriending sinners than in separating himself from them. Just as the sick need healing, so sinners need repentance and forgiveness: "Heal me, physician of souls. … I am very sick and weak." Jesus gives comfort to all in need: "Be gone, all you evildoers, my Jesus comforts me. … May he grant us all everlasting happiness."

Year C   Luke 6:39-49

BWV 185   *Barmherziges Herze der ewigen Liebe*

"Merciful heart of everlasting love, move and stir my heart." Jesus' warning about the blind leading the blind is reflected in the cantata, as are more general admonitions to a godly life of mercy, charity, forgiveness, generosity, and non-judgmentalism: "Practice charity and strive while still on earth to become righteous like the Father. … Pull out the beam in your own eye, then concern yourself with the mote in your neighbor's eye." To claim loyalty to Jesus without thinking and acting like him is as foolish as building one's house without a secure foundation: "How can one blind man with another walk along the straight and narrow?"

Alternate: BWV 45 *Es ist dir gesagt, Mensch, was gut ist*

"It is stated for you what is good." Those who follow Jesus should not condemn others, but do good and share God's blessings: "What does the Lord require of you but to do justice, and to love kindness, and to walk humbly with your God?" This is the solid foundation of faith: "I might prove to be a faithful servant… So shall my heart and my mouth be my judges." Such faith yields its fruits: "Grant that I do with zeal what it befits me to do."

TRANSFIGURATION OF OUR LORD

Year A   Matthew 17:1-9

BWV 130   *Herr Gott, dich loben alle wir*

"Lord God, we all praise you … for your creation of the angels. … They are around you, Lord Christ, and around your poor little company; how necessary is this watch indeed amidst Satan's fury and might." The transfiguration of Jesus is a confusing if fleeting vision of his divine glory. However, the disciples' reaction is one of awe and worship, and that response is magnified in the cantata: "O prince of cherubim, let this exalted host of heroes forever minister to your believers, that on Elijah's chariot they may carry them to you in heaven." The majesty of the transfigured Christ is enhanced by a vision of angels overthrowing Satan, of the conquered serpent of primordial chaos, of Daniel's escape from lions and flames, and of Elijah's chariot into heaven. The title hymn is set to the familiar 'Old Hundredth' tune.

Alternate: BWV 225 Singet dem Herrn ein neues Lied
Not long after being reprimanded for their earth-bound mentality, Peter, James, and John witness an appearance of Moses and Elijah with the transfigured Christ. They are overwhelmed and fall down in worship: "Sing a new song to the Lord, let the community of the holy praise him." Jesus raises them and sends them on their way: "As a father takes pity on his young children, so does the Lord with all of us. ... He knows how little strength we have. ... God, be our shelter and our light. ... Praise him for his great majesty."

Year B   Mark 9:2-9

BWV 225   Singet dem Herrn ein neues Lied
"Sing a new song to the Lord. ... Let the children of Zion be happy in their king." Midway through his ministry Jesus is revealed briefly to some of the disciples in heavenly splendor: "Be our shelter and light." This metamorphosis fills them with amazement and fear, and with God's assurance that Jesus is indeed the divine Son. The motet celebrates the glory of Christ in words from Psalm 149 and 150 (see also *BWV 190*): "Praise the Lord for his deeds; praise God for his great majesty." The brevity of the Transfiguration is reflected in lines of the hymn *My Soul, Now Praise Your Maker.* "God knows we are only dust, like the grass that is raked, like flowers and falling leaves." This is all the more reason to sing to God: "Let all that breathes praise the Lord: Hallelujah!"

Alternate: BWV 128 Auf Christi Himmelfahrt allein
In the midst of his ministry Jesus momentarily reveals his divine glory to three disciples. This vision prefigures his resurrection and the heavenly glory promised to all believers: "On Christ's ascent to heaven alone shall I base my own journey to him. ... There, in Salem's tent, shall I dwell transfigured. There shall I see God face to face. ... My eyes shall see him most clearly." Followers of Christ are assured of God's presence throughout life: "Ah, that I could build a tabernacle in advance. ... God does not dwell on mountains or in valleys, the Almighty is visible everywhere."

Year C   Luke 9:28-36

BWV 50   Nun ist das Heil und die Kraft
"Now have come the salvation and the power and the kingdom of our God, and the authority of his Messiah." The illusive vision of a transfigured Christ is not elaborated in any of the cantatas, but this glorious chorus praises God and God's Messiah, whose reign has been revealed to the faithful. Quoting Revelation 12, this signals the ultimate defeat of Satan "who accused them day and night before our God."

Alternate: BWV 22 Jesus nahm zu sich die Zwölfe
"Jesus took the twelve aside and said to them, 'See, we are going up to Jerusalem, and everything that is written about the Son of Man by the prophets will be

[22] accomplished"'. The disciples' human instincts desire to remain secure in the blessed glow of the Transfiguration, but they are yet unable to understand the passion yet to come: "For flesh and blood cannot comprehend at all, like your disciples, the words you spoke. They desire, when you are transfigured, to erect a mighty fortress on Tabor's mountain, but not to gaze on Golgotha." Once again, Jesus himself leads the way to repentance and forgiveness: "My eternal treasure, reform my heart, transform my courage. ... Then draw me to you in peace."

JOSEPH, GUARDIAN OF JESUS
March 19

Matthew 1:16, 18-21, 24*a*

BWV 36   *Schwingt freudig euch empor*
"Soar joyfully to the stars on high." By virtue of his loyalty to Mary and his obedience to God, Joseph is given genealogical and legal status as father of Jesus. Like any parent, and aware of God's special purposes, he rejoices at the child's birth: "For he approaches you in person, the Lord of Glory. ... Now come, Savior of the Gentiles, known as the virgin's child; all the world marvels that God has ordained for him such a birth. ... Even with subdued, weak voices God's majesty is honored."

ANNUNCIATION OF OUR LORD
March 25 *

Luke 1:26-38

BWV 147   *Herz und Mund und Tat und Leben*
"Heart and mouth and deeds and life must bear witness of Christ, without fear and hypocrisy, that he is God and savior." When the angel Gabriel visits the Virgin Mary, to tell her that she will give birth to the Son of God, she is fearful, amazed, and submissive. The cantata, which twice presents the hymn known as *Jesu, Joy of Man's Desiring*, portrays the overwhelming power of God's Spirit and the total yielding of Mary: "Mary makes known the innermost part of her soul through thanks and praise. ... Do not be ashamed, O soul, to acknowledge your savior. ... Prepare the way to you, O Jesus, even now; my Savior, choose the believing soul, and look upon me with the eyes of grace." Through this lowly maiden, God's greatest victory will be won over satanic and worldly forces: "The almighty wonder-hand of the Highest works in the secret places of the earth. ... Jesus remains my joy." This power and victory will be given to Jesus and all who follow him.

---

* If this coincides with Palm/Passion Sunday, *BWV* 182 may be used.

Alternate: BWV 1 Wie schön leuchtet der Morgenstern
The gospel of Gabriel's announcement to Mary is read on the annual festival of the Annunciation, the day for which this cantata was composed. "How beautifully gleams the morning star." Because this day nearly always falls in Lent, the sacramental and salvific dimensions of the Annunciation may be considered: "O heavenly bread, which neither grave, danger, nor death can tear out of our hearts. ... Our souls feel the most powerful impulses of the most ardent love and taste on earth heavenly delight. ... How heartily glad I am indeed that my treasure is the alpha and omega, the beginning and the end."

Ash Wednesday

Year A   Matthew 6:1-6, 16-21

BWV 199   Mein Herze schwimmt im Blut
"My heart swims in blood, for sin's brood in God's holy eyes turns me into a monster ... and I must hide from him before whom even the angels cover their faces." The self-giving disciplines of alms, prayer, and fasting represent a heart that is completely resigned to the will of God: "Silent sighs, quiet laments, you may express my sorrows, for my mouth is closed. ... God be gracious to me, a sinner!" The cantata shows the regret and penitence human sin may cause, but does not lose sight of the unfailing mercy of God, who reaches out to rescue the sinner: "God is reconciled, and ... no longer excludes me from eternal blessedness, nor from his heart."

Alternate: BWV 26 Ach wie flüchtig, ach wie nichtig
"Ah, how fleeting, how trifling is human life." Jesus is insistent that his followers' acts of devotion, such as fasting, prayer, and almsgiving be done with discretion and humility, lest they appear self-serving: "To set one's heart on earthly treasures is a seduction of the foolish world." The quest for riches, admiration, or other reward leads nowhere: "Whoever sat enthroned as a god does not escape dust and ashes, and when his last hour strikes and he is carried to the earth and the foundation of his dignity is shattered, he will be quite forgotten."

Year B   Matthew 6:1-6, 16-21

BWV 135   Ach Herr, mich armen Sünder
"O Lord, do not punish me, a poor sinner." Acts of piety include almsgiving, prayer, and fasting. However, Jesus warns that any of these must be done in humility, not for public display: "Kindly forgive my sins and show mercy." The cantata expresses the sufferings of a most humble penitent, who seeks forgiveness of sins and relief from pains internal and external: "My soul is torn with fear and terror. ... Bring comfort,

[135] Jesus, to my spirit." The combined forces of evil cannot prevail against the comfort that comes from Jesus: "After tears and after weeping he makes the sun of joy shine again." The familiar tune 'Passion Chorale' is heard.

Alternate: BWV 181 Leichtgesinnte Flattergeister
Acts of worship and charity must come forth from hearts of sincerity and love, not from self-serving motives: "Insincere and fickle spirits sap the world's strength. ... Hearts of rock which spitefully resist will forfeit their own salvation and meet at last their doom. ... The endless numbers of harmful thorns ... by these will our strength be choked." Only heaven's values will withstand to the end: "The noble seed will lie unfruitful if we do not live according to the Spirit."

Year C   Matthew 6:1-6, 16-21

BWV 32   Liebster Jesu, mein Verlangen
"Beloved Jesus, my desire, tell me where may I find you?" Although the feelings of separation and alienation from God are all too common among Christians, and the desire to express faith in God can be strong, nevertheless Jesus warns against outward expressions of piety. Lessons on almsgiving, prayer, and fasting are appropriate for the church at the beginning of Lent. "You can be happy if heart and soul are kindled out of love for me." To the faithful who seek a closer relationship with Christ, the cantata directs them to the house of the Lord: "Love me and lead me on, that I may as best I can embrace and love you too and no more be sad."

Alternate: BWV 136 Erforsche mich, Gott, und erfahre mein Herz
The practices of faith require discipline, humility, and sincerity of heart: "Search me, O God, and know my heart." At the beginning of Lent, Christians examine the realities of their own lives and the pains of the world: "The curse which strikes the earth has also smitten the hearts of mortals." In faith, they turn to the Lord: "A day shall come that will pass sentence on what is hidden. ... Though we may be stained by the sins that Adam's fall has brought upon us, if we have found refuge in Jesus' wounds, that merciful stream of blood, we shall be purified."

FIRST SUNDAY IN LENT

Year A   Matthew 4:1-11

BWV 40   Dazu ist erschienen der Sohn Gottes
Jesus is baptized by John, and then his commitment to his mission is tested by the devil: "For this the Son of God has appeared: that he may destroy the works of the devil. ... Sin causes suffering; Christ brings joy, for he has come into the world for our comfort." Depicting the devil as the serpent of destruction, the cantata celebrates Jesus' victory

over evil and the final victory of all the faithful: "The serpent, which in Paradise on all of Adam's children let the poison of souls fall, brings us no more danger; the woman's seed is manifest."

Alternate: BWV 48 Ich elender Mensch, wer wird mich erlösen
When the Lord Jesus himself is tempted by Satan, the tragedy of human sinfulness is underscored. The cantata raises the penitential cry of Lent: "Wretched man that I am, who shall redeem me from the body of this death? ... When the cross's cup tastes bitter to the soul, this cup drives from the soul a fervent cry." Only a return to God can alleviate the burden of guilt: "Lay down the Sodom of my sinful members. ... Forgive me, O Jesus, my sins."

Year B   Mark 1:9-15

BWV 178   Wo Gott, der Herr, nicht bei uns hält
"If God the Lord is not on our side when our enemies rage against us ... then all is lost for us." Following his baptism in the Jordan River, Jesus' ministry begins in the desert with forty days of testing by the devil. Although the gospel does not give the details of this testing, each Christian can imagine the worst temptations he or she has fought. As described in the eight stanzas of the title hymn, which echo Psalm 124, demonic attacks of doubt, deceit, despair, or even persecution can be resisted only under the protection of God: "God almighty is on our side and frees us from their snares. ... He leads his people with a forceful hand across the sea of suffering to the promised land. ... For those who put their trust in Jesus the door of grace is ever open."

Alternate: BWV 80 Ein feste Burg ist unser Gott
"A mighty fortress is our God." As Jesus is tempted by Satan, the supernatural power of evil is manifest: "The ancient wicked enemy truly now besets us. ... We can do nothing with our own might." Fallen humanity can rely only on God's protection: "Let not Satan and his vices enter your soul. ... Drive out Satan and the world. ... And if the world were filled with devils, about to devour us, that would scarcely frighten us, for we shall conquer." The 'good news' is the final victory of Christ: "A single word can destroy him."

Year C   Luke 4:1-13

BWV 54   Widerstehe doch der Sünde
"Stand firm against all sinning. ... Be not blinded by Satan." Jesus' divine sonship is tested by the devil at the onset of his ministry: "Vile sinning seems, in truth, outwardly wonderful. ... But if we look more closely, we see it is but an empty shadow." In the cantata the satanic contest for every Christian is the temptation to sin, recalling the hypocrites of Jesus' time, wicked Sodom, and Eden's forbidden fruit: "Those who commit sin are of the devil, for he invented sin, but if one resists his vile shackles with true devotion, sin will take flight."

Alternate: BWV 179 Siehe zu, daß deine Gottesfurcht nicht Heuchelei sei
The temptations for Jesus are those for everyone: to doubt the reality of God's grace, and to trust in something else: "Do not disobey the fear of the Lord; do not approach him with a divided heart." Reliance on one's own strength or virtue leads to disaster: "Most Christians in the world are lukewarm Laodiceans or puffed-up Pharisees. ... Hypocrites, though outwardly fair, cannot stand before God." Instead, those are justified who come before God in humility: "My God of mercy, have mercy on me."

SECOND SUNDAY IN LENT

Year A   John 3:1-17

BWV 176   Es ist ein trotzig und verzagt Ding
The cantata title is an unflattering quote from Jeremiah 17, describing the human spirit, which no one can make sense of: "There is something perverse and desperate about all human hearts." Nicodemus comes to Jesus at night, seeking answers to the mysterious ways of God: "Nicodemus ventured to meet Jesus not by day but by night." In metaphors Jesus describes the gifts of the Spirit and the Son, given by the mystery of God's love: "Rouse yourselves, fearful and diffident spirits, recover, hear what Jesus promises: that I gain heaven through faith." So too, the merciful ways of God are often beyond comprehension. The people of God will live only by trusting God.

Alternate: BWV 68 Also hat Gott die Welt geliebt
Jesus tells Nicodemus that the kingdom of God is a wholly new form of existence, based on God's love for humanity: "God so loved the world that he gave us his Son . ... My believing heart, exult, sing, jest: your Jesus is here!" As the Savior, Jesus brings redemption, not condemnation: "Whoever believes in him is not condemned."

Year B   Mark 8:31-38

BWV 56   Ich will den Kreuzstab gerne tragen
"Gladly shall I bear the cross; it comes from God's beloved hand." In what may be Jesus' most defining words on discipleship, he speaks to his followers of self-denial for the sake of witnessing to God's reign. Just as he would eventually carry his own cross to Calvary, so they should prepare themselves for hardship and persecution: "Sorrow, affliction, and distress engulf me like waves." With the cross of Christ in hand, the cantata's disciple is willing to face the storms of life, and eager to follow Christ to the peaceful shores of heaven: "Then shall I find strength in the Lord. ... I stand here ready and prepared. ... Then shall my savior wipe the tears from my eyes."

Alternate: BWV 22 Jesus nahm zu sich die Zwölfe
"Jesus took the twelve aside." He speaks to his disciples about his death and resurrection not once but three times. "They understood none of these things." He invites them to take up their cross and follow: "I am prepared and will go from here to Jerusalem, to your passion." Peter resists and is rebuked: "Strike down everything that resists this denial of the flesh."

Year C   Luke 13:31-35

BWV 46   Schauet doch und sehet, ob irgendein Schmerz sei
"Look and see if there is any sorrow like my sorrow. ... Lament, then, devastated city of God." Jesus' heart breaks for Jerusalem, because the people there seem unable to heed God's prophets. The cantata's opening lines from Lamentations 1 reflect that disappointment: "You did not heed the tears of Jesus." Jerusalem will soon be forsaken, like ancient Gomorrah: "Since you do not mend your ways but grow more sinful each day, you must perish." As in all divine warnings, the goal is that sinners turn from their ways, repent, and return to fellowship with God: "Jesus gathers the righteous most lovingly, as his own sheep and chickens ... to dwell in safety."

Alternate: BWV 40 Dazu ist erschienen der Sohn Gottes
Amidst growing hostilities, Jesus laments over Jerusalem. His prophetic mission points toward conflict: "The Son of God was revealed for this purpose: to destroy the works of the devil. ... The light of the world illumines the earth. ... Sin brings sorrow." In the end, Jesus' compassion will be vindicated: "Christ brings joy, for he has entered this world to console. ... Jesus, who can save, will gather his chickens under his wing. ... He is the sun of grace."

THIRD SUNDAY IN LENT

Year A   John 4:5-42

BWV 170   Vergnügte Ruh, beliebte Seelenlust
"Contented rest, beloved pleasure of the soul! You cannot be found in hell's sins but rather in heavenly concord." Jesus meets, talks to, and befriends a Samaritan woman at Jacob's well: "Righteous God, how far man is alienated from you! ... I too should love my enemy like my best friend." For the disciples it is a powerful lesson in kindness and outreach, and remains so for every reader of the gospel. The cantata illuminates the inner peace this woman receives as the message of God's love is extended to her and her people, formerly treated as outcasts: "Let me find this dwelling-place where I may be at peace." When reconciled to God in Christ, the sinner can withstand even abuse from enemies and criticism from friends.

Alternate: BWV 162 Ach, ich sehe, jetzt, da ich zur Hochzeit gehe
"Ah, I see, now as I go to the marriage, happiness and misery." Religious and social laws separate the Samaritan woman from Jesus, but the common need for water and for spiritual refreshment brings them together: "Jesus, help me endure it. ... How has human flesh come to such honor, that God's Son has for ever taken it upon himself? ... Jesus, fountain of all grace ... refresh my soul. ... Come, unite with me."

Year B   John 2:13-22

BWV 102   Herr, deine Augen sehen nach dem Glauben
"Lord, your eyes look for faith." When he enters the temple, Jesus drives out the merchants and money changers, whose enterprises are overshadowing its proper religious purposes: "You strike them but they do not feel it. ... Where is the power of his word if all improvement retreats from the heart?" The cantata sees this perversion of the Jerusalem establishment as a continuation of ancient abuses, quoting a prophetic indictment from Jeremiah 5 and an apostolic warning from Romans 2: "Do you not know that God's goodness entices you to repentance? ... God, who was formerly gracious, can easily lead you before his judgment seat." Matthew, Mark, and Luke place this event later in Jesus' ministry, shortly before his arrest and trial. As always, the hope is for Christians to repent, turn to Jesus, and escape self-destruction.

Alternate: BWV 90 Es reißet euch ein schrecklich Ende
Jesus sees the neglect and misuse of the temple and drives out the money changers and merchants, leading him into conflict with the religious leaders: "A terrible end shall sweep you away, you disdainful sinners." Casting himself in a prophetic role, Jesus foretells his own death and resurrection and God's ultimate justice: "God's kindness is renewed every day, but ingratitude always sins against mercy. ... In peril the Word's power is all the more recognized and revealed."

Year C   Luke 13:1-9

BWV 124   Meinen Jesum laß ich nicht
"I shall not forsake my Jesus, since he gave his life for me." Recent victims of Pilate's purge and of a collapsed tower are reminders of the fate of all sinners who do not repent. "What grave hardship does my soul still suffer here? ... But my soul looks up with faith to that place where faith and hope shine radiant." Yet, as the parable of the fig tree shows, God is willing to forbear whenever possible. With its title inspired by Jacob's statement to the angel in Genesis 32, the cantata expresses a sincere determination to remain faithful to Jesus, despite life's many trials: "Withdraw swiftly from the world, O heart. ... And be contented in Jesus. ... Christ shall ever guide me to the springs of life."

Alternate: BWV 46 Schauet doch und sehet, ob irgendein Schmerz sei

Although suffering cannot always be proportionally related to sinfulness, all are sinful and in danger of judgment: "O sinners, you must not suppose that Jerusalem alone is more than others filled with sin." God seeks repentance, so that divine mercy and patience might allow the fruits of faith: "Yet Jesus shall, even while dispensing punishment, protect and help the righteous. ... When storms of vengeance reward the sinners, he helps the righteous to dwell in safety." In God's love alone is there hope for humanity: "O great God of faithfulness ... spare us for his sake and do not reward us for our sins."

FOURTH SUNDAY IN LENT

Year A   John 9:1-41

BWV 38   *Aus tiefer Not schrei ich zu dir*

"Out of deep distress I cry to you, Lord God." Jesus' miracles of healing, especially giving sight to the blind, and specifically this extended account, illustrate divine compassion for all who suffer and power over the forces of darkness. "In Jesus' grace alone will there be comfort and forgiveness for us. ... How often must new signs soften my heart? ... How soon the morning of comfort appears after the night of distress and cares!" The human condition, exemplified by blindness and sickness, is vividly portrayed in this cantata, which is based on Luther's hymn paraphrase of Psalm 130, *Out of the Depths I Cry to You.*

Alternate: BWV 23 Du wahrer Gott und Davids Sohn

"O true God, son of David." The man blind from birth receives physical sight and spiritual light, able to confess Jesus as 'Messiah': "You, the salvation of all mankind, have indeed appeared to serve the sick and not the healthy." On the other hand, the Pharisees, who think they can see, are blind, and their sin remains: "The eyes of all wait upon you, Lord. ... Grant them strength and light; do not leave them forever in darkness."

Year B   John 3:14-21

BWV 68   *Also hat Gott die Welt geliebt*

"God so loved the world that he gave us his Son." In a nighttime conversation with Nicodemus, Jesus presents a classic, perhaps the greatest summary of the gospel. "My faithful heart, rejoice, sing, be glad. ... He did not just come into the world to judge." Comparing the cross to the bronze serpent in the wilderness, a sign of both punishment for sin and salvation from sin, Jesus makes clear the moral expectations incumbent on the children of God: "He who believes in him is not condemned."

Alternate: BWV 174 Ich liebe den Höchsten von ganzem Gemüte
At the cross, the world is divided between light and darkness, and people are judged according to their faith. Those who respond to God's love come to eternal life: "I love the Almighty with all my heart, he loves me also exceedingly. ... O love without compare! ... God so loved the world ... Jesus gives his heavenly kingdom and requires but this of you: maintain your faith until the end."

Year C   Luke 15:1-3, 11*b*-32

BWV 5   *Wo soll ich fliehen hin*
"Where shall I flee?" The gospel parable commonly known as 'The Prodigal Son' contains many themes. The general desperation expressed in the cantata is common to the sick seeking healing, the persecuted hoping for relief, and the sinful begging for forgiveness: "Seeing that I am burdened by so many grievous sins." Repentance and restoration are depicted vividly by the parable's younger son, who, only after hitting rock bottom, comes to his senses and returns to his loving father: "Sin's turmoil has ... covered my whole spirit, so that God would have banished me as unclean." They are also depicted inconclusively by the older brother, who remains obedient but lacks the gratitude and joy of the father's house, and who has difficulty welcoming back his lost brother. His final response remains to be fulfilled by the reader. The cantata invites each one to return to God, to see Jesus as refuge for all those in trouble: "My dear Savior comforts me. ... However great my crime, he frees and liberates me."

Alternate: BWV 55 Ich armer Mensch, ich Sündenknecht
Only when the run-away son comes to his senses and realizes his self-induced misery, can he begin to be restored: "I, wretched man, a slave to sin, I come before God's presence with fear and trembling. ... I have offended against God." Repentance and forgiveness remain God's good news for all people: "I shall not stand trial, but rather go before the throne of grace to my righteous Father. ... Though I have turned aside from you, I shall return."

FIFTH SUNDAY IN LENT

Year A   John 11:1-45

BWV 156   *Ich stehe mit einem Fuß im Grabe*
Jesus weeps at the grave of his friend Lazarus, and then raises him to life: "I stand with one foot in the grave; deal with me, O God, according to your loving kindness." The cantata reminds all mortals that they stand near the gates of death, and also that in Christ they stand at the gates of resurrection and life: "My life and my death lie, dearest God, in your hands. ... Grant me also that in my living body my soul too may be without sickness and remain ever healthy."

Alternate: BWV 95 Christus, der ist mein Leben

Jesus Christ, 'the resurrection and the life', gives life to Lazarus and confidence to all mortals: "Christ, he is my life; to die is my gain. ... With delight of the heart I would depart from this place. ... I am willing and ready to bring my poor body...back to earth." Martha expresses hope in future resurrection: "I know this and believe it is quite certain that from out of my grave I have access to the Father. ... I will not remain in the grave."

Year B　　　John 12:20-33

BWV 1083　Tilge, Höchster, meine Sünden

"Savior, blot out my transgressions ... my sins are a sore affliction. ... I am but a sinner here." Jesus describes the meaning of his impending death to Greek disciples in terms of a buried seed and of himself raised in victory: "Make me to feel joy and gladness .... for your cross assures me." The paraphrase of Psalm 51 expresses the humility of faith before the Savior, who gives himself out of love for the people of the world: "Give my heart, O Lord, your solace. ... Help me keep your word in mind."

Alternate: BWV 114 Ach, lieben Christen, seid getrost

Followers of Jesus need not fear death: "Ah, dear Christians, be comforted, how despondent you are!" Jesus' own ministry of salvation leads him to the cross: "Endure with patience what you through your own fault have brought upon yourself. ... Prepare your heart that it shun neither death nor the grave, and you shall by a blessed death pass through this sinful corruption into innocence and majesty." Like a seed placed in the earth, Jesus dies in order to bring forth new life: "The grain of wheat will bear no fruit unless it fall into the earth."

Year C　　　John 12:1-8

BWV 227　Jesu, meine Freude

"Jesus, my joy, the pleasure of my heart ... apart from you, nothing on earth matters for me." When Mary of Bethany anoints Jesus' feet, Judas is scandalized by her extravagance. Jesus, however, sees this deed as an act of loving devotion. The motet features all six stanzas of the hymn *Jesus, Priceless Treasure* and intersperses them with verses from Romans 8: "There is, then, no condemnation for those who are in Christ Jesus." Jesus remains the ultimate source of joy and object of adoration among those who are filled with God's Spirit, even in the face of hardship or death: "Away with all treasure! Jesus, you alone are my delight and my desire. ... Good night, those of you whom the world favors; you do not please me."

Alternate: BWV 150 Nach dir, Herr, verlanget mich

"To you, Lord, I lift up my soul." Although Mary of Bethany is criticized for the extravagance of her anointing Jesus, he interprets it as preparation for his own burial. This is an act of devotion, not to be condemned, but honored: "I

[150] am and shall remain content, though cross, storm and other trials may rage here on earth. ... You are the God of my salvation; on you I wait all the day. ... If God remains my faithful jewel, I shall ignore human affliction."

SUNDAY OF THE PASSION
PALM SUNDAY

Year A   Matthew 26:14 – 27:66

BWV 244   St. Matthew Passion: *Kommt, ihr Töchter, helft mir klagen*
"Come, O daughters, help me lament. ... O spotless Lamb of God, sacrificed on the cross." The passion account in Matthew includes some unique and highly dramatic details of the arrest, trial, death, and burial of Jesus. Jesus appears as the royal captive, the apocalyptic Son of Man, whom even the tomb might not be able to hold. "The Son of Man will be delivered up to be crucified. ... One of you is going to betray me." The elaborate setting portrays the effects of Christ's suffering and death on individual believers and on the community: "O man, bewail your grievous sin. ... Behold how my heart and eyes weep bitterly for you. ... My God, why have you forsaken me? ... Make yourself pure, my heart." Several hymns stanzas are included, most notably, four to the 'Passion Chorale' tune of *O Sacred Head, Now Wounded*.

> *Alternate: BWV* 182 *Himmelskönig, sei willkommen*
> The passion narrative is preceded by Jesus' triumphal entry into Jerusalem on 'Palm Sunday' (Matthew 21:1-11). The cantata echoes this greeting: "King of heaven, you are welcome. ... Enter in, you have won our hearts." His truest kingship is seen in his self-sacrifice on the cross: "It is your mighty love, O great Son of God, that has driven you from the throne of your majesty, and made you offer yourself as a sacrifice." The way of the cross remains the way into the reign of God: "Though the world shouts 'Crucify!', let me not abandon, Lord, the banner of your cross. ... Jesus, your passion is unalloyed joy to me."

Year B   Mark 14:1 – 15:47

BWV 247   St. Mark Passion: *Geh, Jesu, geh zu deiner Pein*
"Go, Jesus, go to your suffering. I will lament forever, as I await your consolation, the peace I shall gain through you." The passion account in the earliest gospel portrays Jesus as the heroic victim of perverted religion and political injustice: "It was two days before the Passover and the festival of unleavened bread. The chief priests and the scribes were looking for a way to arrest Jesus. ... Treacherous world, your flattering kiss to the pious soul is a poison." The Christian turns to the suffering Jesus as the ultimate blessing and comfort: "My God, my God, why have you forsaken me? ... God has never forsaken the soul that always trusts... Your death bestowed the light on me and took me from my sinful plight, for Jesus now dwells within me." This passion setting exists only in conjectural reconstruction.

Alternate: BWV 56 Ich will den Kreuzstab gerne tragen
In the passion according to Mark Jesus is singularly desolate, betrayed by his friends and abandoned by God, and the disciples are particularly distant. This tragic portrayal intensifies the call to discipleship for believers in every generation: "I would gladly bear the cross. … It leads me, after my torments, to God, into the promised land. … At last my yoke shall fall from me. … Then shall I, like an eagle, rise up from this earth without ever growing weary."

Year C   Luke 22:14 – 23:56

BWV 106   Gottes Zeit ist die allerbeste Zeit

"God's own time is the very best of times. … Lord, teach us to number our days." The passion according to Luke portrays Christ as a martyr, an innocent victim who witnesses to his faith even at his unjust death. "This is the ancient law, O man: you must perish. Even so, come, Lord Jesus." Besides quotations from Psalms 31 and 90, Sirach 14, Acts 17, 1 Corinthians 15, and Revelation 22, the cantata features two of Jesus' words from the cross which are unique to this gospel: his promise of paradise to the repentant thief and his final self-commendation to the Father: "Into your hands I commend my spirit. … Today you will be with me in paradise." Also heard is the first stanza of Luther's hymn *In Peace and Joy I Now Depart.*

Alternate: BWV 22 Jesus nahm zu sich die Zwölfe
"Jesus took the twelve aside" to say it is necessary that he enter Jerusalem to face his suffering, death, burial, and resurrection: "See, we are going up to Jerusalem, and everything that is written about the Son of Man by the prophets will be accomplished." Believers of every age are invited to follow him, and to find salvation: "My Jesus, draw me to you … to Jerusalem, to your passion."

MONDAY IN HOLY WEEK

John 12:1-11

BWV 227   Jesu, meine Freude

"Jesus, my joy, my heart's pleasure!" Mary's anointing of Jesus foreshadows his death and burial. It also leads to death threats for him and for Lazarus: "Lamb of God, my bridegroom, besides you, nothing on earth becomes preferable for me." Jesus does not fear death, and his disciples need not fear it either: "There is nothing condemnatory for those in Christ Jesus, who walk not after the flesh but after the Spirit. … You are not of the flesh but of the Spirit. … Depart, sad spirits, for my master of happiness enters."

Alternate: BWV 39 Brich dem Hungrigen dein Brot
When Mary's anointing evokes a protest from Judas, Jesus compares this act of devotion to ongoing concern for the poor: "Is it not to share your bread with

[39] the hungry? ... Then your light shall break forth like the dawn." These words from Isaiah 58 call for service to both God and humanity. "How can I, Lord, give you due reward? ... I have nothing but my soul to give to my neighbor. ... Blessed are they, who out of pity attend to others' sufferings."

TUESDAY IN HOLY WEEK

John 12:20-36

BWV 22 *Jesus nahm zu sich die Zwölfe*

In Jerusalem at festival time, Jesus speaks of his own death and resurrection. In these events God's purposes will be fulfilled: "Everything that is written about the Son of Man by the prophets will be accomplished." Greeks and Jews alike are invited to follow Christ into the light and glory of God: "My Jesus, draw me on, and I shall come ... draw me to you in peace."

Alternate: BWV 159 Sehet, wir gehn hinauf gen Jerusalem
Jesus struggles to face the cross: "See, we are going up to Jerusalem. ... Your cross is already prepared for you. ... If you would remain behind, I myself would have to go not up to the heavenly Jerusalem, but alas down to Hell." Nevertheless he foresees his death as the opening of God's glory to Greeks and the entire world and the path on which all his followers might come to eternal life: "I will still embrace you on the cross. ... It is accomplished, suffering is over; from our sinful fall we have been justified in God. ... Jesus, your passion is to me pure joy."

WEDNESDAY IN HOLY WEEK

John 13:21-32

BWV 12 *Weinen, Klagen, Sorgen, Zagen*

As he bids farewell to his disciples, Jesus is troubled, and announces that one of them will soon betray him. This causes confusion and distress, and Judas is sent out into the night. "Weeping, lamenting, grieving, trembling, anguish, and distress are the Christian's bread of tears: they who bear the mark of Jesus. ... Cross and crown are bound together ... I kiss the reproach of Christ, I will embrace his cross."

Alternate: BWV 44 Sie werden euch in den Bann tun
"They shall put you out of the synagogues." At the last supper Jesus recognizes the mounting forces of evil and a growing tension among the disciples, and he speaks to them of their fears and eventual betrayal: "The time will come when whoever kills you shall think he does God a service thereby." Suffering is the fate not only of Christ but also of those who follow him: "The Antichrist ... seeks to persecute the members of Christ. ... It remains the Christian's comfort that God watches over his church."

MAUNDY THURSDAY

John 13:1-17, 31*b*-35

BWV 180   *Schmücke dich, o liebe Seele*

"Adorn yourself, O dear soul … for the Lord, full of salvation and grace, lets you be invited now as his guest." At his farewell dinner Jesus washes the feet of his disciples, as a reminder both of cleansing from sin and of loving servitude: "How precious are the gifts of the sacred meal!" The joys of God's table are offered to all who will come, who will open the door when the Savior knocks: "How souls are nourished here who array themselves in faith." The gifts of forgiveness and love transform human sadness into eternal joy: "Jesus, true bread of life … let me through this souls' meal estimate your love aright."

Alternate: BWV 184 *Erwünschtes Freudenlicht*

On the night before his betrayal, Jesus demonstrates God's covenant of love. By his foot-washing and holy supper, and through his cross and resurrection, the light of eternal life shines: "Desired light of joy that dawns with the new covenant through Jesus, our shepherd … who nourishes our soul … who gives himself for his flock; he loves them to the grave and to death. … He does not shrink from bitter death on the cross."

GOOD FRIDAY

John 18:1 – 19:42

BWV 245   St. John Passion: *Herr, unser Herrscher*[*]

"Lord, our master, whose name in all lands is majestic, show us through this your passion that you, the true Son of God, are to be exalted in every age, even in your deepest woe." The passion account in the fourth gospel underscores the power and majesty of Christ throughout the proceedings, for example, in the contest of nerves between Jesus and Pilate, and in Jesus' unaided carrying of the cross. The setting incorporates a note of triumph in Jesus' dying words, 'It is finished': "It is fulfilled; Judah's hero wins the battle. … I will praise you eternally." Included is the earthquake episode borrowed from Matthew's gospel.

Alternate: BWV 159 *Sehet, wir gehn hinauf gen Jerusalem*

"See, we are going up to Jerusalem." Every step of Jesus' passion is in accordance with the Father's will: "Your cross is already prepared for you. … If you would remain behind, I myself would have to go not up to the heavenly Jerusalem, but alas down to Hell." In his death, victory and hope are accomplished: "I will still embrace you on the cross. … It is accomplished, suffering is over, from our sinful fall we have been justified in God. … Jesus, your passion is to me pure joy."

---

[*] The second (1725) version opens with the chorale text *O Mensch, bewein dein Sünde groß,* "O man, bewail your great sin; for this, Christ, from his Father's bosom went forth and came to earth." It concludes with the chorale text *Christe, du Lamm Gottes,* "O Christ, Lamb of God, who take away the sins of the world, have mercy on us."

RESURRECTION OF OUR LORD
VIGIL OF EASTER

Year A   John 20:1-18

BWV 66   *Erfreut euch, ihr Herzen*

"Rejoice, you hearts; vanish, you sorrows. The Savior lives and reigns among you."
The excitement and joy of the disciples at the triumph of Christ overwhelm believers in
every age. "The grave is broken and therewith our distress; my mouth shall show forth
God's deeds. The Savior lives." The dialog between tenor and alto parallels the conversation between Christ and Mary Magdalene: "Jesus calls us to live with him. ... My
resur-rection is your comfort. ... You who conquer death, for you the grave's stone
yields, the seal breaks."

> *Alternate:* BWV 31 *Der Himmel lacht! Die Erde jubilieret*
> "The heavens laugh, the earth rejoices. ... The creator lives! ... He who chose
> the grave for rest, the holiest, will not be able to see corruption." Mary is the
> first among the apostles to meet the risen Christ: "The Lord was dead, and,
> see, he lives again." In love for him she rushes to tell the others what she has
> seen and heard: "Rise up from dead works; let your Savior live in you. ... You
> must be resurrected in spirit and leave the graves of sin. ... Lead me to life
> everlasting."

Year B   John 20:1-18

BWV 145   *Auf, mein Herz, des Herren Tag*†

"Rise up, my heart. ... If you acknowledge Jesus with your mouth, that he is Lord, and
believe in your heart that God raised him from the dead, then you shall be blessed. ... I
live, my heart, to your delight; my life raises your life on high." Mary Magdalene first
discovers the empty tomb, and only later meets the risen Christ: "You live, my Jesus, to
my delight; your life raises my life on high." Her conversation with and personal
attachment to Christ is dramatized in the cantata's duet, and its descriptions of the joy
that fills her heart: "I am redeemed, I am freed and live now with God in peace and
unity. ... The grave's darkness raises me to heavenly glory. My Jesus lives!"

> *Alternate:* BWV 137 *Lobe den Herren, den mächtigen König der Ehren*
> Mary Magdalene is transformed by meeting the risen Christ, and she hurries to
> tell the good news to the other apostles. Resurrection hallelujahs ring out
> among Christians in every generation: "Praise the Lord, the mighty king of
> honor ... who governs all things so gloriously, who leads you safely on his
> eagle's wings ... who has adorned you so exquisitely ... has rained down love
> from heaven; consider what the Almighty can do, who treats you with love."

---

† = *So du mit deinem Munde bekennest = Ich lebe, mein Herze, zu deinem Ergötzen*

Year C   John 20:1-18

BWV 249   Easter Oratorio: *Kommt, eilet und laufet*

"Come, hasten and run. ... Make for the cave where Jesus lies hidden!" The empty tomb, two angels, and Jesus himself testify to his resurrection, and evoke a wide range of emotions from those who come: "Laughter and joking accompany our hearts, for our salvation is awakened." The oratorio dramatizes the Easter excitement by the soloists' speaking for the men and women at the tomb: "Here is the grave and here the stone that closed it, but where can my Savior be? He has awakened from death. ... Tell me where to find Jesus. ... We are overjoyed that our Jesus is alive again."

> *Alternate:* BWV 4 *Christ lag in Todesbanden*
> "Christ lay in bondage to death, given for all our sin. He is once more arisen and has brought us true life." Based on all seven stanzas of Luther's Easter hymn, *Christ Jesus Lay in Death's Strong Bands*, the cantata expresses both the mystery and the exaltation of that hymn, which itself evolved from an ancient plainchant and a medieval hymn. Mary Magdalene, Peter, and the beloved disciple find Jesus' tomb empty on Easter morning. Later, Mary is greeted by two angels and by the risen Christ. Her sadness quickly turns to joy, and she returns to tell the others. It is her triumphant joy that echoes throughout the cantata: "He has risen again. ... Jesus Christ, Son of God ...did away with sin. ... Here is the true Easter lamb. ... Thus we celebrate the feast with joy of heart. ... Hallelujah!"

RESURRECTION OF OUR LORD
EASTER DAY

Year A   Matthew 28:1-10

BWV 4   *Christ lag in Todesbanden*

The resurrection of Christ is depicted as a cosmic battle of God and the forces of life against Satan and the powers of death, between captivity and liberation: "It was an awesome thing that strife, when death and life wrestled, and life won the victory." The triumphal theme, ending each stanza with the victory cry 'Hallelujah!', as do so many Easter hymns, is particularly prominent in this resurrection account. Recalling the contest between Moses and Pharaoh, Matthew underscores semi-apocalyptic elements in the passion narrative and the comparative impotence of the Roman guards at the tomb. "So let us keep the great high feast. ... Hallelujah!"

> *Alternate:* BWV 145 *Auf, mein Herz, des Herren Tag* †
> The earth trembles as an angel removes the stone to reveal an empty tomb, overcoming the guards. The women hear the angel's message that Christ has

---

† = *So du mit deinem Munde bekennest* = *Ich lebe, mein Herze, zu deinem Ergötzen*

[145] been raised, and that they should tell all this to the disciples. As they return with fear and great joy, they meet Jesus: "I live, my heart, to your delight; my life raises your life on high." Soon the good news is carried to Galilee: "You live, my Jesus, to my delight; your life raises my life on high. ... I am redeemed, I am freed and live now with God in peace and unity. ... The grave's darkness raises me to heavenly glory. My Jesus lives!"

Year B   Mark 16:1-8

BWV 31   *Der Himmel lacht! Die Erde jubilieret*

"The heavens laugh, the earth rejoices." Mark's account of the empty tomb offers the fewest details and no appearances at all of the risen Christ. This in no way, however, dampens exultation over the resurrection, as the cantata clearly expresses: "The creator lives ... and is freed from the bonds of death. ... The Lord was dead, and, lo, he lives again." The mystery of God's triumph over death and re-creation of life for the human race can only evoke endless praise to God and eager devotion to Christ: "Rise then, O God-devoted soul, with Christ in spirit. ... Adam must decay in us, if the new Adam shall recover, who is created in God's image. ... Jesus Christ, the Son of God, will unlock the door of heaven and lead me to eternal life."

Alternate: BWV 249 Easter Oratorio: *Kommt, eilet und laufet*
"Come, hasten and run, you who are fleet of foot, make for the cave where Jesus lies hidden." The women arrive at the tomb of Jesus, only to find his body gone: "A weak woman must put you to shame." They have only the word of an unknown messenger who announces that Jesus is raised and has gone to Galilee: "He has risen from the dead. ... Tell me where I might find Jesus. ... We rejoice that our Jesus lives again."

Year C   Luke 24:1-12

BWV 137   *Lobe den Herren, den mächtigen König der Ehren*

"Praise the Lord, the mighty king of honor ... who governs all things so gloriously, who leads you safely on his eagle's wings ... who has adorned you so exquisitely ... who has rained down love from heaven." Women from Galilee come to the tomb on Easter morning and are reminded by the heavenly messengers of Jesus' earlier words: He would be raised from death. In the words of the hymn *Praise to the Lord, the Almighty*, the cantata praises God for wondrously raising Jesus and calling the new creation into being: "Consider what the Almighty can do, who treats you with love."

Alternate: BWV 66 Erfreut euch, ihr Herzen
"Rejoice, every heart." The women of Galilee arrive at the tomb of Jesus, finding it open and his body gone. Angels remind them that Jesus spoke earlier that he would rise again: "The grave is rent asunder, and our woe is ended. ... To rejoice in the life of Jesus brings bright sunshine to our hearts. ... I shall be triumphant in God. ... Hallelujah!"

RESURRECTION OF OUR LORD
EASTER EVENING

Luke 24:13-49

BWV 158   *Der Friede sei mit dir*

"Peace be with you, you uneasy conscience. Your mediator stands here." On the evening of his resurrection, Jesus appears to the disciples, eats with them, explains to them the scriptural precedents for these events, and promises them the power of the Holy Spirit. "World, farewell, I am weary of you; Salem's refuge suits me." Fears, guilt, and doubts will pass away, the cantata demonstrates, as the risen Christ sends his peace: "I may be a child of peace. ... Here is the true Easter Lamb. ... Its blood marks our door."

> *Alternate: BWV 149 Man singet mit Freuden vom Sieg*
> The risen Christ appears to his followers and renews their understanding and joy: "They sing with the joy of victory in the tabernacles of the righteous. ... Power and strength be sung to God, to the Lamb who has conquered and driven away Satan." Their faith launches the world-wide mission of which Jesus has so often spoken. "Then awaken me from death, that my eyes may see you in all joy, O God's Son, my Savior and throne of grace."

EASTER MONDAY

Matthew 28:9-15*a*

BWV 134   *Ein Herz, das seinen Jesum lebend weiß*

"A heart that knows its Jesus to be alive feels Jesus' goodness afresh." As Jesus' enemies had once plotted his death, now they conspire to cover up his resurrection. It is futile, as the faithful have already met the risen Christ and are no longer afraid to proclaim God's victory: "How the believing mind rejoices! Rise up, believers. ... A splendid renewed light shines in you. ... The Savior lives and conquers with might. ... To prepare my victor's crown you accepted the crown of thorns, my Lord, my God, my risen salvation. ... After your resurrection we do not die, even though we die temporally."

> *Alternate: BWV 50 Nun ist das Heil und die Kraft*
> The apocalyptic vision of the cantata belittles the desperate attempt of the Jerusalem authorities to cover up the actual resurrection of Christ: "Now have come the salvation and the power and the kingdom of our God, and the authority of his Messiah, for the accuser of our comrades has been thrown down."

SECOND SUNDAY OF EASTER

Year A   John 20:19-31

BWV 67   *Halt im Gedächtnis Jesum Christ*

The cantata opens with a call to remembrance, quoted from 2 Timothy 2: "Remember Jesus Christ, raised from the dead." The appearance of the risen Christ to the disciples on Easter evening and again a week later and his gift of the Spirit and peace assure them of his presence and love. They are enabled to take his mantle and become a community of resurrection faith: "My faith knows the Savior's victory, yet my heart feels war and fighting. ... Peace be with you!" The new life of faith will have its trials, but the Spirit of Christ will lead all believers past fears, hardships, and death into triumph and eternal peace: "Jesus summons us to peace and refreshes in us weary ones spirit and body at once. ... In your name do we cry to your Father."

> *Alternate: BWV 134 Ein Herz, das seinen Jesum lebend weiß*
> Unbelief becomes belief as the risen Christ appears to his disciples: "A heart that knows its Jesus to be alive feels Jesus' goodness afresh. ... The living Savior causes blessed times. ... The Savior appears and comforts us again, and through himself strengthens the church militant. ... Your favor and faithfulness —your resurrection makes them new again. ... Therefore praise and thanks be given to you."

Year B   John 20:19-31

BWV 42   *Am Abend aber desselbigen Sabbats*

The first lines of the gospel are quoted, and the promise of Jesus' presence with his followers is recalled: "Then the same evening, being the first day of the week ... Jesus came and stood in the midst ... and utters his Amen." The appearance and words of the risen Christ calm their fears and bring to them the peace of God: "Do not despair, little flock. ... He would protect his church. ... Jesus shields his own people, whenever persecution strikes them." The prayer for that peace and harmony rises from every generation: "Graciously grant us peace, Lord God, in our time."

> *Alternate: BWV 158 Der Friede sei mit dir*
> "Peace be unto you." With these words the risen Savior greets the disciples: "Your intercessor stands here." His presence and divine *shalom* restore their faith and disperse their fears: "Now, O Lord, govern my thoughts, that in this world, for as long as it pleases you to let me stay, I may be a child of peace. ... Here is the true Easter Lamb that God has offered. ... His blood marks our door; faith holds it up in the face of death."

Year C   John 20:19-31

BWV 149   *Man singet mit Freuden vom Sieg*

"There are songs of glad victory in the tents of the righteous." The victory of the Pass-over Psalm 118, which opens the cantata, expresses the power of the resurrection, as it transforms the believer and the angels of heaven: "The right hand of the Lord does valiantly. ... Might and power be sung to God, the Lamb, who has defeated and banished Satan." The disciples are hiding in fear after the crucifixion of Jesus, but when they see the risen Christ, they are filled with joy, peace, and the Holy Spirit: "Honor and victory have come to the devout through the blood of the Lamb. ... Lord Jesus Christ, hear me, hear me, I will praise you eternally."

> *Alternate: BWV 42 Am Abend aber desselbigen Sabbats*
> The first lines of the gospel are quoted, and the promise of Jesus' presence with his followers is recalled: "Then the same evening, being the first day of the week ... Jesus came and stood in the midst ... and utters his Amen." The appear-ance and words of the risen Christ calm their fears and bring to them the peace of God: "Do not despair, little flock. ... He would protect his church. ... Jesus shields his own people, whenever persecution strikes them." The prayer for that peace and harmony rises from every generation: "Graciously grant us peace, Lord God, in our time."

THIRD SUNDAY OF EASTER

Year A   Luke 24:13-35

BWV 6   *Bleib bei uns, denn es will Abend werden*

"Remain with us, for it is towards evening and the day has drawn to a close." A quote from the disciples on the road to Emmaus on the evening of the first Easter Sunday leads to the opening of their eyes and hearts to the risen Christ: "Your divine word, that bright light, let it indeed not be extinguished. ... Let your word shine brightly for us." Like theirs, the faith of every generation is undergirded by the Word and Sacrament, and the presence of the risen Lord gives power to overcome evil and to spread the good news: "Shield your Christendom, that it may praise you in eternity."

> *Alternate: BWV 66 Erfreut euch, ihr Herzen*
> "Rejoice, every heart." Traveling to Emmaus the evening of the resurrection, two disciples are blessed by the presence of the risen Christ, as he teaches them the scriptures and breaks bread with them: "The grave is broken, and therewith our distress. ... Since I have heavenly refreshment here, my spirit seeks here its delight and repose. ... Conquer me and my spirit of doubt ... so that it takes heed of the risen Jesus."

Year B   Luke 24:36*b*-48

BWV 134   *Ein Herz, das seinen Jesum lebend weiß*

"A heart that knows its Jesus to be living feels Jesus' new kindness. ... Arise, believers, sing the sweet songs. ... The Savior lives and conquers with might to bring you salvation." Jesus appears to the disciples after his resurrection, to assure them he is really risen and that these things are in accordance with the scriptures, and to prepare them for what is to come: "The Savior appears and comforts us. ... May your hand embrace us, that we may clearly perceive what your death and victory gain for us." The cantata rejoices in the presence of the risen Christ, whose love gives strength and hope to all Christians: "Each soul sees and tastes our living Lord's infinite kindness."

> *Alternate: BWV 67 Halt im Gedächtnis Jesum Christ*
> "Remember that Jesus Christ was raised from the dead." Jesus appears fully alive to the disciples on the evening of his resurrection. He recalls the scriptures and helps them understand all that has taken place: "My faith knows the Savior's triumph, but my heart feels strife and war." The good news they hear will be carried to all people, bringing peace and salvation: "My Savior, I beg you, appear.   ... Jesus summons us to peace, and restores in us weary ones soul and body alike."

Year C   John 21:1-19

BWV 93   *Wer nur den lieben Gott läßt walten*

"If you but permit God to prevail and hope in him all your days, God will protect you wondrously. ... God comes before we know it and bestows much bounty on us." Even after Jesus' resurrection the apostles are confused and hesitant regarding their mission: "Though Peter toiled all night in vain and caught nothing, at the word of Jesus he was able to catch a great haul of fish." The cantata is based on the hymn *If You But Trust in God to Guide You*, encouraging all disciples to remain faithful to Christ in all their work: "It is he who can work true miracles."

> *Alternate: BWV 6 Bleib bei uns, denn es will Abend werden*
> "Abide with us, for it is almost evening." After eating with his disciples on the lakeshore, the risen Christ questions Peter's loyalty, and commissions him to feed the flock. Peter pledges faithfulness: "Highly praised Son of God, may it not displease you that now before your throne we ask, 'Stay, O stay with us as our light.' ... Jesus, let us see you, that we might not tread the paths of sin. ... Prove your might, Lord Jesus Christ."

MARK, EVANGELIST
April 25

Mark 1:1-15

BWV 30   *Freue dich, erlöste Schar*

St. Mark announces 'the beginning of the good news of Jesus Christ, the Son of God' by introducing the ministry of John the Baptist: "Rejoice, O redeemed host, rejoice in Zion's tabernacles. ... The burden of the law is abolished. ... The herald comes and announces the king." John, in turn greets Jesus, who is baptized and tested before extending the good news: "Your savior calls and cries. ... For now is the time of grace." All are invited to repent and believe: "I will not grieve you, but rather heartily love you, since you are so gracious to me. ... My heart and mouth shall both exalt you, according to the covenant made with you, with well-deserved praise."

PHILIP AND JAMES, APOSTLES
May 1

John 14:8-14

BWV 74   *Wer mich liebet, der wird mein Wort halten*

Philip seeks a vision of the Father, and Jesus himself provides that revelation: "Whoever loves me will keep my word, and my Father will love him, and we will come to him and make our abode with him. ... For whoever seeks, fears, loves, and honors you, to him the Father is attached." Jesus' eventual departure will never remove his presence: "Though he goes away, he comes back again, the highly praised Son of God."

FOURTH SUNDAY OF EASTER

Year A   John 10:1-10

BWV 175   *Er rufet seine Schafen mit Namen*

"He calls his sheep by name and leads them out." As he describes himself as savior of the people, Jesus portrays sheep seeking the safety of the shepherd in the sheepfold, the leader who knows the way home and whose voice they will recognize: "Come, lead me ... my shepherd, my joy. ... True shepherd, I know your kind voice, which is full of love and meekness." The believer who feels lost or confused at times is heard in the cantata, praying for the protection and the way of Christ, the way to God: "He destroys devil and death."

> *Alternate: BWV 104 Du Hirte Israel, höre*
>
> "Give ear, Shepherd of Israel." Like the shepherd of sheep, Jesus describes himself as the gatekeeper and the very gate into God's salvation: "The highest shepherd cares for me. ... Gather up, O good shepherd, us poor and straying ones ... and lead us into your sheepfold." The believer trusts and follows the Savior: "The Lord is my faithful shepherd."

Year B   John 10:11-18

BWV 85   *Ich bin ein guter Hirt*

"I am the good shepherd: the good shepherd lays down his life for the sheep." As a good shepherd Jesus is willing to risk his life for the safety of the people in his care: "He has already given his life for his sheep. … This shepherd will keep the wolf's jaw shut." The cantata focuses on the sacrificial death of Jesus for the welfare of his people: "Behold what love can do: my Jesus takes good care of his flock, and has shed on the cross his precious blood for them."

> *Alternate: BWV 184 Erwünschtes Freudenlicht*
> "Longed-for light of joy, which dawns with the new covenant through Jesus our shepherd. … He loves us, his flock." Like faithful kings of old, like God himself, Jesus shepherds the people like a flock: "Blessed Christians, O happy flock, come, draw nigh to Jesus with gratitude. … Good shepherd, comfort of your people, grant us only your holy word."

Year C   John 10:22-30

BWV 112   *Der Herr ist mein getreuer Hirt*

The title hymn, on which the cantata is based, is a paraphrase of Psalm 23: "The Lord is my faithful shepherd; he has me in his care." Jesus' protective role as 'good shepherd' becomes important as he faces growing hostility between his people and the religious authorities: "It is the Lord's Holy Spirit that makes me light in heart. … I feel no misfortune. … You prepare a table for me before my enemies on every side." God gives blessings and security to the faithful, even against evil forces and death itself: "After death I shall be with Christ my Lord."

> *Alternate: BWV 85 Ich bin ein guter Hirt*
> "I am a good shepherd" says Jesus, who knows and leads his flock in safety: "The good shepherd lays down his life for the sheep … which no one shall steal from him." As one with the Father, Jesus assures his followers of divine protection: "Retreat, all who are my enemies. … I have God as friend."

FIFTH SUNDAY OF EASTER

Year A   John 14:1-14

BWV 229   *Komm, Jesu, komm*

"Come, Jesus, come, my body is weary, my strength is ebbing. … I long for your peace." In his farewell discourses Jesus encourages the disciples to regard him as the key to heaven: "You are the right path, truth, and life." If people know him as the way, the truth, and the life, they most assuredly have found the way to God, ultimate truth, and eternal life: "My spirit has found a good lodging. It will soar beside the Creator, because Jesus is and remains the true path to life." In times of sorrow and loss, even at death, the presence of Jesus gives assurance, peace, and hope.

Alternate: BWV 99 Was Gott tut, das ist wohlgetan
In his farewell speech, Jesus assures his disciples that he speaks the truth and leads them to eternal life with God: "What God deals is dealt bountifully, his will remains just. … His word of truth stands sure. … It leads me on the path of life." Those who follow Christ will see miracles of faith: "Now the covenant contracted from eternity remains the ground of my faith. … I let God alone govern me."

Year B   John 15:1-8

BWV 148   *Bringet dem Herrn Ehre seines Names*

"Give to the Lord the glory due his name." In the words of Psalm 96 the cantata calls on all disciples to praise God, who gives divine life and power. Jesus describes himself as a vine and his disciples as branches on the vine: "I hasten to hear the teachings of life. … I in you and you in me; faith, love, forbearance, hope shall be my bed of rest." An intimate and enduring relationship with God assures the believer of everlasting life: "My God, remain in me and give me your Spirit, governing me according to your word." This connection assures them of life in him, as well as the power to bring forth the fruits of faith, by which God is glorified.

Alternate: BWV 31 Der Himmel lacht! Die Erde jubilieret
"Heaven laughs, and earth rejoices." Jesus, as a life-giving vine, unites and nourishes all who are joined to him: "He lives again; if our head lives, then our members live too. … The vine that now blooms bears no dead grapes. The tree of life lets its branches flourish." The new life of resurrection is already and forever bestowed on the children of God: "So can nothing separate me from Jesus."

Year C   John 13:31-35

BWV 95   *Christus, der ist mein Leben*

"Christ is my life; to die is my reward. … According to God's will I am consoled in heart and mind, calm and quiet." As he prepares to leave the disciples, Jesus gives them the 'new commandment' to love one another. That love will be a public witness to their transformation as his followers: "False world, now I have nothing more to do with you. … If a shepherd seeks his lost sheep, why should Jesus not find me again?" The cantata, beginning with an echo from Philippians 1, highlights the 'farewell' aspect of Jesus' words. This is reflected in the farewell of every believer, filled with hope since Christ is risen from the dead: "So I can now with joyful mind found my resurrection upon my Savior."

Alternate: BWV 76 Die Himmel erzählen die Ehre Gottes

On the eve of his crucifixion Jesus speaks of God's glory at its peak: "The heavens declare the glory of God. ... There is no speech or language where their voice is not heard. ... Listen, you nations, to the voice of God. ... Lord, you have summoned us ... and given us your Spirit." Beginning with lines from Psalm 19, the cantata proclaims that divine love, the ultimate glory, will be seen as the disciples love one another: "May God bless the faithful throng, that they may show forth and increase his honor by their faith, love, and holiness ... so that among us here on earth brotherly devotion may be ever strengthened and renewed."

SIXTH SUNDAY OF EASTER

Year A John 14:15-21

BWV 108 Es ist euch gut, daß ich hingehe

"It is good for you that I go away, for if I do not go away, the Comforter will not come to you. But if I go, I will send him to you." In preparing the disciples for his departure, Jesus promises the Holy Spirit, to confirm and spread the truth which Jesus has taught and to strengthen commitment to the commandment of love. The cantata affirms the presence of the Spirit by faithfulness to the word of Christ and a confident look to the future: "Your Spirit will so lead me that I walk on the upright path. ... He will guide you into all truth."

Alternate: BWV 145 Auf, mein Herz, des Herren Tag †

As he bids farewell to his disciples, Jesus promises his continuing spiritual presence, to know the nearness of God and to be guided into lives of truth: "Rise up, my heart. ... If you acknowledge Jesus with your mouth, that he is Lord, and believe in your heart that God raised him from the dead, then you shall be blessed." Unity with Christ means eternal life with God: "I am redeemed; I am freed and now live with God in peace and unity. ... My Jesus lives! ... I am certain and have trust that the grave's darkness raises me to heavenly glory."

Year B John15:9-17

BWV 172 Erschallet, ihr Lieder, erklinget, ihr Saiten

"Resound, songs, ring out, strings, O happiest hours." Jesus is known to the disciples as the source or channel of love from God, and he summons them to exercise that same love to one another: "God wishes to prepare our souls as temples. If someone loves me, he will keep my words, and my Father will love him, and we will come to him

---

† = *So du mit deinem Munde bekennest* = *Ich lebe, mein Herze, zu deinem Ergötzen*

and make our abode with him." With that refrain from John 14 the cantata celebrates God's love poured out in the Holy Spirit: "Most precious love, enter in." Christ continues to live in and among his faithful.

Alternate: BWV 57 Selig ist der Mann
Repeating his new commandment of loving one another, Jesus pledges his love and friendship to the disciples. This encouragement to face responsibility and hardship is also a promise of God's protection and guidance: "Jesus, if I did not know that you will comfort me, my courage and my heart would fail. ... Believe that I shall be your close friend forever, who shall delight you and bring you to heaven."

Year C   John 14:23-29 *or* John 5:1-9

BWV 59   *Wer mich liebet, der wird mein Wort halten*
In his farewell discourses to the disciples, Jesus instructs them in obeying his word, his commandment of love, and his personal example of humility and faith (John 14:23-29): "Those who love me will keep my word, and my Father will love them, and we will come to them and make our home with them." To understand and meet these challenges, they would receive the Spirit of God: "Come, come, my heart is open to you ... devoted to you alone. ... I am going away, and I am coming to you." The cantata, one of two with this first line (see *BWV* 74), celebrates the coming of the Spirit, to transform and enrich the lives of all believers: "If you loved me you would rejoice. ... I laugh at hell's anger."

Alternate: BWV 48 Ich elender Mensch, wer wird mich erlösen
"Wretched man that I am! Who will rescue me from this body of death?" After waiting many years by the Bethesda Pool to be healed, the sick man was restored by a word from Jesus (John 5:1-9): "Here the hand of the Savior shows wonders also to the dead. ... He can make their body sound, their soul strong. ... Lord Jesus Christ, my only comfort, I will turn to you. ... I am yours and shall remain so."

ASCENSION OF OUR LORD

Year A   Luke 24:44-53

BWV 128   *Auf Christi Himmelfahrt allein*
"On Christ's ascension to heaven alone shall I base my own journey to him." Jesus departs from his disciples on the Mount of Olives. The cantata brings into focus the hope that Christians also shall ascend into heaven, to be forever with God: "There shall I see God face to face. ... I shall gaze on your majesty for all eternity." Christ's resurrection and ascension are a vision of the transfiguration of human existence in eternity.

Alternate: BWV 11 Ascension Oratorio: *Lobet Gott in seinen Reichen*
"Praise God in his kingdoms!" The ascension of Christ forty days after his resurrection is recorded only by Luke (Luke 24:44-53 and Acts 1:1-11). In the Ascension Oratorio, the evangelist narrates the story, and the chorus and soloists respond with praise, separation anxiety, hopeful anticipation of Christ's return, and faith until that happens. "The Lord Jesus lifted up his hands and blessed his disciples. ... He departed from them. ... He was visibly lifted up and went up to heaven." Hymn stanzas praise the triumphant Christ: "Now all lies under you ... at your service ... Jesus, your glances of grace I can indeed see constantly. Your love stays behind."

Year B   Luke 24:44-53

BWV 11   Ascension Oratorio: *Lobet Gott in seinen Reichen*
"Praise God in his kingdoms!" The ascension of Christ forty days after his resurrection is recorded only by Luke (Luke 24:44-53 and Acts 1:1-11). In the Ascension Oratorio, the evangelist narrates the story, and the chorus and soloists respond with praise, separation anxiety, hopeful anticipation of Christ's return, and faith until that happens. "The Lord Jesus lifted up his hands and blessed his disciples. ... He departed from them. ... He was visibly lifted up and went up to heaven." Hymn stanzas praise the triumphant Christ: "Now all lies under you ... at your service ... Jesus, your glances of grace I can indeed see constantly. Your love stays behind."

Alternate: BWV 43 Gott fähret auf mit Jauchzen
Jesus interprets the scriptures to the disciples in light of his own death and resurrection, and sends them out with the promise of the Holy Spirit, to preach repentance and forgiveness throughout the world. Then he departs into heaven. The cantata begins with words from Psalm 47, now fulfilled in Jesus: "God has gone up with a shout, the Lord with the sound of a trumpet. Sing praises!" The ascension proclaims the power of God and the triumph of God's Son: "He has led captivity captive. ... He was received up into heaven and sat at the right hand of God. ... Jesus has now completed his work of salvation." Heaven's gates are opened to all people, as the power of evil has been broken. "I stand here on the way and call on him gratefully."

Year C   Luke 24:44-53

BWV 43   *Gott fähret auf mit Jauchzen*
Jesus interprets the scriptures to the disciples in light of his own death and resurrection, and sends them out with the promise of the Holy Spirit, to preach repentance and forgiveness throughout the world. Then he departs into heaven. The cantata begins with words from Psalm 47, now fulfilled in Jesus: "God has gone up with a shout, the Lord with the sound of a trumpet. Sing praises!" The ascension proclaims the power of

God and the triumph of God's Son: "He has led captivity captive. ... He was received up into heaven and sat at the right hand of God. ... Jesus has now completed his work of salvation." Heaven's gates are opened to all people, as the power of evil has been broken. "I stand here on the way and call on him gratefully."

> *Alternate:* BWV 128 *Auf Christi Himmelfahrt allein*
> "On Christ's ascension to heaven alone shall I base my own journey to him." Jesus departs from his disciples on the Mount of Olives. The cantata brings into focus the hope that Christians also shall ascend into heaven, to be forever with God: "There shall I see God face to face. ... I shall gaze on your majesty for all eternity." Christ's resurrection and ascension are a vision of the transfiguration of human existence in eternity.

SEVENTH SUNDAY OF EASTER

Year A   John 17:1-11

BWV 152   *Tritt auf die Glaubensbahn*

"Walk the path of faith." Jesus prays for his disciples on the night before his betrayal and arrest, that they might be united in their faith and their mission: "Blessed is a chosen Christian who lays his faith's foundation on this cornerstone." The cantata calls disciples to follow the Lord along the road of faith, as he leads them through death and resurrection: "Come, soul, and walk through suffering to joy." Despite impediments of the world, Christ is a strong foundation, providing a way to eternal life: "I will give you the crown after grief and shame."

> *Alternate:* BWV 43 *Gott fähret auf mit Jauchzen*
> "God has gone up with a shout." At the last supper Jesus prays passionately for God's protection of the disciples: "It is he who quite alone has trodden the winepress ... to bring salvation to the lost." All that has been given to Jesus from the Father is now given to them: "He would prepare for me a dwelling by his side."

Year B   John 17:6-19

BWV 100   *Was Gott tut, das ist wohlgetan*

"Whatever God does is well done. ... He is my God, who sustains me when I am in distress. ... He will not forget me. ... He is my light, my life." On the eve of his death Jesus prays for the disciples, that God will continue to protect them and keep them united. The cantata, one of three with this title (see BWV 98 and BWV 99), features all six stanzas of the title hymn. It expresses sincere and abiding confidence in God's care: "Though I am cast onto the rough road by affliction, death, and misery, God shall hold me just like a father in his arms."

Alternate: BWV 98 Was Gott tut, das ist wohlgetan

As he prepares to depart from his disciples, Jesus prays for them, entrusting them to God's care: "His will is just and lasts forever. … The Lord is close to all who trust in his might." May God protect them from evil and keep them holy: "God the Father still lives, forsaking none of his people. … God has a heart that brims with mercy."

Year C   John 17:20-26

BWV 125   *Mit Fried und Freud ich fahr dahin*

"In peace and joy I go forth, according to God's will." Although Jesus' farewell to his apostles is sad, his high-priestly prayer is filled with peace and joy. Assured of God's unfailing love, he extends his petition to all who will come to faith through the work of the apostles, praying for the unity of the church: "Even with failing eyes I shall look to you, my faithful savior. … God, the creator of all things, is salvation and life." The cantata recalls the joy- and peace-filled valediction of Simeon in Luke 2, and of any Christian approaching death: "A word of promise fervently desired echoes mightily on and on."

Alternate: BWV 126 Erhalt uns, Herr, bei deinem Wort

Jesus entrusts to his disciples the faith and unity granted by God, so that the world might see the glory of God through them. He prays for their strength and guidance: "Uphold us, Lord in your Word. … Send down your might from heaven … to fill your church with gladness. … Human might and favor shall be of little avail if you will not protect your poor flock. … Make your people to be of one accord on earth, that we, members of Christ's body, may be one in faith and united in life. … Graciously grant us peace."

MATTHIAS, APOSTLE
May 14

Acts 1:15-26

BWV 177   *Ich ruf zu dir, Herr Jesus Christ*

"I call to you, Lord Jesus Christ." After the ascension of Jesus, otherwise-unknown Matthias is elected to fill the vacant seat of Judas, and becomes one of the apostles. With the others, he is sent to carry forth the gospel in word and deed: "to live for you, to be of use to my neighbor, and to abide in your word. … Pardon me too at this hour, give me a new life. … Grant me constancy to the end: you alone have it in your hands. … Help me, a weak one, O Lord Christ."

John 7:37-39

BWV 173   *Erhöhtes Fleisch und Blut*

Early in his ministry Jesus promises the Spirit in terms of rivers of living water. A new day dawns as God floods the world with this life-giving power: "Raised flesh and blood which God takes upon himself. … A sanctified disposition sees and tastes God's goodness." The cantata praises the exalted Christ for the blessings of redemption, grace, joy, and help: "He gives us his Son, to partake of the gifts of grace that flow like rich streams." For these, Christians pledge their lives and worship: "We would bring, then, our heart as an offering. … Stir, O Most High, our spirit, that the gifts of the highest Spirit may have their effect in us."

> *Alternate: BWV 170 Vergnügte Ruh, beliebte Seelenlust*
> Compared to a fountain of drinking water, Jesus is the source of God's life-giving Spirit: "Contented rest, beloved pleasure of the soul, you cannot be found in hell's sins, but rather in heavenly concord. You alone strengthen the weak breast. …Therefore nothing but virtue's gifts shall have their dwelling in my heart. … My heart flees from anger and resentment and wishes only to live with God, who is himself called Love."

PENTECOST

DAY OF PENTECOST

Year A   John 20:19-23

BWV 34   *O ewiges Feuer, o Ursprung der Liebe*

"O eternal fire, O source of love, enkindle our hearts and consecrate them." As the risen Christ met with his disciples on the evening of the resurrection and breathed into them the Holy Spirit of resurrection and peace, so fifty days later on the day of Pentecost the Spirit is poured out on a great company. The Spirit appears as flames on each of the believers, and this image dominates the cantata: "Let heavenly flames penetrate and well up. … Let our souls please you in faith … our hearts keep your Word of truth." The prayer is that the Spirit of God infuse the human spirits, filling the people with love, faith, and peace: "Blessed are you … whom God has selected for his dwelling. … His blessing works mightily to send peace upon Israel, peace upon you."

> *Alternate: BWV 59 Wer mich liebet, der wird mein Wort halten*
> In the fourth gospel Jesus imparts his Spirit on the day of his resurrection, blessing the disciples with divine peace: "Whoever loves me will keep my word, and my Father will love him, and we will come to him and make our abode with him. … He promises, together with the Father and the Holy Spirit, to dwell in our hearts." The coming of the Holy Spirit continues and guarantees the presence of God in every time and place: "Come, Holy Spirit, Lord God, fill with the goodness of your grace the heart, will, and mind of your believers."

Year B   John 15:26-27; 16:4*b*-15

BWV 226   Der Geist hilft unsrer Schwachheit

As Jesus meets with the disciples for the last time before his death, he promises blessings for them in the future, when the Holy Spirit will come upon them: "The Spirit helps our weakness, for we do not know for what we should pray." In words from Romans 8 the motet recalls the outpouring of the Spirit at Pentecost: "He knows what is the mind of the Spirit, for he makes intercession for the saints according to the will of God." One stanza of Luther's Pentecost hymn *Come, Holy Ghost, God and Lord* prays that such spiritual power may come to every generation of believers: "Holy fire, sweet comfort, now help us joyfully and comforted to remain constant in your service."

> *Alternate: BWV 34 O ewiges Feuer, o Ursprung der Liebe*
> In preparing the disciples for his departure, Jesus promises an 'Advocate' who will confirm all that has been said and will guide them more deeply into the truth: "Let heavenly flames penetrate and well up . ... Let our souls please you in faith. ... Blessed are you ... whom God has selected for his dwelling. ... His blessing works mightily to send peace upon Israel, peace upon you."

Year C   John 14:8-17, 25-27

BWV 74   Wer mich liebet, der wird mein Wort halten

Jesus affirms keeping his commandment to love one another as an indication of loving him: "Those who love me will keep my word." To help his disciples do this, he gives the gift of his Spirit, the divine Advocate, who will provide the understanding and peace that they need: "I am going away, and I am coming to you." The cantata, one of two with this first line (see *BWV 59*), opens the believer's heart to the Spirit, and looks forward joyfully to the blessings God will bestow: "Come, hasten, tune your strings and sing lively, happy songs. Though he leaves, he shall return, the highly exalted Son of God."

> *Alternate: BWV 172 Erschallet, ihr Lieder, erklinget, ihr Saiten*
> "Resound, O songs, ring out, O strings." With the coming of the Holy Spirit, the disciples have the full revelation of God, which Jesus himself is, united in truth and glory: "Those who love me will keep my word. ... O paradise of souls, through which God's Spirit breathes, the Spirit that blew at creation. ... Prepare yourself, the Comforter draws near. ... Your Word, your Spirit, your body and blood restore my heart."

THE HOLY TRINITY

Year A   Matthew 28:16-20

BWV 129   *Gelobet sei der Herr, mein Gott*

"Praised be the Lord, my God, my light, my life, my creator. ... Praised be the Lord ... the Father's dearest Son ... who has redeemed me with his precious blood. ... Praised be the Lord ... the Father's priceless Spirit, who ... counsels me, comforts and helps me." Jesus' great commission includes the instruction to baptize in the name of the Father, the Son, and the Holy Spirit. These three names of the one God have been included in the baptismal formula ever since, invoking the Holy Trinity. The cantata presents all five stanzas of the title hymn, giving honor to each person of the Trinity, who is eternal and most holy: "Praised be my God in all eternity!"

> *Alternate: BWV* 176 *Es ist ein trotzig und verzagt Ding*
> "There is something stubborn and faint-hearted." With all the authority of God, Jesus commissions his disciples to proclaim the gospel to all nations. Whatever fears or reservations they may have, Jesus will always be present with them: "I fear that by day my powerlessness cannot endure. Yet I comfort myself ... for all who but believe in you shall not be lost." The triune God is impressed on lives through teaching and baptism: "I shall there above with thanks and praise glorify Father, Son, and Holy Spirit, which are called triune ... one essence, three persons."

Year B   John 3:1-17

BWV 174   *Ich liebe den Höchsten von ganzem Gemüte*

"I love the Almighty with all my heart; he loves me also exceedingly." Jesus speaks to Nicodemus about God's salvation in terms of Father, Son and Holy Spirit. That mixture of terms has developed into the church's teaching about the Trinity. The cantata focuses primarily on the divine love that has been shown in the coming of the Son as a Savior from sin: "The Father has delivered his Son's life up to death for the sake of sinners. ... God so loved the world!" In return, the believer can only respond with appreciation and devotion: "Grasp salvation, you hands of faith."

> *Alternate: BWV* 68 *Also hat Gott die Welt geliebt*
> "God so loved the world that he gave us his Son." By water and the Holy Spirit the miracle of the cross opens God's kingdom to all believers: "Whoever trusts that Jesus was born for him shall be forever unforsaken." The pledge of the triune God is the salvation of the world: "He did not come into the world to judge. ... He who believes in him is not condemned."

Year C   John 16:12-15

BWV 165   *O heiliges Geist- und Wasserbad*

"O sacred spring of water and the Spirit, which admits us to God's kingdom and inscribes us in the book of life!" Jesus teaches the disciples about the Spirit and the

[165] Father, both in connection to himself. The cantata, remembering that the Holy Trinity is celebrated on the octave of Pentecost, speaks of the coming of the Holy Spirit through the waters of baptism: "How blest is a Christian … who becomes a child of grace and bliss … when baptized." The church continues to administer baptism in the triune name, in which alone come forgiveness, salvation, and eternal life: "Grant that I may be joyful and renew this bond of mercy. … His word, his baptism, his supper help to thwart every disaster."

Alternate: BWV 108 Es ist euch gut, daß ich hingehe
"It is good for you that I go away." In his valediction Jesus identifies his ministry with that of the Father and the Holy Spirit: "If I do not go away the Comforter will not come." By the power of the Spirit, disciples can continue to hear and understand the Father's word, the word they know in Christ: "No doubt can deter me from heeding, Lord, your word. … Your Spirit will so govern me that I may tread the proper path. … When the Spirit of truth comes, he will guide you into all truth."

SUNDAY 8
May 24-28 *

Year A   Matthew 6:24-34

BWV 187   *Es wartet alles auf dich*
"These wait all upon you, that you may give them their food in due season." In comforting words from his Sermon on the Mount, Jesus assures the disciples that they need not be anxious about the future: "When you open your hand, they are filled with good things. … Therefore you should not worry or say, 'What shall we eat? What shall we drink?'" Whatever comes, it is in God's care. The cantata's opening lines, recalling Psalm 104, are joined by verses from the gospel, together showing the expansiveness both of the created world and also of God's careful attention to everyone's needs: "For your heavenly Father knows that you have need of all these things."

Alternate: BWV 51 Jauchzet Gott in allen Landen
"Shout with joy to God, all lands." Jesus' lessons in godly devotion and trust are examples of faith that brings forth confident hope. For this, humankind can raise hymns of gratitude and praise: "We praise what he has done for us. … A grateful spirit in return shall show through its devout life, that we are called your children."

Year B   Mark 2:13-22

BWV 103   *Ihr werdet weinen und heulen*
"You shall weep and lament, but the world shall rejoice." When criticized for his association with sinners, Jesus contrasts their spiritual needs, which he has come to serve, to the needs of the self-righteous. He draws similar contrasts between the penitence of the

---

* If this occurs *after* Holy Trinity Sunday

unforgiven with the joy of those who know the reality of salvation: "And you shall be sorrowful, but your sorrow shall be turned into joy. … No physician but you can be found … who shall heal the wounds of my transgressions." The cantata describes an ironic reversal, quoting John 16, when the faithful suffer temporarily at the hands of the world. Even then, they know a new day is coming and theirs will be the final joy: "I shall make ready for your coming, I have trust in your promise."

Altenate: BWV 135 Ach Herr, mich armen Sünder
"O Lord, do not punish a poor sinner. … Kindly forgive my sins and show mercy." Jesus is more interested in meeting and befriending sinners than in separating himself from them. Just as the sick need healing, so sinners need repentance and forgiveness: "Heal me, physician of souls. … I am very sick and weak." Jesus gives comfort to all in need: "Be gone, all you evildoers, my Jesus comforts me. … May he grant us all everlasting happiness."

Year C   Luke 6:39-49

BWV 185   Barmherziges Herze der ewigen Liebe
"Merciful heart of everlasting love, move and stir my heart." Jesus' warning about the blind leading the blind is reflected in the cantata, as are more general admonitions to a godly life of mercy, charity, forgiveness, generosity, and non-judgmentalism: "Practice charity and strive while still on earth to become righteous like the Father. … Pull out the beam in your own eye, then concern yourself with the mote in your neighbor's eye." To claim loyalty to Jesus without thinking and acting like him is as foolish as building one's house without a secure foundation: "How can one blind man with another walk along the straight and narrow?"

Alternate: BWV 45 Es ist dir gesagt, Mensch, was gut ist
"We have told you what is good." Those who follow Jesus should not condemn others, but do good and share God's blessings: "What does the Lord require of you but to do justice, and to love kindness, and to walk humbly with your God?" This is the solid foundation of faith: "I might prove to be a faithful servant. … So shall my heart and my mouth be my judges." Such faith yields its fruits: "Grant that I do with zeal what it befits me to do."

SUNDAY 9
May 29 – June 4 *

Year A   Matthew 7:21-29

BWV 45   Es ist dir gesagt, Mensch, was gut ist
Jesus concludes his Sermon on the Mount with the parable of houses built on sand and on rock, indicating the foolish and wise listener, respectively. The cantata opens with

---

* If this occurs *after* Holy Trinity Sunday

[45] words of Micah 6, summarizing that prophet's vision of the faithful life: "You have been told, O man, what is good and what the Lord requires of you … his word as a plumb line by which my foot shall be intent at all times to proceed." Since there is therefore no excuse for not knowing God's will and purpose, what is right and wrong, Jesus' own words are harsh to those who say one thing and do another: "There will be many who say to me on that day, 'Lord! Lord!' … The will of the Lord must be done; yet his assistance is also certain. … When I do it, then grant that it prospers."

> *Alternate: BWV 109 Ich glaube, lieber Herr, hilf meinem Unglauben*
> How easy it is to deceive oneself by believing in something false: "I believe, dear Lord, help my unbelief." Without faithfulness there is only eventual disaster: "I already sink to the earth from worry, which casts me down to destruction." Jesus' words reveal the Father's will and offer a secure foundation: "Eyes of faith shall behold the salvation of the Lord. … Whoever builds on this rock … I have yet never seen that person fall."

Year B   Mark 2:23 – 3:6

BWV 76, part 1   *Die Himmel erzählen die Ehre Gottes*

"The heavens declare the glory of God." That Jesus interprets the Sabbath laws in favor of performing deeds that are necessary and helpful arouses opposition from the Pharisees. Although these issues are not addressed directly, the cantata, beginning with a quote from Psalm 19, demonstrates that the entire cosmos is of God, and that the welfare of human beings supersedes hard-hearted legalism: "God does not fail to manifest himself … and calls through messengers without number: Rise up and come to my feast of love. … Hasten to his throne of grace. … You have illumined and quickened us, refreshed and nourished us with yourself, and given us your Spirit."

> *Alternate: BWV 101 Nimm von uns, Herr, du treuer Gott*
> To reveal his critics' hypocrisy, Jesus raises issues of Sabbath observances, namely, that the needs of humanity supersede ritual observances. God's mercy alone brings forgiveness, righteousness, and peace: "Take from us, faithful God, the grave punishment and great distress that we with our countless sins have truly merited. … Through your faithfulness … appear to us with solace and deliverance. … Show me too mercy for evermore, O merciful God."

Year C   Luke 7:1-10

BWV 25   *Es ist nichts Gesundes an meinem Leibe*

The Centurion comes to Jesus, begging him to heal his dear slave: "There is no soundness in my flesh because of your indignation." Though he is a man of authority, he has no power over sickness and no immunity from death, and feels unworthy even to receive Jesus into his house. "The entire world is but a hospital, where countless human beings and even children in the cradle lie gravely ill." The cantata describes the sense of worthlessness and desperation the man feels: "You alone, Jesus Christ, my physician, know the best cure for my soul. … Have mercy, O healer and helper of all who ail." He departs justified, and the slave is healed.

Alternate: BWV 17 Wer Dank opfert, der preiset mich
"Whoever gives thanks glorifies me." In this incident of healing, it is Jesus who is amazed. The humility and trust of the Centurion are laudable: "To those who go the right way I will show the salvation of God." Such faith permits health and wholeness: "What abundance of goodness you give me! … So the Lord does to us wretches, if we fear him with pure childlike awe."

VISIT OF MARY TO ELIZABETH
May 31

Luke 1:39-57

BWV 10   Meine Seele erhebt den Herren
"My soul magnifies the Lord, and my spirit rejoices in God, my Savior." The praise that Mary sings following her visit to Elizabeth is a joyful response to her becoming the mother of the Savior, and to his actual arrival: "You have done so much for me, that I cannot count or note it all." It also foretells the tone of the Savior's mission, as envisioned by Luke: "Those who are full of pride and arrogance his hand will scatter like chaff." The greatness of God, seen primarily in divine mercy and justice, receives more emphasis than the momentous events which evoked this song: "The Savior was born, the eternal Word appeared in the flesh. … God's Word is full of grace and truth." In the cantata Mary's great song *Magnificat* appears in its German paraphrase, with a traditional melody being heard in three of the movements.

Alternate: BWV 243 Magnificat anima mea
"My soul proclaims the greatness of the Lord." Overwhelmed with her super-natural pregnancy, Mary visits her relative Elizabeth, who is also expecting a child. Afterwards Mary praises God for the miracle: "You, Lord, have looked with favor on your lowly servant. From this day all generations will call me blessed. You, the Almighty, have done great things for me … the promise made to our forebears, to Abraham and his children forever." The Christmas interpolations of this *Magnificat* setting would be omitted on this occasion.

SUNDAY 10
June 5-11 *

Year A   Matthew 9:9-13, 18-26

BWV 2   Ach, Gott, vom Himmel sieh darein
"O God, look down from heaven and take pity on us." Psalm 12, appointed for use on St. Bartholomew's Day but not on any Sunday, is paraphrased in a hymn by Luther. The first and last stanzas of the hymn open and close the cantata, the other stanzas adapted as recitatives and arias. Although the gospel recounts the call of the disciple

---

* If this occurs *after* Holy Trinity Sunday

[2] Matthew, it is the need for physical and spiritual healing that colors the cantata: "Faith is quite extinguished among all the children of men. ... They resemble the graves of the dead." As the ruler whose daughter had died and as the hemorrhaging woman, those in affliction continue to cry out for help and to cling faithfully to God in times of doubt, opposition, and pain. "Therefore God says, 'I must be their helper.' ... The bright sunshine of pure truth shall, with new strength that brings comfort and life, refresh and delight them."

> *Alternate: BWV 103 Ihr werdet weinen und heulen*
> When Jesus heals a sick woman and restores life to a girl, he is touched by the suffering of many. As a physician he comes to make people well, physically and spiritually: "You shall weep and lament, but the world shall rejoice. ... Now you shall be sorrowful, yet your sorrow shall be turned into joy. ... No physician is to be found other than you." Through faith, suffering yields to joy: "Your brief suffering shall be turned into joy and everlasting welfare."

Year B   Mark 3:20-35

BWV 76, part 2   Die Himmel erzählen die Ehre Gottes ... Gott segne

"May God bless the faithful throng." Baffled by Jesus' amazing words and deeds, people accuse him of being demon-possessed. He points out the folly of that possibility, of Satan's fighting against himself. Rather, Jesus is on the side of all who do the will of God. The second part of the cantata opens with a blessing on the true family of God. The Christian is aware of hostility on all sides, but celebrates the love of God revealed in the community of faith: "To embrace Christ with my faith I shall relinquish all pleasure. ... Love, O Christians, in your deeds. Jesus dies for his brothers, and they die for each other, for he has joined them together."

> *Alternate: BWV 80 Ein feste Burg ist unser Gott*
> The scribes from Jerusalem accuse Jesus of being in league with the devil, and he shows them the blasphemy of their claim. "A mighty fortress is our God, a sure defense and sword. ... The ancient wicked enemy truly now besets us." Jesus and his followers are, rather, destroying the powers of evil by doing God's will: "Come into my heart's abode, Lord Jesus, my desiring. Drive out Satan and the world, and let your image gleam in me anew. ... And if the world were filled with devils, that would scarcely frighten us, for we shall conquer."

Year C   Luke 7:11-17

BWV 161   Komm, du süße Todesstunde

"Come, sweet hour of death. ... World, your delights weigh heavily." Moved with pity for a bereaved mother, Jesus restores her son to life: "Pale death is my dawn. ... My desire is ... soon to be with Christ." The cantata illustrates that, as Jesus overcomes death, occasionally during his ministry and definitively by his own resurrection, so

Christians need no longer fear the power of death, because it is only temporary, and from it arises eternal life: "Let the spirit, the body's guest, dress in immortality. ... How can death then harm me?"

Alternate: BWV 156 Ich stehe mit einem Fuß im Grabe
"I stand with one foot in the grave." Despite the funeral ceremonies, Jesus raises a dead man to life: "At my soul's departure, receive it, Lord, into your hand. ... Only let my end be a blissful one." In giving life, Jesus glorifies God and brings joy and hope to humanity: "My life and my death are all in your hands. ... Let my affliction not last long. ... Grant to me as well that in my living body my soul be free from sickness and healthy at all times."

BARNABAS, APOSTLE
June 11

Matthew 10:7-16

BWV 126   Erhalt uns, Herr, bei deinem Wort
"Uphold us, Lord, by your word." Armed only with the gospel, the apostles are sent to extend the kingdom of heaven: "Man's favor and might would be of little use, if you would not protect this poor little band of men." Their lives are in themselves witnesses to both the grace and the urgency of the word: "Grant your people one mind on earth, that we, the members of Christ's body, may be one in faith, united in life." Proceeding with integrity and care, apostles bring God's blessing to the world: "Your word and truth will be manifest ... so that you make the teaching of the holy word fruitful in blessing."

SUNDAY 11
June 12-18 *

Year A   Matthew 9:35 – 10:23

BWV 104   Du Hirte Israel, höre
"Shepherd of Israel, give ear. ... The highest shepherd cares for me: what are my cares?" Jesus sees a world ready and waiting for the gospel, and he gathers and sends the apostles to proclaim it. Their work will evoke opposition, but must be dispatched quickly. The opening section of the cantata invokes God as 'shepherd' in the words of Psalm 80, and prayers follow for guidance and protection in any challenge of the future: "If the wilderness makes me too anxious, still my weak step hurries on. ... Ah, gather up, O Good Shepherd, us poor and straying ones...and lead us into your sheepfold."

---

* If this occurs *after* Holy Trinity Sunday

Alternate: BWV 177 Ich ruf zu dir, Herr Jesu Christ

Jesus gives his disciples instructions, which are stern and urgent: "I call upon you, Lord Jesus Christ ... to live for you, to be of use to my neighbor, and to abide by your word. ... Grant that from the bottom of my heart I may forgive my enemies." Through their work, healing and teaching would come to the towns and villages of Palestine: "Let your word always be my food to nourish my soul, to defend me when misfortune comes. ... Help me, a weak one, O Lord Christ."

Year B   Mark 4:26-34

BWV 188   *Ich habe meine Zuversicht*

The cantata speaks of trusting in God's power and purpose, even when outward evidence is slim: "I have placed my trust in the faithful God." In parables of seed germination and growth, Jesus teaches the disciples about the mysterious spread of the gospel: "Though he at first conceals his love, his heart, which he can never withdraw, in secret cares." Beneath the surface, God stirs new life, even when worldly powers falter: "He does not and cannot wish us evil. ... Unfathomable is the way in which the Lord guides his people. ... Blessed be all who trust in God."

Alternate: BWV 69a Lobe den Herrn, meine Seele

"Praise the Lord, my soul." Like a seed secretively growing, God's influence miraculously unfolds in the world: "O my soul, rise up and tell what God has shown to you. ... I cannot, O Lord, count your wonders any more than I can count the stars." Divine mysteries are revealed only as people trust the power and mercy of God: "What God has done is well done; to this I shall be constant."

Year C   Luke 7:36 – 8:3

BWV 150   *Nach dir, Herr, verlanget mich*

"To you, Lord, I lift up my soul." The woman who anoints Jesus, who in Luke's account is a repentant sinner, is honored for her humility and generosity: "O my God, in you I trust; do not let me be put to shame; do not let my enemies exult over me." The cantatas do not address this event directly, but this cantata, based on Psalm 25, illustrates the faith, contentment, and confidence which Jesus praises, and the joy and victory that come from God: "For you I wait all day long. ... Entrust both thought and deed to God. ... Christ, who stands by us, helps me daily win the battle."

Alternate: BWV 39 Brich dem Hungrigen dein Brot

Through her extravagant acts of repentant devotion, an unwelcomed guest is forgiven of her many sins. All present learn that true love finds ways of compassionate service: "Share your bread with the hungry, and bring the homeless poor into your house. ... Then your light shall break forth like the dawn, and your healing shall spring up quickly; your vindication shall go before you, the glory of the Lord shall be your rear guard. ... Do not neglect to do good."

SUNDAY 12
June 19-25 *

Year A   Matthew 10:24-39

BWV 114   *Ach, lieben Christen, seid getrost*

"Ah, dear Christians, be of good courage." Comparing the fate of the disciples to his own, Jesus forewarns them of ridicule and persecution to come, once they embark on their mission. His principal message is that they be fearless and resolute, knowing that their work will finally be vindicated by God: "To Jesus' fatherly hand alone I will turn in my weakness. ... Well then, prepare your breast so that it shuns not death and grave." The cantata assures sinners that they can return to God forgiven and renewed: "Consider your soul and present it to the Savior. ... Whether we wake or sleep, we are the Lord's; in Christ we are baptized."

Alternate: BWV 112 *Der Herr ist mein getreuer Hirt*
"The Lord is my faithful shepherd." Sending his disciples out 'like sheep into the midst of wolves', Jesus tells them to have no fear: "It is his Holy Spirit that makes me cheerful. ... I fear no misfortune in persecution, suffering, tribulation, and the world's malice." Although hardship or persecutions may come, God always watches over his people as a shepherd cares for his flock: "I will remain always in the house of the Lord, on earth in the Christian community, and after death I shall be there with Christ my Lord."

Year B   Mark 4:35-41

BWV 81   *Jesus schläft, was soll ich hoffen*

"Jesus sleeps, what hope is there for me?" Caught in a storm on the lake, the disciples cry in fear to Jesus, who was asleep in the boat: "The foam-crested billows of Belial's waters redouble their rage. ... The raging flood seeks to weaken the power of faith." He stills the storm and gently upbraids them for their panic: "O you of little faith, why are you so afraid? ... Be still, storm and wind." The cantata speaks of fears in human life, whenever God seems remote or uncaring. The word of peace that is heard from Jesus brings comfort and confidence: "Happy am I, my Jesus speaks. My helper has awakened; the raging waves, misfortune's night, and all sorrows must now end. ... Jesus will protect me."

Alternative: BWV 14 *Wär Gott nicht mit uns diese Zeit*
"If God were not with us ... we should have despaired." Matthew's parallel for today's gospel inspired the cantata. The wind and waves terrify the disciples: "Their rage, like violent floods, would have drowned us with foaming waters." Jesus calms the storm and rouses awe and faith in his disciples: "As violent waves rage against us, your hands will still protect us. ... Our help is in the name of the Lord, the God of heaven and earth."

---

* If this occurs *after* Holy Trinity Sunday

Year C   Luke 8:26-39

BWV 127   *Herr Jesu Christ, wahr' Mensch und Gott*

"Lord Jesus Christ, true man and God … have mercy on me for all my sins." When Jesus heals the man at Gerasene, the exorcized demon recognizes him as 'Jesus, Son of the Most High God.' The title of this cantata reflects that confession, as well as the probable message that the man later proclaimed throughout the whole city. Jesus' true humanity is seen vividly in his own suffering, and his true divinity, in his final redemption of all the faithful: "My soul is at rest in the hands of Jesus. … May it be your wish, O Jesus, to intercede for me and speak with comfort to my soul."

Alternate: BWV 78 *Jesu, der du meine Seele*

The man at Gerasene, from whom Jesus drove out demons, begged to follow him, but Jesus sent him back to his home: "Jesus, you have rescued my soul … from the devil's dark cavern. … Hear us as we raise our voices to beg you for help." In his city the healed man proclaimed God's wondrous power: "When a terrible judge lays a curse upon the condemned, you change it into a blessing. … Lord, I believe; help my weakness."

JOHN THE BAPTIST
June 24

Luke 1:57-80

BWV 167   *Ihr Menschen, rühmet Gottes Liebe*

"You people, celebrate God's love and praise his goodness." The divinely predicted and miraculous birth of John to Elizabeth and Zechariah amazes everyone. Zechariah prophesies that his son will be great and will prepare the way for one even greater: "Blessed be the Lord God of Israel, who turns to us in grace and sends us his Son … a redeemer of the world." The cantata calls on Christians to worship God who, after eons of preparation and waiting, has now prepared the way for the Savior: "First John appeared and had to prepare the path and highway for the Savior. … A mute Zechariah praises God with a loud voice."

Alternate: BWV 121 *Christum wir sollen loben schon*

"Christ we shall praise splendidly." Even before his miraculous birth, John praises the unborn Jesus: "John's joyful leaping recognized you, my Jesus, already." John's entire ministry becomes preparation of the way of the Savior by turning people to God: "My heart sighs. … It presents its grateful offering."

Year A   Matthew 10:40-42

BWV 111   *Was mein Gott will, das g'scheh allzeit*
"Whatever my God wills, may that happen always. … He is ready to help those who have firm faith in him." Jesus reminds his followers to place a high value on faithfulness, as it serves as a channel of divine grace: "Blessed is he who chooses this protection in faithful trust." God's way is indeed the way to blessedness. The cantata reiterates that in God the faithful are set free from the power of sin, and all blessings are made available: "Let me not lose heart. Help guide and defend, O God, my Lord, to the honor of your name."

Alternate: BWV 184 Erwünschtes Freudenlicht
As the "longed-for light of joy", Jesus identifies completely with his disciples and with the poor whom they serve: "Jesus, our shepherd … who nourishes our soul, and through word and Spirit turns our steps to the right ways." This gives courage, gratitude, and joy to all who follow him: "Come, appear alongside Jesus with gratitude. … Fortune and blessing are ready to crown the dedicated throng."

Year B   Mark 5:21-43

BWV 109   *Ich glaube, lieber Herr, hilf meinem Unglauben*
"Lord, I believe; help my unbelief." Each miracle of Jesus is a miracle of faith, as in the cases of Jairus and his daughter and of the bleeding woman: "He must soon hasten to help you, to heal your distress. … The eye of faith shall witness the healing power of the Lord." The cantata emphasizes the role of faith, first by quoting the father of an epileptic boy in Mark 9, and then by urging steadfastness even while beset by doubts: "That faith shall finally triumph."

Alternate: BWV 26 Ach wie flüchtig, ach wie nichtig
"Ah, how fleeting, how trifling." Continually confronting sickness and death, Jesus demonstrates God's power of life. Where faith and hope remain, the reign of God flourishes: "Joy turns to sadness, beauty fades like a flower. … Whoever fears God shall live forever."

Year C   Luke 9:51-62

BWV 12   *Weinen, Klagen, Sorgen, Zagen*
"Weeping, wailing, fretting, fearing, anxiety, and distress are the tearful bread of Christians who bear the sign of Jesus." Focusing his attention on Jerusalem, Jesus speaks strong words of warning to any who would follow him there. The hindrances, internal and external, to discipleship are real and may cause unexpected hardship. The cantata reminds modern disciples of the same difficulties that were part of Jesus' call and his own experience: "Cross and crown are bound together. … I shall embrace his cross. I shall follow after Christ." It also turns sorrow into joy with the promise of God's reign.

Alternate: BWV 146 Wir müssen durch viel Trübsal
Whenever Jesus calls people to follow, it is with life-and-death urgency, and not all can be disciples: "It is through many persecutions that we must enter the kingdom of God. I desire to go to heaven." Through whatever difficulties arise, the grace of God must be carried to all: "How this evil world oppresses me! ... I am prepared to bear my cross with patience. ... Soon the time will come when my heart shall rejoice."

PETER AND PAUL, APOSTLES
June 29

John 21:15-19

BWV 93   Wer nur den lieben Gott läßt walten
Three times Jesus asks Peter, 'Do you love me?' and three times Peter affirms his loyalty. Peter is called to follow as a shepherd of Jesus' flock: "Whoever just lets our dear God govern and hopes in him at all times will be wonderfully supported by him in all cross-bearing and sorrow." The apostles find their security in the resurrected Christ: "God's sense of mercy will never forsake us in counsel or deed. ... I will look to the Lord and constantly trust in my God."

SUNDAY 14
July 3-9

Year A   Matthew 11:16-19, 25-30

BWV 113   Herr Jesu Christ, du höchstes Gut
"Lord Jesus Christ, you highest good, you fountain of grace, see how in my spirit I am burdened with sorrows." Jesus upbraids the people for their lack of cooperation, gives thanks to God that at least a few had come to understand him, and invites the disciples to let him bear their burdens. The cantata responds to this invitation, rejoicing especially in the forgiveness of sins: "I know that my heart would break, if your word did not promise me comfort. ... Jesus receives sinners: sweet words full of comfort and life! He gives true rest to the soul and calls to everyone consolingly, 'Your sin is forgiven you'." The redeemed find strength for the present and hope for the future.

Alternate: BWV 155 Mein Gott, wie lang, ach lange
"My God, how long?" Jesus sends his followers into a confused, sometimes hostile society, and offers them support and guidance for their mission: "Jesus knows the right time to delight you with his help. ... He makes your heart weep in troubled times, so that the light of grace may appear all the lovelier to you. ... Let his word be more certain for you."

Year B   Mark 6:1-13

BWV 126   *Erhalt uns, Herr, bei deinem Wort*

"Uphold us, Lord, in your word." As Jesus commissions his disciples for their future work, recalling his own rejection, he warns them of possible opposition: "Send down your might from heaven ... to fill your church with gladness ... that we members of Christ's body may be one in faith and united in life." The cantata features Luther's hymn *Lord, Keep Us Steadfast in Your Word*. It offers disciples in every generation the support of the word of God and the presence of the Holy Spirit who brings it to life: "Your word and truth are made manifest. ... Bless and bring to fruition the teachings of your sacred word." So, divine truth will ultimately triumph wherever the gospel is proclaimed.

> *Alternate:* BWV 183 *Sie werden euch in den Bann tun*
> "They will put you out of the synagogues." Jesus himself is evicted from his hometown, and the disciples begin to see they are called to a difficult mission: "Indeed, an hour is coming when those who kill you will think that by doing so they are offering worship to God." They are, however, sent by one who protects and strengthens them: "Because the arm of Jesus shall protect me, I will follow gladly and willingly. ... Holy Spirit, you who show me the path on which I should journey, help my weakness." Cantata *BWV* 44 opens with the same title.

Year C   Luke 10:1-11, 16-20

BWV 44   *Sie werden euch in den Bann tun*

"They will put you out of the synagogues." When Jesus sends his disciples into the surrounding towns and villages, he warns them of the frustrations and dangers they will encounter: "Indeed, an hour is coming when those who kill you will think that by doing so they are offering worship to God." The cantata, one of two with this first line (see *BWV* 183), begins with this statement from John 16. "Christians on earth must be Christ's true disciples." Through all this, God protects and prospers the faithful, and will bring them finally to heaven: "God watches over his church. So, even though tempests gather ... the sun of gladness has always soon appeared."

> *Alternate:* BWV 139 *Wohl dem, der sich auf seinen Gott*
> "Happy is he who, just like a child, can trust his God." When Jesus sends out the seventy disciples, it is with a sense of urgency that they are to prepare people to receive him. Their confidence and faith are their power and their protection: "Envy and hatred do not upset me. ... The Savior sends his own people into the very midst of raging wolves. ... But a helping hand suddenly appears. ... God is my shield, my help and counsel."

John 14:1-7

BWV 229   *Komm, Jesu, komm*

"Come, Jesus, come ... I will surrender myself to you." In humility Thomas, the reputed doubter, seeks a way to God, not realizing that Jesus himself is the way: "You are the right path, truth, and life. ... Even if my span of life is hastening to its end, my spirit has found a good lodging. ... Jesus is and remains the true path to life."

SUNDAY 15
July 10-16

Year A   Matthew 13:1-9, 18-23

BWV 18   *Gleichwie der Regen und Schnee vom Himmel fällt*

"Just as the rain and snow fall from heaven ... so too shall be the word that goes forth from my mouth." The opening recitative quotes from Isaiah 55, setting the hopeful tone of the gospel parable, for which, albeit in Luke's version, this cantata was composed. "My God, here shall my heart be: I open it to you in Jesus' name; then scatter your seeds in it as if on good ground. ... Let it bring forth fruit a hundredfold." Aware of the world's temptations and hostilities, the Christian prays for protection, assurance, and faith: "Father, forbid that I or any Christian be perverted by the devil's deceit ... and fall away like rotten fruit. ... My soul's treasure is God's word."

> *Alternate: BWV 181 Leichtgesinnte Flattergeister*
> "Frivolous flibbertigibbets deprive themselves of the word's strength." The seed of God's word falls onto many soils, bearing or not bearing fruits of faith: "Hearts of stone that maliciously resist will forfeit their own salvation. ... The infinite number of harmful thorns, the concern of pleasure to increase one's treasures: these shall feed the fire of hellish torment in eternity." By the grace of God, some of the word is heard, believed, and followed: "You can by your almighty hand alone prepare good, fruitful ground in our hearts."

Year B   Mark 6:14-29

BWV 60   *O Ewigkeit, du Donnerwort*

"Eternity, O word of thunder ... I do not know which way I should turn." The cantatas bypass the death of John the Baptist, but the power of God's eternal word and the boldness with which John faced all opposition and death are not lost in this cantata, one of two with this first line (see *BWV* 20): "My help is at hand, for my Savior is at my side. ... I sacrifice my body before the Lord. ... Blessed are the dead who die in the Lord. ... It is enough."

Alternate: BWV 20 O Ewigkeit, du Donnerwort
"O eternity, O word of thunder." John's words of judgment against King Herod cost him his life. "I do not know which way I should turn." Herod remains under judgment, however, as do all godless tyrants, for the saving message of Jesus continues to spread throughout the land. "There is no misfortune in the world that endures forever. ... Ah, if only the world would heed this! Our time is short, death is swift. ... Awake, lost sheep, awake, rouse yourselves from the sleep of sin."

Year C   Luke 10:25-37

BWV 164   Ihr, die ihr euch von Christo nennet
"You who call yourselves after Christ ... your hearts should be rich in love." One of the Samaritans, a people long despised by the Judeans, turns out to be the most merciful and helpful towards a wounded man by the roadside: "The priest and Levite, who here step aside, are indeed an image of loveless Christians; they act as if they knew nothing of another's misery. They pour neither oil nor wine into their neighbor's wounds." This parable shows the real meaning of keeping the commandments regarding neighbor-liness: "Samaritan-like hearts let themselves feel pain at another's pain and are rich in mercy." The cantata explains that kindness and compassion are not only signs of obedience to ancient commandments, but also demonstrate the faithful following of Christ.

Alternate: BWV 77 Du sollt Gott, deinen Herren, lieben
"You shall love the Lord your God ... and your neighbor as yourself." The Samaritan, by offering unconditional mercy to a fallen traveler, shows himself to be a true neighbor: "Grant me besides, my God, the heart of a Samaritan, that I may also love my neighbor, and in his pain be distressed over him, so that I do not pass him by and leave him in his need."

SUNDAY 16
July 17-23

Year A   Matthew 13:24-30, 36-43

BWV 98   Was Gott tut, das ist wohlgetan
"Whatever God deals is dealt bountifully; his will remains just." In this parable Jesus teaches against condemning others, but rather leaving final judgments to God: "The Lord is near all those who trust his might and his favor." Judgmentalism may lead to erroneous conclusions, and is itself harmful. The cantata, one of three based on the hymn *What God Ordains Is Always Good* (see *BWV 99* and *BWV 100*), trusts God to protect believers from destruction and to hear their daily prayers: "God has a heart that abounds in mercy. ... He alone shall be my defense in all the evil that can befall me."

Alternate: BWV 14 Wär Gott nicht mit uns diese Zeit

"Were not God with us at this time … we should have been dismayed." Jesus' parable, allowing weeds to grow up amid the wheat, may appear submissive to evil, but rather it insists on being nonjudgmental and trusting in God alone: "Had God but allowed it, we would have been alive no more. … The Lord's name stands by us, the God of heaven and earth."

Year B   Mark 6:30-34, 53-56

BWV 13   Meine Seufzer, meine Tränen

"My sighs, my tears cannot be numbered. … My sorrow increases and robs me of all rest." In two episodes the disciples return from their first missionary trip, get rested, and then go with Jesus to meet the crowd. This cantata is a reminder of the sickness, suffering, and sadness experienced by the masses then and now: "My soul, take comfort in your distress: God can with ease turn bitterness into joyful wine." The believer's resignation to God for comfort exemplifies bringing the sick people of Galilee to Jesus for healing: "Your Father on high counsels well in everything."

Alternate: BWV 3 Ach Gott, wie manches Herzeleid

The crowds appear like sheep without a shepherd: "O God, what deep affliction befalls me." They bring their sick to Jesus for healing: "You, Jesus, are everything to me. … Your faithful mouth and your boundless loving…still preserve me." The disciples carry this divine healing throughout the region. The cantata gives them and everyone confidence and hope: "When cares oppress me, I shall in joyfulness sing."

Year C   Luke 10:38-42

BWV 3   Ach Gott, wie manches Herzeleid

"Ah God, how much heartbreak do I encounter at this time!" Although the cantata, one of two with this first line (see *BWV 58*), makes no direct allusion to the gospel, it expresses some of the tension raised by it: "How hard it is for flesh and blood, which mind only earthly and vain things and value neither God nor heaven, to be husbanded to the eternal good." For many modern Christians, whose lives are not necessarily ridden with sorrow and grief or with immediate terror, poverty, and famine, the contrasting images of Mary and Martha may still be apt. The struggle between flesh and Spirit, earthly and heavenly, sacred and secular, is real and common to many. "Keep my heart pure in faith, so that I live and die to you alone." Jesus remains the ultimate value, the only true comfort, strength, and hope.

Alternate: BWV 186 Ärgre dich, o Seele, nicht

"Do not be offended, O soul, that the Most High Light … disguises himself in a servant's form." Martha and Mary serve the Lord in distinctively different ways: "Alas, that a Christian should take such care over his body. … He could indeed choose the best part, which would never deceive his hopes: the salvation of souls that lies in Jesus." Jesus warns against distractions and approves their devotion: "... when Christians show through faith that Christ's word is their greatest treasure."

MARY MAGDALENE, APOSTLE
July 22

John 20:1-2, 11-18

BWV 145   *Auf, mein Herz, des Herren Tag* †

Mary, the first to see the risen Christ is touched and transformed from sadness to joy: "Rise up, my heart. ... If you acknowledge Jesus with your mouth, that he is Lord, and believe in your heart that God raised him from the dead, then you shall be blessed. ... I live, my heart, to your delight ... I am redeemed; I am freed and now live with God in peace and unity." She, as an 'apostle to the apostles', carries the good news to the others: "My Jesus lives. ... I am certain and have trust that the grave's darkness raises me to heavenly glory."

SUNDAY 17
July 24-30

Year A   Mathew 13:31-33, 44-52

BWV 71   *Gott ist mein König*

"God is my king from of old." In the parables of the leaven, treasure, pearl, and net the 'kingdom of heaven' is mentioned each time. The cantata makes clear that it is indeed God who is the king: "Day and night are yours. You cause both sun and stars to have their appointed course." Although nearly all the biblical references are from Psalm 74 and other ancient Hebrew texts, nevertheless the reign of God pertains to the contemporary world and the lives of all believers who pray 'Your will be done on earth as in heaven': "To every land you set its borders. ... Here peace must radiate, though murder and the storm of war everywhere arise."

Alternate: BWV 69 Lobe den Herrn, meine Seele
"Praise the Lord, my soul." In several down-to-earth parables, Jesus encourages his hearers to recognize the presence of God's activity in the world around them: "He brought us to the light, and he still sustains us. ... Consider, my spirit, the unhidden trace of the Almighty, which even in small things proves to be very great. ... The land bears fruit and improves; your word has succeeded well.".

---

† = *So du mit deinem Munde bekennest = Ich lebe, mein Herze, zu deinem Ergötzen*

Year B   John 6:1-21

BWV 21, part 1   *Ich hatte viel Bekümmernis*

"My heart was deeply troubled, but your comforting words revived my spirit." The feeding of the crowd, Jesus' most popular miracle, is recounted six times. John's version links the event to previous healing miracles, the Passover, and the crowd's perception of Jesus as a prophet and king. Afterwards Jesus comes walking across the water to the disciples in their boat, calming their fears. It is this inner fear and the distress of the diseased and hungry crowd that are reflected in part 1 of the cantata: "Do you not hear the wailing of those who are bound to you in faith and truth? ... Why are you troubled, my spirit, and so unquiet within me?" As always, in Christ there are comfort and strength: "Wait upon God, for I shall yet give him thanks. He is the help of my countenance and is my God."

> *Alternate: BWV* 177 *Ich ruf zu dir, Herr Jesu Christ*
> Besides spiritual nourishment, Jesus provides the multitudes with bread and fish, that they may know God's care: "I call upon you, Lord Jesus Christ. ... Let your word always be my food with which to nourish my soul, to defend me when misfortune comes near." Both temporal and eternal life depend entirely on the grace of God: "Whoever receives your gifts, receives them free: Through works no one can inherit or acquire your mercy, which saves us from dying."

Year C   Luke 11:1-13

BWV 86   *Wahrlich, wahrlich, ich sage euch*

"Truly, truly I say to you, if you ask something of the Father in my name, he will grant it to you." That Jesus teaches his disciples to pray by addressing God as 'Father' underscores his own faith, as well as the faith he instills in them: "My prayer and supplication certainly go to God's heart, for his word promises it to me." Such faith is well-founded, as God exceeds the ideals of even the best earthly father: "God's help is secure ... therefore we should trust him." The opening quote of the cantata is from John 16. It is an assurance that God is more trustworthy than anything that can be expected of the world.

> *Alternate: BWV* 87 *Bisher habt ihr nichts gebeten in meinem Namen*
> Prayer, as an expression of faith in Jesus, is rightly offered in his name: "Till now you have asked nothing in my name." To approach God as 'Father' can open the believer to unexpected blessing. "Forgive, O Father, our guilt, and still have patience with us when we pray with devotion."

JAMES, APOSTLE
July 25

Mark 10:35-45

BWV 98   *Was Gott tut, das ist wohlgetan*

"Whatever God does is done well." When James and his brother ask for privileges, Jesus teaches them about the responsibilities of discipleship: "Cease, eyes, from weeping. Indeed, I bear my heavy yoke with patience." Christ-like service is the criterion of 'greatness': "Therefore let us from now on, when we hover in the greatest distress, raise our hearts to God alone. ... He alone shall be my defense in all the evil that can befall me."

SUNDAY 18
July 31 – August 6

Year A   Matthew 14:13-21

BWV 196   *Der Herr denkt an uns*

"The Lord is mindful of us and blesses us ... those who fear the Lord, both small and great." The most popular miracle of Jesus is the feeding of the great crowd, reported six times in the gospels. The entire cantata consists of quotes from Psalm 115 (which is otherwise not included in the lectionary). The loving care of God is seen among all the people: "You are the blessed of the Lord, who has made heaven and earth." Miracles of the past are promised to future generations as well.

> *Alternate: BWV 186 Ärgre dich, o Seele, nicht*
> To be fed by Jesus is more that food. It is also his teaching and example: "Do not be offended, soul, that the Most High Light ... disguises himself in a servant's form. ... Blessed is he who sees in the scriptures how through his teaching ... he sends a spiritual manna." Multitudes are invited to know and love God through him: "Taste and see how friendly Jesus is."

Year B   John 6:24-35

BWV 21, part 2   *Ich hatte viel Bekümmernis... Ach, Jesu, meine Ruh*

The crowds follow after Jesus, in search of direction and encouragement in doing the will of God: "Ah, Jesus, my repose, my light, where are you? ... O soul, I am with you." As when he feeds them bread and fish, Jesus offers spiritual refreshment to those who come in faith: "Your struggle shall be crowned with sweet refreshment. ... You shall inherit salvation through the juice of this vine. ... I come and refresh you with my gaze of grace. ... Jesus consoles me with heavenly joy."

> *Alternate: BWV 113 Herr Jesu Christ, du höchstes Gut*
> The feeding of the multitude is a great example of God's work in Christ: "Lord Jesus Christ, you highest good, you fountain of grace, see how in my spirit I am

85

[113] burdened with sorrows." As 'the bread of life', Jesus provides forgiveness and life to the world: "I know that my heart would break, if your word did not promise me comfort. ... Jesus receives sinners: sweet words full of comfort and life! He gives true rest to the soul and calls to everyone consolingly, 'Your sin is forgiven you'."

Year C   Luke 12:13-21

BWV 94   *Was frag ich nach der Welt*

"What do I ask from the world?" The powerful parable of temporal vs. eternal values answers a request for Jesus to settle a family dispute over property. The cantata underscores the poverty of mere earthy wealth, the shortness of mortal existence, and the delusion of mammon: "The world is like smoke or a shadow that soon vanishes and passes away. ... A proud man builds the most splendid palaces ... and not once does he consider how soon these things slip away." Not only do these things provide no lasting security, they corrupt and dishonor life. Only in Jesus can people find the true values of God's kingdom: "Jesus alone shall be my soul's wealth."

> *Alternate: BWV 20 O Ewigkeit, du Donnerwort*
> "Eternity, O thunder-word." Words of warning are directed toward any who store up earthly riches with no regard for things of enduring value: "As mortals in the world have been from the very beginning, yet at last its time would be determined and measure laid: It would have to cease one day. ... The time is short; death is swift."

SUNDAY 19
August 7-13

Year A   Matthew 14:22-33

BWV 228   *Fürchte dich nicht, ich bin bei dir*

The disciples of Jesus are continually thrown into panic, nowhere more dramatically than the incident when Jesus comes to them across the water: "Do not be afraid, I am with you." Jesus speaks these words from Isaiah 43: "I am your God; I will strengthen you, I will also help you, I will sustain you with the right hand of my justice," words which are echoed throughout the New Testament. Fear of the unknown and fear of the known undermine Christian faith and paralyze the worship and service of the Savior: "You are mine because I grasp you and, O my light, will not let you out of my heart. ... Do not fear, you are mine."

> *Alternate: BWV 92 Ich hab in Gottes Herz und Sinn*
> Surprised and frightened when he sees Jesus walking across the water, Peter attempts to do the same: "I have surrendered to God's heart and mind my own

heart and mind. ... His heart remains kind and well-disposed." The wind, however, frightens him, and he loses faith and begins to sink: "When the waves lay hold of me and with fury drag me to the ocean's bed, it is only because he wishes to test me, to see whether I remember Jonah, whether I, like Peter, shall remember him."

Year B   John 6:35, 41-51

BWV 84   *Ich bin vergnügt mit meinem Glücke*
As the living bread from heaven, Christ offers assurance and contentment to his followers: "I am content with my good fortune ...I do not go to bed hungry." The believer, whose sentiments are portrayed by the cantata, gladly partakes of this bread and is indeed contented to serve Christ throughout life: "I eat my meager bread with joy. ... In the sweat of my countenance I shall meanwhile savor my bread. ... I am satisfied whatever God decrees."

> *Alternate: BWV 196 Der Herr denkt an uns*
> Jesus' heavenly origin is difficult to understand, and the identification of his flesh with life-giving bread is too much for some to swallow. Only by faith is it possible to believe and accept such abundant grace: "The Lord has been mindful of us. He will bless us. ... He will bless them that fear the Lord, both small and great. ... The Lord will increase you more and more, you and your children."

Year C   Luke 12:32-40

BWV 115   *Mache dich, meine Geist, bereit*
"Make ready, my spirit; watch and pray, that the evil time does not unexpectedly come upon you." Jesus prepares the faithful for an uncertain future, that they will be ready at all times for the glorious arrival of the kingdom: "God, who watches over your soul...would but have from you open spiritual eyes." The cantata seeks to counteract apathy and ignorance with prayer and watchfulness: "The whole world and its members are nothing but false brothers." God responds with mercy to those who come to him in faith: "We are victorious through God's strength, since his Son ... gives us courage and strength."

> *Alternate: BWV 140 Wachet auf, ruft uns die Stimme*
> The disciples are urged to remain watchful and ready for the Lord's return, confident of God's fatherly care: "Awake! We are called by the voice of the watchman. ... Rise up, the bridegroom comes." For the faithful, reuniting with Christ will be a time of great blessedness: "Forget now, O soul, the fear, the pain that you have had to endure. ... No eye has ever seen, no ear has ever heard such joy."

SUNDAY 20
August 14-20

Year A   Matthew 15:10-28

BWV 51   *Jauchzet Gott in allen Landen*

In the spirit of Psalm 66, all the nations are invited to praise God: "Shout for joy to God in all lands ... for in cross-bearing and distress he has at all times stood by us." Jesus teaches that many popular theories of defilement and purity are misguided, and the divisions between good and evil are false. It follows that faith and righteousness can be found outside Israel, as his conversation with the Gentile woman demonstrates. Her joy and praise are the essence of the cantata: "We praise what he has done for us .   ... A grateful spirit in return shall show through its devout life, that we are called your children."

> *Alternate:* BWV 152 *Tritt auf die Glaubensbahn*
>
> Jesus demonstrates that a life of moral, humanitarian faithfulness overrides concerns for social exclusion or ritual purity: "Walk on the path of faith." To the chagrin of the misguided Pharisees, Jesus finds 'great faith' in the Canaanite woman and is able therefore to display divine mercy and power: "It is a stumbling block to the world's wisdom that God's Son leaves his high throne of honor.....and suffers as a human being. ... Acknowledge me in faith and do not fret. ... I shall grant you a crown after affliction and shame."

Year B   John 6:51-58

BWV 27   *Wer weiß, wie nahe mir mein Ende*

"Who knows how near my end is? Dear God alone can know." Having given the multitude fish and bread to eat, Christ offers himself as living bread, a gift of eternal life. The people, although miraculously fed, feel oppressed by their mortality, and the cantata expresses this human despair with life and a resignation to death: "'Welcome' is what I shall say when death comes to my bedside." Christ's promise of eternal life through his flesh and blood brings renewal to the weary Christian and hope for final peace and happiness: "I have desire to depart, and with the Lamb, the bridegroom of all innocents, to savor blessedness."

> *Alternate:* BWV 186 *Ärgre dich, o Seele, nicht*
>
> "Fret not, O soul." By feeding the multitude, Jesus compares himself to the manna from heaven which Moses mediated to ancient Israel: "If you, like that crowd, are not fed quickly, you sigh: 'Ah, Lord, how long will you forget me?' ... He proves himself easily able to instruct weak souls, to nourish weary bodies; this satisfies body and soul." All people are hereby invited to receive life and salvation: "The Word feeds us and quenches our thirst."

Year C   Luke 12:49-56

BWV 146   *Wir müssen durch viel Trübsal*

"We must through much tribulation enter into the kingdom of God." Jesus speaks of conflicts and divisions that will arise, as his message confronts the ordinary ideas and institutions of the world. The cantata quotes Paul and Barnabas in Acts 14, reporting persecution resulting from their work. The Christian shares a defiance of evil powers with a sad weariness over the on-going struggle: "I would go to heaven. ... My continuing city is not here. ... How the wicked world oppresses me! ... How I will rejoice ... when all passing tribulation is gone!" Of course, God's ways will finally prevail.

> *Alternate: BWV* 116 *Du Friedefürst, Herr Jesu Christ*
> "Prince of Peace, Lord Jesus Christ ... you are a strong helper in distress." Jesus sees clearly the difficulties that lie in the way his mission: "Ah, unspeakable is the distress!" Christians should discern good from evil and turn to Christ for rescue and reconciliation: "Stretch out your hand on the terrified, plagued land; it can conquer the enemy's might and bring us lasting peace."

MARY, MOTHER OF OUR LORD
August 15

Luke 1:46-55

BWV 1   *Wie schön leuchtet der Morgenstern*

"How brightly shines the morning star." Commemoration of the Virgin Mary on this date, designated as her Assumption in other traditions, prescribes the reading of Mary's *Magnificat*, calling forth humility, ecstasy, and determination. These are reflected in the cantata: "My king and my bridegroom, you have taken possession of my heart... A joyful light from God has arisen for me... Heart and mind are raised as long as I live in singing, great king, to your praise."

SUNDAY 21
August 21-27

Year A   Matthew 16:13-20

BWV 92   *Ich hab in Gottes Herz und Sinn*

"To God's heart and mind I have yielded my own heart and mind. ... His heart remains well-disposed to me. It can fail me nevermore." At a pivotal moment in his ministry, Jesus queries his disciples' understanding about himself. Peter confesses his faith and is

[92] commissioned as the foundation rock for the church: "With Peter I will direct my mind towards him. ... My foot shall firmly—till the last remnant of my days—be grounded here upon this rock." The cantata probes the personal meaning of such a faith in terms of surrender, confidence in God's unfailing love, resolution, forbearance, and reverence: "Your heavenly kingdom must come to light within me."

> *Alternate:* BWV 174 *Ich liebe den Höchsten von ganzem Gemüte*
> Speaking for the disciples, Peter confesses Jesus to be 'the Messiah, the Son of the living God': "I love the Most High with all my mind." In response, Jesus promises God's support and protection: "Before this mighty standard even hell's gates tremble. ... Grasp your salvation, you hands of faith." Such trust and conviction give the church its foundation: "You are yet my confidence, my salvation, and my heart's comfort ... my God and Lord."

Year B   John 6:56-69

BWV 49   *Ich geh und suche mit Verlangen*

"With longing I go and seek you, my dove, my fairest bride. ... My feast is prepared and my marriage-table ready." Jesus' suggestion that people eat his flesh and drink his blood scandalizes many in the audience, and only a few remain as his followers. In the spirit of the Song of Solomon, the cantata dramatizes the response of the faithful, who hear the banquet invitation of Jesus, and who join him with passion and devotion: "You shall enjoy my sumptuous meal. ... The fallen generations might be guests in the hall of heaven at our Savior's meal. ... And so I draw you to me." Stanza 7 of the hymn *O Morning Star, How Fair and Bright* is heard in the final section: "Come O lovely crown of joy ... I wait for you with longing."

> *Alternate:* BWV 163 *Nur jedem das Seine*
> "To each only his due. ... My God, you are the giver of every gift. ... I would gladly give you, O God, my heart." Few crises of faith are as clear-cut as loyalty to God or mammon, to Jesus or Caesar. Many believers struggle with faith and reason, with belief and unbelief, as do Jesus' disciples when they hear his difficult teaching: "Fill, therefore, my heart with your blessing. ... Lead both my heart and mind ... that I may ever remain a member of your body."

Year C   Luke 13:10-17

BWV A160   *Jauchzet dem Herrn, alle Welt*

"Praise the Lord in every land; serve the Lord with joy." The synagogue leader cannot bring himself to rejoice at the woman's good fortune, because her healing took place on the Sabbath. "Come and contemplate him with gladness." The motet expresses the praise of the restored woman and the joy of those who saw her: "May we in faith believe him, put all our trust in him. ... And so we sing this day: Amen!" Words from Psalm 100 call all the faithful, wherever and whenever, to glorify God.

Alternate: BWV 148 Bringet dem Herrn Ehre seines Names

Jesus demonstrates the true meaning of the Sabbath, as he heals a crippled woman. She praises God: "Bring to the Lord the honor of his name. ... For my repose is no one but you. How holy and how precious, Most High, is your Sabbath feast!" The religious leaders, however, see only a transgression of the law, and fail to realize God's mercy and power: "Oh, if only the children of the present darkness might consider that loveliness. ... Faith, love, endurance, hope shall be my bed of peace."

BARTHOLOMEW, APOSTLE
August 24

John 1:43-51

BWV 79   *Gott der Herr ist Sonn und Schild*

"The Lord God is a sun and shield. ... No good thing will he withhold from those who walk uprightly." After Philip meets Jesus, he introduces him to Bartholomew (aka Nathaniel), 'truly an Israelite in whom there is no deceit', as the fulfillment of the scriptures. The cantata quotes Psalm 84, giving thanks for past and present blessings: "Our thankful souls therefore praise his goodness, which he fosters for his little band." Even greater are the good news of Jesus and the assurance of his eternal blessings: "We know the proper path to blessedness, for, Jesus, you have shown it to us through your word. ... Let your word shine on us brightly."

SUNDAY 22
August 28 – September 3

Year A   Matthew 16:21-28

BWV 22   *Jesus nahm zu sich die Zwölfe*

"Jesus took unto him the twelve and said to them, 'Behold we go up to Jerusalem'." Reflecting on the first of Jesus' passion predictions, the cantata recognizes the disciples' incomprehension of what lies ahead in Jerusalem: "And they understood none of these things." Christians can see the connection between the transfiguration on Tabor and the crucifixion on Golgotha and can rely on Jesus for final peace: "My Jesus, draw me on, and I shall come, for flesh and blood cannot comprehend at all. ... Reform my heart, transform my courage. ... Mortify us through your goodness, awaken us through your grace."

Alternate: BWV 166 Wo gehest du hin
Peter, who recently confessed profound faith in Jesus, here is scolded for failing to see the serious implications of discipleship. "Quo vadis? Where are you going?" To follow Jesus to Jerusalem means bearing the burdens and responsibilities of the cross, as well as its saving power: "I would be mindful of heaven. … Let my thoughts not stray."

Year B   Mark 7:1-8, 14-15, 21-23

BWV 131   Aus der Tiefen rufe ich, Herr, zu dir
"Out of the depths I cry to you, O Lord. Lord, hear my voice. … If you, Lord, should mark iniquities, who shall stand?" The scribes and Pharisees criticize Jesus and the disciples for their lack of purity. Jesus counters them with a prophetic critique of their hypocrisy, citing that moral purity has more to do with one's living habits than with ceremonial rubrics. The cantata is based on Psalm 130: "My soul waits for the Lord from one morning watch to the next." Its description of true need, repentance, and trust is in direct contrast to smug self-righteousness: "I am a troubled sinner … and would gladly in your blood be washed clean of sin. … With the Lord there is mercy."

Alternate: BWV 132 Bereitet die Wege, bereitet die Bahn
The scribes and Pharisees, though scrupulous about hand-washing, are guilty of evil thoughts and desires. Citing Isaiah 29, Jesus warns them of hypocrisy, lest they miss God's gracious call altogether: "Prepare the way, prepare the path. … The Messiah draws near. … Who are you? Question your conscience. … Consult the commandments. … Although my mouth and lips have called you Lord and Father …I have denied you by my life. … Mortify us through your goodness. Awaken us through your grace."

Year C   Luke 14:1, 7-14

BWV 47   Wer sich selbst erhöhet, der soll erniedriget werden
"Whoever exalts himself shall be abased, and whoever humbles himself shall be exalted." Jesus' own demeanor and instructions regarding meekness take focus during dinnertime when people jostle for prominence: "Humility comes from Jesus' kingdom." The cantata is mindful of the dangers of arrogance, in which one can so easily overlook one's own weaknesses and sins: "Jesus, bow down my heart. … Grant me a lowly mind, that I may be pleasing to you." The willingness to step aside in favor of one's neighbors becomes possible, when one relies on God's approval and ultimate vindication.

Alternate: BWV 114 Ach, lieben Christen, seid getrost
Humility before God requires hospitality to God's children, even the most humble: "Ah, dear Christians, be of good courage. … Pride once ate of the forbidden fruit to become like God; how often you exalt yourself with grandiloquent gestures, so that you have to be abased."

September 4-10

Year A   Matthew 18:15-20

BWV 177   *Ich ruf zu dir, Herr Jesu Christ*

"I call to you, Lord Jesus Christ ... grant me peace at this time ... that I might live for you, serve my neighbor well, in short, uphold your word." Jesus gives his disciples the responsibility of forgiving sins and reconciling people: "Grant that I, from the depths of my heart, may forgive my enemies; forgive me also at this hour, give me a new life." Their purpose is always to rebuild broken relationships and restore a sense of community among the alienated. When this work is effective, the will of God is done on earth. The cantata engages five stanzas of the title hymn, a prayer for personal grace to receive courage and strength, for effective forgiving of enemies: "Help, O Lord, my weakness! I cling to your mercy alone."

Alternate: BWV 42 Am Abend aber desselbigen Sabbats
Discipline within the church, especially the forgiving and retention of sins, is always based on the authority and Spirit of Jesus: "The same day at evening, being the first day of the week ... Jesus came and stood in their midst. Where two or three are gathered together in Jesus' precious name, there Jesus appears in their midst." The presence of Christ remains the strength and protection of the Christian community: "For them the sun must shine with the golden heading: 'Jesus is a shield of his own people.' ... May we lead a peaceable and quiet life in all godliness and honesty."

Year B   Mark 7:24-37

BWV 35   *Geist und Seele wird verwirret*

"Spirit and soul become confused, when they gaze on you, my God." Of the gospel miracles, the healing of the deaf man is explicitly referred to in the cantata: "To the deaf you give hearing, to the dumb the gift of speech. ... You open at a word the eyelids of the blind." The faith expressed throughout is descriptive of the woman who asked that her daughter be cleansed of an evil spirit: "Touch too my tongue with your mighty hand, that I may praise these signs of wonder in sacred worship."

Alternate: BWV 51 Jauchzet Gott in allen Landen
After healing a demon-possessed girl and a deaf man, Jesus is proclaimed far and wide, despite his efforts to avoid notoriety: "Rejoice in God in all lands. ... He has always stood beside us in affliction and distress. ... Most High, renew your goodness each morning. ... May he increase in us what he pledges in his mercy."

Year C   Luke 14:25-33

BWV 8   *Liebster Gott, wann werd ich sterben*

"Dearest God, when shall I die?" The high cost of discipleship includes detachment from possessions, earthly hopes, and human relationships, and involves complete submission to the call of Jesus. Confrontation with death was far more common in Bach's day than today, and is thematic to many of the cantatas, including this one: "My body daily inclines itself towards earth, and there its resting-place must be. ... Yet retreat, you mad, vain cares!" In Christ the believer can live and die in confidence of God's supporting love and final release from death: "Enough that out of God's abundance the highest good must yet befall me."

Alternate: BWV 3 Ach Gott, wie manches Herzeleid
"Ah, God, how much heartbreak I encounter!" This may be the first reaction of those called to follow Christ. The cost of discipleship is high. "The flesh is weak, yet the spirit is willing; so help me. ... My Jesus will be my treasure and wealth."

SUNDAY 24
September 11-17

Year A   Matthew 18:21-35

BWV 89   *Was soll ich aus dir machen, Ephraim*

"How shall I give you up, Ephraim? How can I hand you over, Israel?" The cantata opens with harsh words from Hosea 11, which both warn and plead for reconciliation. "Surely God should speak a word of judgment. ... The sum of your sins is endless. ... Vengeance will begin with those who have shown no mercy. ... My heart shall lay wrath, wrangling, and discord aside; it is prepared to forgive its neighbor." A man cannot be forgiven of his great debt while he is unwilling to forgive someone else of a small debt. Jesus tells this parable in hopes that all God's people will readily forgive others, as taught in his prayer: 'Forgive us our sins, as we forgive those who sin against us.'

Alternate: BWV 115 Mache dich, meine Geist, bereit
"Prepare yourself, my soul, watch, beseech, and pray, lest the evil day overtake you unawares." When asked about the extent of forgiveness, Jesus tells a parable of an unforgiving servant: "He sends you the light of his grace. ... Beseech in your grievous guilt your judge for his forbearance." As God forgives his debtors, so they must forgive their debtors: "We are victorious through his strength: for his Son, through whom we pray, gives us courage and strength, and would come to us with help."

Year B   Mark 8:27-38

BWV 159   *Sehet, wir gehn hinauf gen Jerusalem*

"Behold, we go up to Jerusalem." At the midpoint of his ministry, Jesus hears Peter's confession of faith, and predicts his own eventual suffering, death, and resurrection: "The cross is already prepared for you." Peter protests the forecast and is reprimanded for obstructing God's mission for Jesus: "Do not enter. If you were to remain behind, I myself would not have to journey to Jerusalem." Instead, disciples must practice sacrifice and self-denial: "I follow your path through spittle and pain." The cantata underscores the same implications of following Jesus, whatever worldly or selfish distractions may interfere: "It is finished, the pain is over, from the fall into sin we are now justly restored to God."

> *Alternate:* BWV 23 *Du wahrer Gott und Davids Sohn*
> At a crucial point in his ministry Jesus asks his disciples who they think him to be. Peter addresses him as the 'Messiah': "True God and son of David." Jesus then teaches them the deeper meanings of their messianic discipleship: "The eyes of all, Lord God almighty, wait upon you, mine above all others. … Lamb of God, you who bear the sins of the world, grant us your peace."

Year C   Luke 15:1-10

BWV 184   *Erwünschtes Freudenlicht*

"Desired light of joy, that dawns with the new covenant through Jesus, our shepherd!" The scribes and Pharisees criticize Jesus for associating with people they consider unacceptable. In response he tells stories about a lost sheep and a lost coin, how the finding of each brings joy to the owner. So heaven rejoices when a sinner returns to God: "We, who formerly strayed in death's valleys, now feel abundantly how God sends to us the long-awaited shepherd, who … turns our steps to the right way." In the cantata Jesus, like the good shepherd, searches out anyone who may be lost: "Remain our God and refuge, you who by your almighty hands turn our path to life." Christians should rejoice, not complain, when people are received into the fellowship of faith.

> *Alternate:* BWV 135 *Ach Herr, mich armen Sünder*
> There is great joy in heaven over sinners who return to God. Rather than rebuke tax collectors and other social outcasts, Jesus welcomes them: "Lord, do not rebuke me, a poor sinner … otherwise all is lost." God's generous mercy should silence the grumbling Pharisees and scribes: "Help me, through your goodness, out of my great spiritual trouble!"

HOLY CROSS DAY
September 14

John 3:13-17

BWV 174   *Ich liebe den Höchsten von ganzem Gemüte*

The cross is the instrument and symbol of salvation, for upon it is the love of God: "I love the Most High with all my mind; he has loved me too in the highest degree. … There I have the eternal source of goodness. … The Father has given his Child's life in death for sinners. … Grasp your salvation, you hands of faith." From the crucified Christ shines the light of eternal life: "You are yet my confidence, my salvation and my heart's comfort; he has redeemed me by his blood: Lord Jesus Christ, my God and Lord."

SUNDAY 25
September 18-24

Year A   Matthew 20:1-16

BWV 144   *Nimm, was dein ist, und gehe hin*

"Take what is yours and go your way." In one of his parables of the great reversal, when the last are made first and the first last, Jesus shocks the disciples with the irrational generosity of God. The cantata, composed specifically for this gospel text, counsels Christians not to complain when others are treated graciously: "Do not murmur … when your wish is not fulfilled; rather be contented with what your God has apportioned you." God's ways are truly just, and generous enough that all might find contentment: "His will is just and lasts forever. … Contentedness is a jewel in this life that can bring pleasure amid the greatest sadness."

> *Alternate: BWV 85 Ich bin ein guter Hirt*
> "I am a good shepherd." The landowner, in need of workers, gathers all those available and pays each of them a full day's wages. More concerned about their welfare than his own profits, he illustrates the pastoral Spirit of Christ: "When the hirelings sleep, this shepherd will watch over his sheep, that each one in longed-for rest may enjoy the mead and pasture, in which life's streams are flowing. … Behold what love can do. My Jesus takes care of his own flock."

Year B   Mark 9:30-37

BWV 166   *Wo gehest du hin*

"Where are you going?" The second time Jesus predicts his arrest, death, and resurrection, the disciples distract themselves by discussing who of them is the greatest: "I would be mindful of heaven and not present my heart to the world. … Lord Jesus Christ, let my thoughts not stray." Jesus holds up to them a child as great in God's sight. The title question referred originally in John 16 to Jesus' departure, but the cantata asks it of each Christian: "Let everyone beware when good fortune laughs, for here on earth things can easily change. ... Time goes by, death approaches." Whatever the future may hold, and whenever the heavenly journey begins, Christ is the assurance of God's presence.

> *Alternate: BWV 159 Sehet, wir gehn hinauf gen Jerusalem*
> "Look, we are going up to Jerusalem." When Jesus predicts his death and resurrection, the disciples struggle to understand their role: "The cross is already prepared for you. ... Do not enter ... I follow your path through spittle and pain." Jesus' own example of humility and willing service shows the way into God's reign: "It is finished, the pain is over, from the fall into sin we are now justly restored to God."

Year C   Luke 16:1-13

BWV 105   Herr, gehe nicht ins Gericht
The parable of the unjust steward can be misleading, but it demonstrates Jesus' insistence on radical, wholehearted commitment to the purposes of God. Any disciple needs to learn the parameters of devotion to Jesus. "Lord, do not enter into judgment with your servant! For before you no one living shall be justified." Beginning with a quote from Psalm 143, the cantata prays for mercy and forgiveness, that believers do not fall into the traps of sinful complicity, greed, or carelessness: "Happy is he who knows his guarantor. ... The handwriting of ordinances is blotted out. ... If only I can make Jesus my friend, mammon will be worth nothing to me."

> *Alternate: BWV 94 Was frag ich nach der Welt*
> "What do I ask from the world and all its treasures, when I can have joy only of you, my Jesus?" In the parable of the dishonest manager, one man's shrewd efforts enable him to achieve his goal. Jesus asks his disciples for even greater singleness of purpose, that earthly distractions might not obscure the kingdom: "Deluded world ... even your riches, wealth, and gold are deceit and false appearances. You may count vain mammon; I instead will choose Jesus."

MATTHEW, APOSTLE AND EVANGELIST
September 21

Matthew 9:9-13

BWV 103   Ihr werdet weinen und heulen
Matthew, a tax collector, is chosen as a disciple not because of his righteousness, but as a sinner: "No physician is to be found other than you ... who will heal the wounds of my sins. ... Leave off your sorrowful beginnings. ... I will set the crown of joy upon you and honor you."

September 25 – October 1

Year A   Matthew 21:23-32

BWV 87   *Bisher habt ihr nichts gebeten in meinem Namen*
"Till now you have asked nothing in my name." In a battle of wits Jesus tries to get the
religious leaders of Jerusalem to understand the faith to which God is calling them:
"You have willfully infringed both law and gospel." Their rejection of that call is
elaborated in the cantata, beginning with quotes from John 16. The repentant soul
prays for forgiveness and relief from life's pains: "Forgive, O Father, all our sins, and be
patient with us yet. ... Speak no more in parables, but rather intercede for us. When our
guilt rises even to heaven, you see and know my heart, that nothing can hide from you."

> *Alternate: BWV 96 Herr Christ, der einige Gottessohn*
> "Lord Christ, the only Son of God, the everlasting Father ... whom David of
> old worshipped in spirit as his Lord." When his authority is questioned, Jesus
> reveals his critics' hypocrisy. True authority is seen in faithfulness to God's
> calling: "Lead me, O Lord, to the path of righteousness. ... Chasten in us the
> old self, that the new may live here upon this earth, turning our mind and
> desires and thoughts to you."

Year B   Mark 9:38-50

BWV 73   *Herr, wie du willt, so schick's mit mir*
"Lord, deal with me as you wish, in living and in dying." Jesus teaches that authenticity
depends on doing good deeds, not on particular human connections: "Your will, in
truth, is a sealed book, which human wisdom cannot read." He condemns those who
cause or encourage destructive behavior, and praises anyone doing even simple deeds of
kindness: "Your Spirit ... shows that your will shall heal us. ... Alas, our will remains
perverse." The cantata laments the perversity of the human heart and prays for the Spirit
to make Christians able to promote God's purposes: "But a Christian, schooled in
God's Spirit learns to submit to God's will. ... To him laud, honor, and praise!"

> *Alternate: BWV 186 Ärgre dich, o Seele, nicht*
> "Fret not, my soul." The disciples are alerted to the evils that surround and
> threaten them: "Oh, Lord, how long will you forget me? ... O soul, do not
> doubt, let mere reason not ensnare you." With guidance and care, they can
> remain faithful and accomplish their purposes: "My Savior reveals himself in his
> works of mercy. ... Christians prove through their faith that Christ's word is
> their greatest treasure."

Year C   Luke 16:19-31

BWV 75, part 1   *Die Elenden sollen essen*
"The poor shall eat so that they shall be satisfied." The story of the rich man Dives and
poor man Lazarus dramatizes the importance of caring for the poor and suffering:

"Wealth, voluptuousness, and luxury make one's spirit over to hell." Ever since the wilderness wandering, food shortages have been a concern of God's people, and morality dictates that resources must be shared fairly. The cantata, beginning with a quote from Psalm 22, indicates the eventual reversal between those who are rich and powerful and those weak and poor: "Whoever has endured Lazarus's torments patiently shall be taken to heaven by the angels. ... There all pains recede."

Alternate: BWV 181 *Leichtgesinnte Flattergeister*
The rich man Dives is condemned for his lack of care for poor Lazarus: "Frivolous flutter-spirits rob themselves of the word's power." The repeated word of God calls all people into faithfulness: "Hearts of stone, that maliciously resist, will forfeit their own salvation."

MICHAEL AND ALL ANGELS
September 29

Revelation 12:7-12

BWV 19   *Es erhub sich ein Streit*
"There arose a great strife ... but Michael conquers, and the host that surrounds him overthrows Satan's cruelty." The cosmic battle between the supernatural powers of good and evil describes so well the fears and hopes of the early Christians under Roman persecution: "There lies the dragon. The uncreated Michael and his host of angels have prevailed over him." The same theme surfaces whenever serious oppression threatens. It spoke against religious opponents at the time of the Reformation, and stands as a warning to the political and moral powers in every age. The angels of God will defend the faithful: "Our body and soul shall be shielded by angels. ... Around us both near and far encamps the angel of our Lord. ... Abide, O angels, abide with me. ... Let us love the face of devout angels."

Alternate: BWV 149 *Man singet mit Freuden vom Sieg*
"Songs of rejoicing and victory sound in the tents of the righteous." Archangel Michael defeats Satan in an apocalyptic battle, portraying the victory of Christ over death. All who follow Christ are promised divine power over evil (Luke 10:17-20), as they extend his reign: "Power and strength be sung to God, to the Lamb who has conquered and driven away Satan. ... God's angels are encamped around me on all sides ... whole hosts of angels." The final outcome of faith is peace and eternal life: "God's angels never retreat: they are with me every-where. ... They shall bear me up in their hands. ... Lord, let your dear angel at my very end carry my soul into Abraham's bosom."

SUNDAY 27
October 2-8

Year A   Matthew 21:33-46

BWV 101   *Nimm von uns, Herr, du treuer Gott*

"Take from us, faithful God, the grave punishment and great distress that we with countless sins have truly merited." Jesus tells a parable with dire consequences for the faithless and sinful. The violent behavior of the wicked tenants recalls Jerusalem's rejection of God's prophets and anticipates the suffering of Jesus. It precipitates divine judgment on any who oppose the coming kingdom of heaven. The cantata prays for repentance, that the fate of Jesus and the martyrs, as well as of Jerusalem, may be avoided, and that the common life may be blessed, not cursed: "Hear our pleading, that we may not through sinful deeds perish like Jerusalem. ... Give proof to us of your great grace, and do not punish us when caught red-handed. ... Forbear with a father's grace with this our feeble flesh."

> *Alternate: BWV 102 Herr, deine Augen sehen nach dem Glauben*
> "Lord, do your eyes not look for truth?" The judgmental parable of the wicked tenants unmasks the evil intents of the Pharisees and chief priests: "They have made their faces harder than rock; they have refused to turn back." Despite God's persistent appeal, sometimes human rejection also persists: "Almighty God seeks indeed to tame us through gentleness, to see if the erring soul might still submit; but if it persists in its obdurate way, he abandons it to the heart's arrogance. ... Do you despise the riches of his goodness and forbearance and long-suffering, not knowing that the goodness of God leads you to repentance?"

Year B   Mark 10:2-16

BWV 139   *Wohl dem, der sich auf seinen Gott*

"Happy is the one who, just like a child, can trust in God." The Pharisees test Jesus' teaching about divorce, and he shows them the greater intentions of marriage, with special attention to the welfare of children: "He remains at peace if only he makes God his friend." Although the cantata speaks, possibly referring to the contentious legalists, of raging foes, angry wolves, lowly rabble, and Satan's craft, the principal focus is on God's friendship: "He protects me even from the world. ... The light of comfort shines on me from afar. ... God is my shield, my help, my counsel." Married relationships and families are blessed by God, and they stand as signs of God's reign.

> *Alternate: BWV 118 O Jesu Christ, meins Lebens Licht*
> Some Pharisees test Jesus with a question about the legality of divorce. They fail to understand that their 'hardness of heart' is what alienates people, contrary to God's intentions for human society: "O Jesus Christ, light of my life, my refuge, my comfort, my trust. I am but a guest on earth, and sore oppressed by the weight of my sins."

Year C Luke 17:5-10

BWV 75, part 2 *Die Elenden sollen essen ... Nur eines kränkt*

Jesus teaches the disciples how to live under the kingdom of God, here regarding temptations, forgiveness, faith, and dedication: "Only one thing grieves a Christian mind: when it thinks of its poverty in spirit. It indeed believes in God's goodness, which makes all things new." The ways of God become possibilities only through Christ: "Therefore I let him alone rule."

Alternate: BWV 180 Schmücke dich, o liebe Seele

"Adorn yourself, beloved soul." A test of faith is one's willingness to work as a dedicated servant, without thought of reward: "Let me through this soul's meal estimate your love aright, that, as now on earth, I may also become a guest in heaven." God, as a noble master, never neglects his children.

SUNDAY 28
October 9-15

Year A Matthew 22:1-14

BWV 162 *Ach, ich sehe, jetzt, da ich zur Hochzeit gehe*

"Ah, I see now, as I go to the marriage, happiness and misery." The king insists that the seats at his marriage feast be filled, if not by the invited guests, then by others: "O great marriage, to which the king of heaven summons humankind!" However, one improperly dressed man is expelled: "How happy are they whom faith leads here, and how cursed are they who disdain this feast!" The cantata recognizes that being invited to heaven does not guarantee that everyone will accept, and unlikely guests may take their places: "My Jesus, let me not come unrobed to the wedding, that your judgment not fall on me." The required wedding garment is equated with faith in Christ and the righteousness that he alone can offer.

Alternate: BWV 180 Schmücke dich, o liebe Seele

God is generous in preparing a banquet for his children, and insistent that the banquet hall be filled: "Adorn yourself, beloved soul. ... Rouse yourself: your Savior knocks." The blessings of heaven are great and are to be received in faith: "How precious the gifts of the sacred supper! ... My heart feels both fear and joy. ... Lord, you are everything to me. You shall see my faithfulness and not despise my belief, which is still weak and fearful. ... Kindle my spirit with love, that it may be directed in faith only to heavenly things, and be ever mindful of your love."

Year B   Mark 10:17-31

BWV 97   In allen meinen Taten

"In all my undertakings I allow the Almighty to counsel. ... I take it as he gives it." The encounter with the rich young man, who is hesitant to divest his wealth, raises the issue of money as an impediment to the kingdom of God. Jesus assures the disciples that God is able to provide for them whatever they need. The cantata is based on the title hymn of nine stanzas, associated with the familiar tune 'Innsbruck'. Throughout, the futility of living and acting apart from God is overcome only by faith and commitment: "May he mercifully deliver me from my sins. ... I have surrendered myself to him, to die and to live."

Alternate: BWV 138   Warum betrübst du dich, mein Herz

"Why are you troubled, my heart? Do you grieve and suffer pain merely for temporal good?" Jesus warns his disciples against both legalism and materialism: "Put trust in your Lord and God, who has created all things." False 'gods' leads to unfulfilled hopes and nagging fear: "Provision for my keeping is somewhat meager. ... I put my trust in God. ... Now no worries can prey upon me, nor can poverty plague me."

Year C   Luke 17:11-19

BWV 17   Wer Dank opfert, der preiset mich

"Whoever offers thanks praises me. ... How should one not praise you constantly?" The cantata quotes from the gospel: "When he saw that he had become healthy, he turned around and praised God with a loud voice ... and he was a Samaritan." Like the healed leper's gratitude, thanks that rise from those richly blessed truly honor and glorify God. "Heal me perfectly in body and soul." Christians, who know forgiveness and salvation, should lead the world in worship of God for such great power and kindness.

Alternate: BWV 72   Alles nur nach Gottes Willen

Cleansed from leprosy, one man returns to thank Jesus and praise God: "All only according to God's will ... this shall be my motto. ... Lord, if you will, I grow healthy and pure." Though this man is a Samaritan, Jesus recognizes his faith: "God is ready to help those who have firm faith in him."

Sunday 29
October 16-22

Year A   Matthew 22:15-22

BWV 163   *Nur jedem das Seine*

"To each only his due. If rulers must have toll, taxes, and tributes, let one not refuse the debt that is owed. But the heart is bound to God alone." In an attempt to trap Jesus in his teaching, the Pharisees question his obedience to Caesar. As always, he exposes their ignorance and malevolence. The cantata affirms loyalty to rulers and willingness to pay proper taxes. Earthly citizenship does not diminish human dependence on God, and may not be allowed to resist complete devotion to God, who gives every good thing: "We have what we have from your hand alone. ... Let my heart be the coin that I pay you, my Jesus ... that my heart and my spirit abide in you forever."

Alternate: BWV 139 *Wohl dem, der sich auf seinen Gott*

"Happy are they who, just like a child, can trust their God." Although Jesus clearly advocates ultimate trust in God, he does not speak of the government as an enemy. Composed to accompany this gospel reading, the cantata focuses instead on the ill-intentioned plotting of the Pharisees: "God is my friend; what does my enemy's rage avail? ... The Savior sends his own people into the very midst of raging wolves." Jesus' words silence their attacks and reveal the wisdom of God: "The evil rabble, with malice and with mockery, has cunningly surrounded him; but since he utters such words of wisdom, he protects me even from the world."

Year B   Mark 10:35-45

BWV 99   *Was Gott tut, das ist wohlgetan*

"Whatever God does is well done. ... However he acts on my behalf, I shall stand by him calmly." Jesus uses the outrageous request of James and John to teach the disciples about the true use of power, not to dominate but to serve others. The cantata, one of three with this title (see BWV 98 and BWV 100), speaks of the bitter cup and points to the sorrows of the cross: "My heart grows calm and contents itself with God's paternal faith and grace. ... Whoever, through false delusion, considers the cross too heavy to be borne will have no pleasure in times to come." As always, God is a refuge and a comfort for any who will trust in him.

Alternate: BWV 56 *Ich will den Kreuzstab gerne tragen*

The disciples quite naturally expect privileges or rewards for their faithfulness, but Jesus says that true greatness is accomplished through humility, service, and suffering: "Gladly shall I bear the cross; it comes from God's beloved hand. ... He calls out to me: I am with you; I shall never leave you nor forsake you. ... I stand here ready and prepared to receive my heritage of bliss with yearning and desire from the hands of Jesus."

Year C   Luke 18:1-8

BWV 157   *Ich lasse dich nicht, du segnest mich denn*

"I will not let you go unless you bless me!" An abused widow persists in her appeal to the judge, though he is unscrupulous, and she finally wins her case, because he yields to her tenacity: "I hold my Jesus firmly, I do not let him go now or ever." Remembering Jacob's refusal to let the angel go, Genesis 32, the cantata (see also *BWV* A159, with the same title) urges the faithful not to give up on or abandon Jesus, but to avail themselves of all the promised blessings: "You are my joy, in unrest my rest, in fear my soft bed. ... Christ lets me forever and ever be led to the stream of life."

> *Alternate: BWV* 143 *Lobe den Herrn, meine Seele*
> "Praise the Lord, my soul." A persistent woman finally receives her request for justice, even though the judge is unsympathetic. In a yet greater way, God hears and answers the prayers of all, especially those in need: "A strong helper in trouble are you, in life and in death. ... O Jesus, deliverer of your flock, continue to be our refuge. ... Graciously help us altogether now at this time."

LUKE, EVANGELIST
October 18

Luke 1:1-4; 24:44-53

BWV 43   *Gott fähret auf mit Jauchzen*

The cosmic exaltation of Jesus opens the way of the gospel to the entire world: "God has gone up with jubilation. ... And the Lord, after he had spoken with them, was lifted up into heaven." Through Christ the reign of God comes to all people: "The Father has indeed ordained for him an eternal kingdom. ... He will prepare for me a mansion next to him, that I may eternally stand at his side, freed from grief and woe."

SUNDAY 30
October 23-29

Year A   Matthew 22:34-46

BWV 96   *Herr Christ, der einige Gottessohn*

"Lord Christ, the only Son of God." The Pharisees challenge Jesus to identify the most important commandment and to establish his own authority, all in hopes of catching him on some religious technicality. He answers them correctly and finally silences them: "O wondrous power of love! ... O incomprehensible, hidden might! ... O rich power of blessing poured out on us!" The cantata proclaims Jesus as Lord, as God's Son whom

David foreshadowed. Affection, obedience and loyalty are the obvious responses to God, whose love has made this gift possible: "I, who am unenlightened ... am so often wont to stray ... now to the right, now to the left. ... Walk with me, my Savior ... that our minds and all desires and thoughts be turned to you."

Alternate: BWV 169 *Gott soll allein mein Herze haben*
When challenged by the Pharisees, Jesus reveals their legalistic perversions and turns the challenge back to them. Of special importance are the intentions of the greatest commandments: "God alone shall have my heart. ... I find in him the highest good. ... Die in me, pride, wealth, lust of eyes, depraved inclinations of the flesh. But this also means be true to your neighbor. ... You shall love the Lord and your neighbor. ... Let us feel the fervency of your love, that we may love each other from our hearts and remain at peace, of the same mind."

Year B   Mark 10:46-52

BWV 23   *Du wahrer Gott und Davids Sohn*
"True God and son of David ... grant through your wondrous hand ... that I be given both help and comfort." Jesus' opening the eyes of the blind demonstrates God's concern to remove the darkness of human hearts. Especially in Mark, the disciples themselves are spiritually blind: "I see you along these paths where people have tried to leave. ... The eyes of all, O Lord, almighty God, wait upon you, mine above all others." Like the blind, all people languish in the sinfulness and darkness of the human condition, waiting for the mercy, light, and strength of the divine Messiah: "Give them strength and light. Leave them not in darkness forever."

Alternate: BWV 38 *Aus tiefer Not schrei ich zu dir*
Blind Bartimaeus cries out to Jesus for mercy and healing: "Out of the depths I cry to you; Lord God hear my calling." He receives his eyesight and is commended for his faith. "I hear in the midst of suffering a word of comfort that my Jesus speaks. ... Though my despair, like chains, fetters one misfortune to another, yet shall my savior free me." Like Bartimaeus, all the faithful may turn to Jesus and be rescued from their suffering: "How soon will comfort's dawn succeed this night of woe and sorrow?"

Year C   Luke 18:9-14

BWV 179   *Siehe zu, daß deine Gottesfurcht nicht Heuchelei sei*
"See to it that your fear of God be not hypocrisy, and do not serve God with a false heart." Jesus approves the penitent tax collector above the self-righteous Pharisee: "puffed-up Pharisees who appear pious from without ... but in their heart is hidden a proud self-glorification ... the publican in the temple ... set this before you, O man, as a laudable example." The cantata's opening quote from Sirach 1 is a guiding theme of Jesus' teaching and pattern of his living. Christians of every generation must be on guard against corruption by pride or by carelessness. Every life is bent by flaws and errors, and all people should join sincerely in the prayer for mercy: "Then you can find grace and help."

Alternate: BWV 131 *Aus der Tiefen rufe ich, Herr, zu dir*
"Out of the depths I cry to you, Lord." No parable shows humble repentance more poignantly than that of the Pharisee and tax collector at prayer. The one who begs for God's mercy is finally justified: "Lord, hear my voice. ... Have mercy on me with such a burden. ... I am also a troubled sinner."

SIMON AND JUDE, APOSTLES
October 28

John 14:21-27

BWV 59   *Wer mich liebet, der wird mein Wort halten*
"Whoever loves me with keep my word." In answer to Jude's question, Jesus promises his continuing presence, guidance, and peace. Through the promised Advocate, believers will be empowered to follow the way of love: "The Almighty says: He will in our souls choose his dwelling place. ... Come, Holy Spirit, God and Lord." It is no longer necessary to live in fear: "The world with all its glory cannot compare with this glory with which our God delights us: that he is enthroned in our hearts."

SUNDAY 31
October 30 – November 5

Year A   Matthew 23:1-12

BWV 169   *Gott soll allein mein Herze haben*
"God alone shall have my heart. ... I find in him the highest good." Jesus warns against the Pharisees' approach to religious life. Although they teach the correct laws of Moses, they do not follow them in spirit: "What is the love of God? Rest for the spirit, delight for the senses." The cantata pledges complete devotion to God in theory and in practice: "My breast may ever practice here on earth the love of God." It is the love of God that enables the faithful to make this commitment and to live in peace: "Give us your grace ... that we may sincerely love each other and dwell in peace."

Alternate: BWV 52 *Falsche Welt, dir trau ich nicht*
Consistent with his own lifestyle, Jesus teaches his disciples to avoid the vanity of status-seeking and privilege: "False world, I do not trust you. ... Your countenance, though outwardly so friendly, secretly plots ruin. ... Honesty has been banished from the world, falseness has driven it out; hypocrisy now remains in its stead." Ultimate exaltation derives from humility: "God is faithful. ... I shall build on his friendship and give my soul, spirit and mind and everything I am into his keeping."

Year B   Mark 12:28-34

BWV 77   *Du sollt Gott, deinen Herren, lieben*
"You shall love the Lord your God with all your heart, and with all your soul, and with all your strength, and with all your mind, and your neighbor as yourself." The scribe commends Jesus for correctly identifying the greatest commandments, and Jesus approves the man's faith: "My God, I love you with all my heart. ... Though I often have the will to accomplish God's commandments, it is yet not possible." Christians struggle every day to live in harmony with these two commandments, and pray for the guiding presence of Christ: "Lord, dwell in me through my faith ... that it may be active in my love."

> *Alternate: BWV 33 Allein zu dir, Herr Jesu Christ*
> The first and greatest commandment is to fear, love, and trust God above all things: "In you alone, Lord Jesus Christ, rests my hope." The second is to love our neighbors as ourselves. Jesus commends the Pharisees for confessing this, despite their difficulties in fulfilling the implications: "I am weak in spirit and devoid of love. ... To obey even the smallest law is much too hard. ... Simply give me out of mercy the true Christian faith. ... Grant that I, from pure impulse, may love my neighbor as myself."

Year C   Luke 19:1-10

BWV 55   *Ich armer Mensch, ich Sündenknecht*
After his encounter with Jesus, Zacchaeus admits his dishonest past and reforms his life: "I, a poor man, a servant of sin, I go before God's presence for judgment with fear and trembling." That repentance is frightening, difficult, and sometimes painful is vividly portrayed in the cantata: "I hold before him his Son. ... I do not deny my wrongs, but your grace and favor are far greater." A paraphrase of Psalm 139 describes God's pursuit of the sinner. The image of Zacchaeus high in the sycamore tree is conveyed by the extraordinarily high vocal range.

> *Alternate: BWV 89 Was soll ich aus dir machen, Ephraim*
> "How can I give you up, Ephraim?" Zacchaeus, a dishonest tax collector, receives Jesus, repents and amends his life. In fulfillment of prophetic hopes, salvation comes to his house: "My heart lays aside wrath, sedition, and strife; it is prepared to forgive my neighbor. ... For the salvation of my soul I will count the drops of the blood of Jesus ... credit that sum to my account!"

REFORMATION DAY
October 31

Romans 3:19-28

BWV 80   *Ein feste Burg ist unser Gott*

"A mighty fortress is our God." Because of the grace shown in Christ, people are justified in God's sight apart from the works of the law: "He saves us freely out of all the trouble that has now befallen us." This grace allows humanity a new sense of freedom and a victory over the forces of evil: "Whatsoever is born of God is elected for victory … is victorious in spirit forever and ever. … Your Savior remains your salvation … your protector." Such freedom is expressed in the cantata as Jesus' expulsion of evil, God's protective strength, and the final crowning of the faithful: "He is indeed with us on the battlefield with his Spirit and gifts." All four stanzas of Luther's hymn *A Mighty Fortress Is Our God* are sung.

> *Alternative: BWV 79   Gott der Herr ist Sonn und Schild*
>
> "God the Lord is sun and shield." Salvation by God's free grace is the enduring theme of the Reformation: "The Lord gives grace and honor. … He will protect us further, though our enemies sharpen arrows." The Word of God, made visible in the life and teaching of Jesus, has secured release from condemnation and freedom to live under divine truth (John 8:31-36): "We know the way to salvation, for, Jesus, you have shown it to us through your word. … Let your word shine brightly for us. … Preserve us in the truth; grant us eternal freedom."

ALL SAINTS DAY
November 1

Year A   Matthew 5:1-12

BWV 107   *Was willst du dich betrüben*

The 'poor in spirit' are proclaimed 'blessed'. To them and other humble and oppressed people Jesus opens the kingdom of heaven: "Why are you so distressed, my dear soul? Devote yourself to love him who is called Emmanuel. … With him you shall achieve that which serves and helps you." This is the pattern of Jesus' words and deeds: "I shall only strive for that which he approves. … With purest mercy you avert want and harm."

Year B   John 11:32-44

BWV 156   *Ich stehe mit einem Fuß im Grabe*

"I stand with one foot in the grave." Jesus is deeply moved at the death of his friend Lazarus. Standing at the tomb, he summons the power of God and calls Lazarus back to life: "Come, dear God, when it pleases you. … My fear and distress, my life and my death lie, dearest God, in your hands." This great miracle foretells the resurrection of Jesus, and of all the dead: "When my body and soul fail, then you, my God, are my comfort and my heart's portion."

Year C   Luke 6:20-31

BWV 78   *Jesu, der du meine Seele*

The blessings on the poor are accompanied by warnings for the rich. God's people in every generation receive divine grace in the midst of their trials and temptations: "Jesus, by whom my soul, through your bitter death, from the devil's dark cave ... has forcibly been torn out, be even now, O God, my refuge." Only the grace of God can sustain people who are both saints and sinners: "May your gracious countenance be gratifying to us. ... Do not count the misdeeds that have angered you. ... When a fearful judgment pronounces a curse on the damned, you change it into a blessing. ... I will trust in your goodness."

SUNDAY 32
November 6-12

Year A   Matthew 25:1-13

BWV 140   *Wachet auf, ruft uns die Stimme*

"Wake up, cries the watchman's voice. ... Where are you, wise virgins?" Five of the bridesmaids are ready when the wedding begins, and five are not: "Make haste, the bridegroom comes." Jesus urges his followers to be awake and watchful for the saving actions of God: "Rise up and take your lamps. ... Go forth, daughters of Zion ... to welcome the bridegroom." The cantata, including the three stanzas of the hymn *Wake, Awake, for Night Is Flying*, reminds all people that the days before the Savior's return are numbered: "We shall follow to the hall of rejoicing and join the Lord's supper. ... So enter in to me, you, my chosen bride." Loyalty to Jesus now and always is assurance of everlasting joy: "I have wedded myself to you for all eternity."

> *Alternate: BWV* 115 *Mache dich, meine Geist, bereit*
> The foolish bridesmaids are not prepared when the bridegroom arrives and are shut out of the wedding: "Prepare yourself, my soul; watch, beseech, and pray lest the evil day overtake you unawares. ... Damnation may suddenly awaken you and, if you are not watchful, cover you with the sleep of eternal death." Stay awake and alert: "We are victorious through his strength: for his Son, through whom we pray, gives us courage and strength, and would come to us with help."

Year B   Mark 12:38-44

BWV 52   *Falsche Welt, dir trau ich nicht*

"False world, I do not trust you." The cantatas neglect the widow and her mite, but this lesson of Jesus underscores the false values that the world teaches: "Honesty has been banished from the world. ... Hypocrisy now remains in its stead." Christians are to

[52] respect generosity more than wealth, and to see sacrificial giving as more God-pleasing than tokenism: "God is faithful. ... I shall build on his friendship and give my soul, spirit, and mind and everything I am into his keeping. ... Thus I can scorn false tongues."

> *Alternate: BWV 139 Wohl dem, der sich auf seinen Gott*
> The poor widow shows herself as a true friend of God, by offering a generous gift, while others are less generous: "Happy is he, who just like a child, can trust God. ... God is my friend. ...My savior permits me to find peace. I render to God what is God's, my innermost soul. ... God is my shield, my help and counsel."

Year C   Luke 20:27-38

BWV 118   O Jesu Christ, meins Lebens Licht
In an effort to discredit Jesus, the Sadducees pose a riddle regarding the complexities of resurrection of the dead. They only succeed in displaying their own ignorance of God's promises and power. The single hymn stanza of this motet speaks of human mortality and the enlightenment and strength received through Jesus Christ: "O Jesus Christ, light of my life, my refuge, my comfort, my trust. I am but a guest on earth, and sore oppressed by the weight of my sins."

> *Alternate: BWV 31 Der Himmel lacht! Die Erde jubilieret*
> In an effort to refute the resurrection, some Sadducees challenge Jesus with a dilemma concerning marriage in heaven. He turns the tables on them and, in anticipation of his own resurrection, speaks to them about eternal life: "Heavens laugh, the earth rejoices ... the Creator lives. ... If our head lives, his members live too. ... Let your Savior live in you, to be felt in your life ... so nothing can separate me from Jesus."

SUNDAY 33
November 13-19

Year A   Matthew 25:14-30

BWV 14   Wär Gott nicht mit uns diese Zeit
"If it had not been the Lord who was on our side ... we should have despaired." The three servants tested in the gospel parable illustrate three different reactions to the apparent absence of God, when people are called to live by faith alone: "Our strength is too weak to withstand our foe." The cantata expresses the struggle of faithfulness due to human weakness. Good and faithful servants are those who continue to trust and praise God: "Your hands will still protect us. ... Our help is in the name of the Lord, the God of heaven and earth."

Alternate: BWV 45 Es ist dir gesagt, Mensch, was gut ist

The three servants respond differently to their lord's investment in them, two wisely and one foolishly. The foolish servant ignores the mandate entrusted to him, and elicits the master's condemnation: "He has told you, O mortal, what is good; and what does the Lord require of you but to do justice, and to love kindness, and to walk humbly with your God? ... So that I might prove to be a faithful servant ... so shall my heart and my mouth be my judges." The warning sounds for all who would serve faithfully: "Grant that I do with zeal what it befits me to do."

Year B   Mark 13:1-8

BWV 26   *Ach wie flüchtig, ach wie nichtig*

"Oh, how fleeting, how trifling is mortal life!" Jesus teaches his disciples that the eventual destruction of the temple will be accompanied by false messiahs and apostasy, by wars, famines, and earthquakes: "Time passes, hours rush past. ... Soon all is over with honor and fame. ... How easily consuming flames are formed, how surging waves rush and roar, until all things shatter and collapse in ruin." All this will be but a prelude to greater calamities coming at the end of the world. The hymn upon which the cantata is based laments the transitory nature of life, especially as it anticipates death and the final cataclysm. Only in God can anyone hope for eternal life: "Whoever fears God shall live forever."

Alternate: BWV 183 Sie werden euch in den Bann tun

Jesus speaks frankly to his disciples, anticipating the opposition and difficulty that lie in the future: "They shall put you out of the synagogues." Although their trials foretell apocalyptic events yet to come, there is no need to fear, as God is the ultimate victor: "I do not fear the terror of death ... because the arm of Jesus shall protect me. ... I draw comfort that your Spirit will stand by me, should there perhaps be too much for me to suffer. ... I know that you care for my welfare."

Year C   Luke 21:5-19

BWV 183   *Sie werden euch in den Bann tun*

"They will place you under a ban, but the time will come when whoever kills you will think he does God a service thereby." The destruction of the temple in first-century Jerusalem was paradigmatic for the political and social upheaval of the time, much of which would be painful for the Christians: "I do not fear death's terror." The cantata, one of two with the same title from John 16 (see *BWV* 44), encourages the believer to remain faithful and courageous, enabled by the Holy Spirit to make whatever sacrifices might be necessary: "I comfort myself that your Spirit will stand by me in the event that it should become too much for me. ... I know you care for my well-being!"

Alternate: BWV 178 *Wo Gott, der Herr, nicht bei uns hält*
Fearing an imminent destruction of the temple, the disciples face an uncertain and ominous future. Only faith in God can sustain and protect them: "If God the Lord does not remain on our side when our enemies rage ... then all is lost. ... Those who embrace God firmly in faith he will never leave nor forsake ... the door of grace stands ever open."

SUNDAY 34
CHRIST THE KING
November 20-26

Year A   Matthew 25:31-46

BWV 116   *Du Friedefürst, Herr Jesu Christ*

"O prince of peace, Lord Jesus Christ." Jesus is pictured as the apocalyptic judge, separating for all eternity the saved from the damned, their fates having been determined by charity practiced during life: "You are a strong helper in need, in life and in death. ... Unutterable is our woe and the menace of the angry judge." The cantata speaks of Jesus as ruler of peace, the same peace he taught to his people: "But remember, O Jesus, you still are called a prince of peace. ... Come then and stretch forth your hand ... and bring us lasting peace." Christians who realize their own failings can always rely on God's mercy, to fill and transform their lives with the Spirit: "Illumine too our hearts and minds. ... You alone can accomplish such things for us."

Alternate: BWV 90 *Es reißet euch ein schrecklich Ende*
"A terrible end shall sweep you away, you disdainful sinners. ... Your wholly stubborn minds have quite forgotten your judge." The terror of final judgment is balanced by the unexpected blessings upon the righteous: "Lead us with your right hand. ... Give us always your holy word. ... Protect us from Satan's guile and murder; grant us one single blessed hour, that we may forever be with you."

Year B   John 18:33-37

BWV 117   *Sei Lob und Ehr dem höchsten Gut*

"Give laud and praise to the highest good, to the Father of all goodness. ... Whatever our God has created, he wishes also to preserve." Jesus is queried by Pilate, who is baffled by a kingdom 'not from this world.' Pilate's question about ultimate truth is answered by a silent Jesus who proceeds to the cross. The cantata presents all nine stanzas of the title hymn, each ending with "Give to our God all honor!" Repeated praises are sung to God for the divine love which has created, redeemed, and sustained all people: "The Lord is not and never was severed from his people. ... When strength and health are lacking, as all the world bears witness, he comes and helps abundantly. ... Give honor to our God."

Alternate: BWV 116 *Du Friedefürst, Herr Jesu Christ*
"O Prince of Peace, Lord Jesus Christ ... you are a strong helper." Responding
to Pilate's summons, Jesus claims for himself an otherworldly kingdom:
"Unspeakable is our distress and the menace of the angry judge. ... We
acknowledge our guilt and ask for nothing but forbearance and your immeasur-
able love. ... You know how in our foe's grim rage what cruelty and wrong
abide." Jesus comes to uphold the truth of God: "Illumine our minds and
hearts with the spirit of your grace, that we may not be a cause for scorn."

Year C   Luke 23:33-43

BWV 182   *Himmelskönig, sei willkommen*
"Heavenly King, welcome!" Jesus shows his mastery over evil by offering words of
forgiveness from the cross, on behalf of those who crucified him and of the repentant
criminal dying beside him: "What strong love, that for the salvation of the world, you set
yourself forth as a sacrifice." The cantata reminds the listener of the true nature of
Christ's royalty, namely, submission to God and compassion for sinners past, present,
and future: "Though the world cries only 'Crucify!', do not let me flee, Lord, from your
cross's banner ... your wounds, crown, and disgrace are my heart's pasture. ... He goes
before us and opens up the way."

Alternate: BWV 106 *Gottes Zeit ist die allerbeste Zeit*
"God's time is the very best time." The repentant thief who is crucified next to
Jesus receives a last-minute promise of eternal life: "In him we die at the right
time, when he wills. ... Into your hands I commit my spirit; you have redeemed
me. ... Today you will be with me in paradise." Even at death, Christ reigns
supreme: "Glory, praise, honor, and majesty be given to you. ... Make us victorious through Jesus Christ."

DAY OF THANKSGIVING

Year A   Luke 17:11-19

BWV 192   *Nun danket alle Gott*
"Now thank the God of all...who does great things for us." Of the ten lepers cured,
only one returns to give thanks, rather than proceed to the priests, as instructed, for rites
of purification: "May the eternally bounteous God grant us in our life an ever-joyful
heart and noble peace. ... And from all trouble redeem us here and there." The heart
richly blessed wants first and foremost to give thanks to the benefactor: "Glory and
honor and praise be to God ... now and evermore." The cantata quotes all three stanzas of the title hymn, *Now Thank We All Our God.*

"God the Lord is sun and shield. ... Therefore our grateful spirit praises the goodness he shows." Like the healed Samaritan everyone has something for which to praise and thank God: "Now thank we all our God with hearts and hands and voices ... who, from our mother's arms, has blessed us on our way with countless gifts of love, and still is ours today." Called and blessed by God, the Christian can go forth in faith: "Grant us eternal freedom to praise your name through Jesus Christ."

Year B   Matthew 6:25-33

BWV 29   *Wir danken dir, Gott, wir danken dir*

"We thank you, God, we thank you and declare your wonders." Jesus says not to be anxious about the future, citing the wild flowers and birds as signs of God's care for all creatures: "God is still our assurance. ... He makes us blessed everywhere." Led by a quote from Psalm 75, the cantata reminds Christians that God has blessed them with protection, help, light, justice, and peace. The prayer asks for God's guidance of those in leadership and for faithful care of the human community: "Remember us with your love, embrace us in your mercy. ... Forget not henceforth with your hand to show us good things. ... May we hold fast our confidence in him, abandon ourselves wholly to him."

Alternate: BWV 187 Es wartet alles auf dich
"Everything waits for you. ... You alone, O Lord, crown the year with your goodness." Jesus comforts the people's anxieties with the assurance of God's constant care: "Your heavenly Father knows that you have need of these things. ... I know that he has set aside my portion for me." Of more value to God than the flowers, birds, and other creatures, humanity most appropriately raises its voice to God in thanksgiving: "We give thanks ... and so we rightly sing 'Gratias'."

Year C   John 6:25-35

BWV 69   *Lobe den Herrn, meine Seele*

"Bless the Lord, my soul, and do not forget his benefits." After feeding a hungry crowd with fish and bread, Jesus presents himself as the bread of life. He directs his followers to God, who supplies everything good and guides the faithful: "How great is God's kindness ... and he sustains us yet." Only gratitude and obedience are fitting responses to such goodness: "If only I were able, mighty God, to bring you a worthy song of thanks! ... Let a happy song of thanks ring out. ... The land bears fruit and mends its ways; your word has prospered well." The cantata, one of three with the opening line from Psalm 103 (see *BWV 69a* and *BWV 143*), concludes with a stanza from Luther's hymn, *May God Bestow on Us His Grace*.

Alternate: BWV 162 Ach, ich sehe, jetzt, da ich zur Hochzeit gehe
After the multitudes are fed, Jesus speaks of himself as the bread of spiritual life: "I see, now as I go to the marriage, happiness and misery, poison of the soul and bread of life." All who are nourished by Jesus do the will of God and are strengthened by him for eternity: "How is our flesh come to such honor, that the Son of God has accepted it forever? ... I rejoice in my God! The power of love has moved him to clothe me in this time of grace through sheer favor with the robe of righteousness."

DEDICATION OR ANNIVERSARY OF A CHURCH

John 10:22-30

BWV 194 *Höchsterwünschtes Freudenfest*

"Most highly desired festival of joy, which the Lord lets us gladly celebrate to his glory in the newly erected sanctuary." At the Jewish Feast of Dedication, the leaders appeal to Jesus to explain his messianic claims. He points to his godly work, and calls on them to see, believe, and follow: "We consecrate our hearts to you publicly as an altar of thanksgiving. You, whom no house, no temple holds ... let this house be pleasing to you." When lives are changed by grace, then temples, altars, songs, and prayers can speak of the presence of God: "Where your glory enters, there the dwelling must be pure and worthy of this guest." At the same time, Christians are reminded that no concept can adequately capture the fullness of God, to whom they are dedicated: "Complete the good work that you have begun. ... May my heart be your tabernacle."

Alternate: BWV 34 O ewiges Feuer, o Ursprung der Liebe
At Hanukkah Jesus speaks of belief and trust as the true dedication which God desires and blesses: "O eternal fire, O source of love, kindle our hearts and dedicate them. ... Happy are you, chosen souls, chosen as God's dwelling-place. ... The Lord pronounces on his hallowed house these words of blessing: Peace upon Israel ... and peace upon you."

SAINTS

Luke 6:20-33

BWV 69 *Lobe den Herrn, meine Seele*

All God's people, living and dead, praise their Creator, Redeemer, and Sustainer: "Praise the Lord, O my soul, and do not forget what good things he has done for you. ... He has brought us to the light, and he still sustains us. ... He maintains and upholds, protects and rules the world." Since God's mercy turns especially to the poor, the saints remain faithful in all situations: "In cross-bearing and necessities you will chasten but not kill us. ... Keep me ever in your care and protection. ... Let the people thank and praise you, O God, with good deeds."

MARTYRS

Mark 8:34-38

BWV 56   *Ich will den Kreuzstab gerne tragen*

"Gladly will I carry the cross." Self-sacrificial living and dying are the best witness one can give to Christ's death and resurrection. The responsibilities and challenges of discipleship allow the reign of God to flourish, as believers follow the way of the cross: "It leads me after my torments to God in the promised land. ... He calls me thus: 'I am with you, I will never leave nor forsake you' ... then I shall gain strength in the Lord. ... There my Savior himself wipes away my tears."

MISSIONARIES

Luke 24:44-53

BWV 44   *Sie werden euch in den Bann tun*

To proclaim the story of Christ, the fulfillment of all that has been written, is the commission given to the disciples. This may bring persecution: "They will place you under the ban. But the time will come when whoever kills you will think he does God a service thereby ... to persecute the members of Christ." Whatever challenges arise, those who witness to the gospel are nurtured and guided by power from above: "Christians resemble palm branches. ... It is and remains the Christian's comfort that God watches over his church."

RENEWERS OF THE CHURCH

Mark 10:35-45

BWV 106   *Gottes Zeit ist die allerbeste Zeit*

True renewal of the church comes not through worldly greatness but by following the footsteps of Jesus: "God's time is the very best time. In him we live, move, and have our being. ... Teach us to remember that we must die, so that we become wise." In humble service a disciple exercises the saving power of God: "My heart and mind are established, meek and quiet. ... May the power of God make us victorious through Jesus Christ."

RENEWERS OF SOCIETY

Luke 6:20-36

BWV 24   *Ein ungefärbt Gemüte*

"An unstained mind ... makes us beloved of God and men." After giving examples of which situations are blessed and which are dangerous, Jesus shows the importance of selfless love, even to one's enemies: "Christians' deeds and business, the whole course of their life should be on this footing. ... Do not make an enemy of your neighbor through falsity, deceit, and cunning." Such Christ-like behavior is expected by and pleasing to God: "Everything that you would that people should do to you, you do to them. ... May faithfulness and truth be the foundation of all your thoughts."

PASTORS AND BISHOPS

John 21:15-17

BWV 6   *Bleib bei uns, denn es will Abend werden*

Preparing the disciples for future hardship and uncertainties, Jesus exhorts them to faithfulness, especially in the earth's final days (Matthew 24:42-47). "Remain with us, for it is towards evening ... highly praised Son of God. ... Darkness has gained the upper hand in many places ... because both small and great without righteousness have walked before you, O God, and acted contrary to their Christian duty." Peter pledges his faithful devotion to Christ: "Let the light of your word shine brightly for us."

THEOLOGIANS AND TEACHERS

John 17:18-23

BWV 71   *Gott ist mein König*

The gifts of knowledge, wisdom, and faith are given to the disciples by Jesus in parables (Matthew 13:47-52) and direct intercession to the Father. Through the continuing work of the Holy Spirit the message of salvation is proclaimed and interpreted to every generation: "God is my king from of old, who works all the salvation that comes to pass on the earth. ... Day and night are yours. You cause both sun and stars to have their appointed course. ... Good fortune, salvation, and great victory must daily anew delight you."

Matthew 13:44-52

BWV 171   *Gott, wie dein Name, so ist auch dein Ruhm*
Those who discover and unfold the treasures of creation expose the greater glory of God: "O God, as your name is, so also is your renown to the ends of the world. Lord, as far as the clouds go, so goes your name's renown. ... Let your word, that bright light, still burn for us pure and clear. ... Turn your blessing toward us, grant peace in all quarters."

MARRIAGE

i   Genesis 2:8-24

BWV 120*a*   *Herr Gott, Beherrscher aller Dinge*
"Lord God, ruler of all things ... through whom all that has breath stirs. ... How marvelous, O God, are your works!" In the midst of the new creation, man needs a fit partner, so God creates woman of the same bone and flesh: "Your goodness was ready when you brought us forth into the world." God's creative love is fulfilled in marriage: "May this love and faithfulness also be renewed today for the betrothed ... that all their deeds may go in, from, and with you." Divine favor continues to bless husband and wife: "Your devout parents' blessing shall lie doubly upon you."

> *Alternate: BWV 197 Gott ist unsre Zuversicht*
> "God is our trust. ... When God governs our hearts, there is blessing without end." From the creation, woman and man were made to complement one another and called into harmonious partnership: "So follow God and his will ... to his holy altar, and joins together heart to heart. ... God's goodness has no end. ... Whoever put their trust in God shall not be forsaken."

ii   Romans 12:1-2

BWV 195   *Dem Gerechten muß das Licht*
"Light dawns for the righteous, and joy for the upright in heart." Paul appeals to his readers that, as they have heard the good news of Christ, so they should be transformed in their attitudes and lifestyles, actually living as children of God: "Light and joy renew themselves." Nowhere is the test of godly living more focused than in marriage: "Form an alliance that prophesies so much well-being." The cantata illustrates that, with Christ as the guide and strength, love and marriage will be a mutual blessing. "Now all give thanks and offer praise ... to God, whose praise the angelic host always proclaims in heaven."

Alternate: BWV 139 Wohl dem, der sich auf seinen Gott
"Happy is anyone who can trust God." As friends of God, people can offer themselves as living sacrifices to God: "God is my friend. … He protects me even from the world." Marriage, as divinely appointed and symbolic of God's love, transforms hearts and lives in accordance with God's perfect will: "The light of comfort shines on me from afar; only then do I learn that God alone is man's best friend. … God is my shield and my counsel; happy are they who have God as a friend."

iii   Matthew 19:4-6

BWV 197   *Gott ist unsre Zuversicht*
"God is our trust, we put our faith in his hands. … At times he guides our actions strangely, yet they end happily in a way we had not intended." In setting a theological trap for Jesus, the Pharisees overlook God's creative intentions and the blessedness of marriage: "Just as God, faithfully and paternally, has meant well by you from your infancy, so would he evermore continue to be your best friend until the end." Hardness of heart too often prevents living in joy and hope: "So journey gladly on God's path, and what you do, do in faith."

Alternate: BWV 120a Herr Gott, Beherrscher aller Dinge
When the Pharisees challenge the legality of divorce, Jesus reminds them of the Creator's original intentions for male and female to live together in life-long marriage: "Lord God, ruler of all things … through whom all that has breath stirs. … How marvelous, O God, are your works! … Through your goodness guide this new bridal couple. Make abundantly clear through them what your word has prescribed for us. … They will for evermore be satisfied and fulfilled with true soul's joy and your abundant blessing, on which everything on earth depends."

CHRISTIAN UNITY

John 17:15-23

BWV 126   *Erhalt uns, Herr, bei deinem Wort*
"Uphold us, Lord, by your word … to delight your church. … Grant your people one mind on earth, that we as members of Christ's body, may be one in faith, united in life." In his 'farewell' discourses to the disciples Jesus prays fervently for unity among them, that the witness of salvation may remain for all generations. Only through faithful followers will the world know of God and of divine peace: "Thus your word and truth will be manifest. … Grant us peace graciously, Lord God, in our times."

HARVEST

Matthew 13:24-43

BWV 14 — *Wär Gott nicht mit uns diese Zeit*

"Were God not with us at this time, we should have been dismayed." Essential to Jesus' 'agricultural' parables is the generous character of God, who sows abundantly and faithfully cares for the crops: "Our strength is too weak to withstand our enemy. ... O God, by your powerful protection we are free of enemies." This is the grace of divine rule: "The Lord's name stands by us, the God of heaven and earth."

DAY OF PENITENCE

Luke 15:11-32

BWV 1083 — *Tilge, Höchster, meine Sünden*

"Savior, blot out my transgressions ... my sins are a sore affliction." The son who wanders away and falls into trouble finally recognizes his failure and his guilt: "I am but a sinner here." His repentance makes reconciliation and restoration possible: "Make me to feel joy and gladness ... for your cross assures me. ... Give my heart, O Lord, your solace ... help me keep your word in mind."

DAY OF MOURNING

Luke 10:25-37

BWV 12 — *Weinen, Klagen, Sorgen, Zagen*

"Weeping, wailing, fretting, fearing." The merciful Samaritan portrays God's care and compassion for all who suffer: "Christ's wounds are their comfort." In answer to the question, 'What must I do to inherit eternal life?', Jesus tells this parable to teach faithfulness and loving service: "I follow after Christ ... in prosperity or affliction, in living or dying." In Christ there is comfort and hope: "After rain, blessing blooms. ... Though I may be driven on a rough road by need, death, and misery, God will hold me quite fatherly in his arms."

NATIONAL HOLIDAY

Mark 12:13-17

BWV 119 — *Preise, Jerusalem, den Herrn*

"Praise the Lord, O Jerusalem. ... He makes peace within your borders. Blessed land! Happy city!" Despite the efforts of the Pharisees and Herodians to entrap him, Jesus advocates paying taxes due to the emperor. God rules and blesses society through good governments: "He never tires of letting righteousness and peace kiss each other. ... Happy shall you be, it shall be well with you. ... What good we see among us happens, next to God, through prudent rulers and through their wise government." Peace on earth is God's glorious gift: "Save your people, Lord Jesus Christ."

Alternate: BWV 163 Nur jedem das Seine

"To each only his due!" Living as a responsible member of society means giving credit where it is due: "If rulers must have toll, taxes, and tributes, let one not refuse the debt that is owed." Christians live in constant gratitude to God, the source ultimate of every good thing: "But the heart is bound to God alone. ... Let my heart be the coin that I, my Jesus, pay you." Whatever demands a higher loyalty becomes idolatrous: "Lead both my heart and mind by your Spirit, that I may shun all things which would sever me from you."

PEACE

John 15:9-12

BWV 67   Halt im Gedächtnis Jesum Christ

"Keep in remembrance Jesus Christ, who is arisen from the dead." The love of God, perfectly embodied in Jesus, creates *shalom* on earth, beginning with those who love one another: "'Peace be with you!' Jesus summons us to peace and refreshes us weary ones spirit and body at once. ... Prince of peace, Lord Jesus Christ ... you are a strong helper in trouble."

STEWARDSHIP OF CREATION

Luke 12:13-21

BWV 20   O Ewigkeit, du Donnerwort

"Eternity, you thunder-word." Like the rich fool of Jesus' parable, all owners, stewards, and servants are warned against trusting in material security alone: "I know not, from great sorrow, where to turn. ... Time, which no one can count, begins at every moment." Care of God-given resources and concern for future generations are dimensions of faithful living: "Deliver your soul, flee from Satan's slavery and make yourself free of sins. ... Rouse yourself from the sleep of sin and improve your life soon."

NEW YEAR'S EVE
December 31

Matthew 25:31-46

BWV 28   Gottlob! Nun geht das Jahr zu Ende

The parable of separating the sheep and the goats wakens the conscience of every listener: "Consider this, my soul: How much good your God's hands have done for you in the old year." Whatever resolutions are needed for the future, true reform comes only from God: "God is a fountain where pure good flows. God is a light where pure grace shines. ... God has so blessed us in the present year, that good deeds and well-being have met together."

Appendices

Appendix 1

Bach Works closely related
to the Psalms

Psalm		*BWV*	
	6		135
	12		2
	19		76
	23		104, 112
	25		150
	42		138
	46		80
	47		43
	51		1083
	62		93
	74		71
	80		104
	84		79
	97		195
	103		69, 69*a*
	104		187
	115		196
	117		230
	119		126
	124		14, 178
	126		110
	130		38, 131
	146		143
	147		119
	149		225
	150		190

Appendix 2

The Bach Cantata as a Liturgical Form in the Twentieth Century
Reuben G. Pirner

This article is the seventh and final chapter of Reuben Pirner's 1963 doctoral thesis, *The Bach Evangelical Church Cantata as a Liturgical Form*, submitted to Ruprecht-Karl Universität, Heidelberg. Twenty-five footnotes, all German references, have been omitted.

The Baroque church cantatas were intended as true liturgical pieces in their day. The question for us today is whether, despite their shortcomings in the light of present-day liturgical principles, pastors and directors of church music should be encouraged to re-introduce them into the divine worship service—especially in those churches which have the necessary resources to perform them.

The question, however, should not be limited to this problem alone. A still more important question is whether the Bach cantatas constitute a liturgical music and a liturgical form that can be and should be used as the basis upon which to lay the foundation for a new evangelical choir music in the Lutheran Church of the 20th century. That Bach's sacred music could and should serve this function was the view taken by Philipp Spitta. Ten years after he had completed his Bach biography, he wrote: "He alone attains the full appreciation of Bach's music who stands in a close relationship to the Church, with the music of its liturgy, with the Bible, and who is at home with the melodies and texts of the chorales." Spitta believed that, instead of the Bach cantatas standing at the periphery of the Church's theology and liturgy, they stood rather at its very core. Therefore, to purge the Lutheran Church of the Cecilian ideal of Roman Catholic Church music and to lay the foundation for a true evangelical church music, he called upon the Protestant church to return to Bach. Just as some evangelical theologians, concerned with the direction 19th century theology was taking, saw the necessity of returning to the theology of Luther and the Reformation for a repristination of evangelical theology, so Spitta and others urged a return to Bach for the establishment of proper evangelical church music.

We desperately need to understand the function of today's church choir. In this context we need to determine whether the Lutheran Church should encourage its poets and composers to write works in the modern idiom, that is, using contemporary texts and music, which would have the role and function in today's divine worship service that Bach's cantatas had in his. The argument that we today are a nervous people, incapable of sitting through a divine worship service greater than an hour in length, is a tenuous one. The passage of time in the human mind has been shown by psychologists to be a relative one. The average motion picture has come to be longer and longer, until, it has been quipped, one can more quickly read the novel than see the movie. Under certain conditions even a worship service of an hour in length can be much too long. Under other conditions it can also be too short. Only in churches with

127

extremely large memberships, in which multiple services are required to accommodate the crowds, does the question concerning the length of the divine worship service need to be answered primarily in terms of practical considerations.

There are some characteristics of the Bach cantata which distinctly commend it over and above the choral selection so frequently heard in the Lutheran churches in the United States today. Not infrequently the "musical selection," the "special music," or the "choral offering" is far less suited to the liturgy of the divine worship service than a Bach cantata. Rarely is this special music chosen with a consideration of the *de tempore* of the Church Year except on major festivals. Very often the "chorale offering" assumes no other function than that of a musical interlude. Occasionally it seemingly serves no other purpose than that of entertaining the members of the congregation.

In the liturgy of the new *Service Book and Hymnal*, which is presently being used by the vast majority of the Lutheran Churches of the National Lutheran Council in the United States, there is no provision made for special choral music. However, nearly all of these churches regularly insert such music into the liturgy each Sunday and festival. The selection of the music and its position in the liturgy are entirely subject to the whim and tastes of the pastor and the director of music. Christians familiar with good liturgical practices frequently find the intrusion of the choir and its music a very disturbing element in the progressive flow of the liturgy. To bring the role and function of the choir into harmony with the role and function of the liturgy is one of today's most pressing liturgical problems.

All persons, therefore, who share in the responsibility of determining the music to be sung in the divine worship service, must be educated to understand the purpose of church music in its close relationship to the divine worship service itself. Only after we have answered the question, "What are the purpose and function of the divine worship service?" can we hope to arrive at a correct answer to the question, "What are the purpose and function of the church choir?"

Can music composed and performed by the church choir serve the function of proclamation? Walter Blankenburg believes that, while the Bach cantatas served to proclaim the Word of God in their day, it is questionable whether they can still do so effectively today. There are several reasons for this. Foremost is the fact that Christians today look upon music in the church in a somewhat different light than did men of the Baroque era. No longer do we subscribe to the Baroque doctrine of affections. We no longer believe that the composer, through the use of particular figures, is capable of expressing particular *Affekte* in music. The concept that music can be a power to influence the conduct of men toward the good or the evil is foreign to our thinking. While we still include music in the curriculum of a liberal education, its inclusion is not for ethical reasons, but for aesthetic reasons alone.

Changed concepts concerning the role of proclamation in the liturgy between Bach's day and our own likewise make the use of music in the role of proclamation problematic. In the churches and court chapels in which the theology was oriented by the tenets of the 17th and 18th century orthodoxy, and in which the church cantata was most highly cultivated, the Church saw little or no mission function in its liturgy for the divine worship service. It was taken for granted that all who entered the church for worship were baptized and confirmed Christians, and therefore in the company of the redeemed and the saved. The stress upon mission work and conversion was largely the result of the efforts of the pietists. The pietists, at the same time, not only rejected figural music in the church, but particularly that music which was associated with the proclamation of the Gospel in its relationship to the sermon. Karl Barth would find many today who would agree with his thesis that music is but poorly suited to aid in the proclamation of the Gospel. It is admirably suited, however, for expressing the congregation's praise and adoration to the Triune God.

The liturgy of the divine worship service cannot afford to ignore those who are strangers to the Christian Church and its teachings, especially in those areas in which large numbers of the population are un-churched. For those who have grown up ignorant of the liturgical tradition of the Church, the question must be repeatedly asked: Does the music used to clothe the Gospel message—be it performing a cantata or the chanting of the lections—aid in communicating that message, or does it distract from the urgency and the poignancy of that message? If the Church is to fulfill the task her Lord has placed upon her, she can ill afford to serve as a museum or a concert hall for the purpose of art and the giving of an aesthetic experience. At the same time, however, the Church must appropriate for its use all areas of art which can aid her in the fulfillment of her mission.

It is unlikely that Bach himself ever questioned the validity of the cantata as a liturgical form. In his letter to the Leipzig city council he wrote that since the death of Kuhnau, his predecessor, the style of music had changed so that he could no longer do justice to the demands of this new style with the singers under his direction.

The Bach cantata enthusiasts frequently go to great lengths in their endeavors to return this form to the liturgy of the divine worship service. Not infrequently their arguments betray a considerable want of under-standing and appreciation for the liturgical principles. Most frequently these enthusiasts argue that it would be a tragedy for Protestants to overlook this great musical heritage. They argue that the Bach cantata performed outside the divine worship service remains but a torso. Here the extent to which purely musical or artistic consider-ations take precedence becomes evident, for sometimes they would gladly arrange the liturgy to suit the cantata. The question whether the liturgy is a torso without the cantata appears not to concern them. It has even been suggested the churches begin a program of re-introducing the Bach cantata by presenting church concerts in which they are performed for the purpose of whetting the appetites of the people for more.

The venture to reclaim the Bach cantata has generally met with little success. In 1931 a plan was carried out whereby one Bach cantata was broadcast each Sunday and festival over the German radio. The broadcast originated in Leipzig and the cantatas were performed by the choir of the *Thomas-Kirche*.

In the *Thomas-Kirche* at Leipzig the Bach cantatas have succeeded more than elsewhere in assuming their former role in the liturgy of the divine worship service. The fact that it was for this church that Bach originally composed the cantatas makes one seriously question the extent to which these performances take place out of liturgical considerations or out of historical considerations. Even if this practice were universally recognized as liturgically desirable, to follow their example would not be easy from a practical point of view. Leipzig has the advantage of having a distinguished choir and orchestra with a 700-year tradition behind them. Through the continued singing of the Bach motets, the congregation, through years of exposure to Bach's music, has developed a certain understanding and love for it.

A similar attempt to incorporate the Baroque cantata into the liturgy of the *Gottesdienst* was made in the *St. Aegidien-Kirche* in Lübeck in 1924. Once a year, beginning in 1893, the University of Heidelberg attempted to have a special "Bach service" at the close of the semester. The special festival service was planned and directed by Prof. Wolfrum and the *Universitätsprediger, Geh. Kirchenrat* Bassermann. Everything that could remind the congregation of a concert was avoided: program notes, highlighting the names of the vocal soloists, the conspicuous director, etc.

Most writers have taken the position that, while the cantata can no longer be returned to the liturgy of the divine worship service, neither can it be performed properly in the concert hall. Many of the earmarks that characterize a public concert—the soloists in formal dress, the gesticulating conductor—vitiate against the message

which the cantata would proclaim. One of the most satisfying solutions arrived at up to the present appears to be that of performing them in the church, but not in the liturgy of the divine worship service. This has led to the institution of the *Kantatengottesdienst* in which the performance of one, two, or even three Bach cantatas is coordinated with Scripture reading and prayer. Such a *Kantatengottesdienst*—occasionally also called *Bach-gottesdienst*—generally takes place in the evening. The music director, therefore, has far greater freedom in selecting the cantatas to be sung, paying less attention to the *de tempore* designations. Members of the congregation who do not care for Bach's music can feel free to absent themselves. An objection which might be made against such special services would be through the injudicious use of other music which stands at variance with the message of the Gospel. The selling of tickets for such performances would be a questionable practice.

One of the most successful undertakings in planning and performing Bach cantatas in a *Kantatengottesdienst* took place at the *Marien-Kirche* in Göttingen beginning in 1930, under the direction of Ludwig Doormann. The Saturday evening *Wochenschlußandacht* served as the setting for performances. The order of service included Scripture readings, congregational singing, prayer, and choir music. The initial difficulty to overcome was that of creating a unity out of the service's various parts. This was finally accomplished by planning the service around the pericope lessons for the following day. For this purpose the Bach cantatas were admirably suited. The service as a whole fell into three parts: The opening consisted of an organ prelude, Scripture verse, and a motet; the second part consisted of the proclamation of the Word with the Gospel lesson, the cantata, and a short meditation; it then closed with prayer, including a Gospel collect, the Lord's Prayer, benediction, and postlude.

The suggestion has been sometimes made that congregations begin the re-introduction of the Bach cantatas by performing them as special music on festival days. Festivals, however, are frequently days in which the Lord's Supper is celebrated. The addition of a cantata would only lengthen the service still more.

Those who object to the cantata on the grounds that its performance in the liturgy makes the service too long, therefore have come forward with another solution: dispense with the spoken sermon and substitute instead the cantata, the "sermon in tones." Since the cantata is most closely related to the sermon, it is only natural that if something must be sacrificed to permit its performance, then it should be the sermon. If the sermon is retained together with the cantata, then it is also the sermon which is put to greatest disadvantage. Karl Glebe states that even the most gifted preacher is put to disadvantage in trying to compete with Bach. A Bach cantata is in itself such a powerful sermon, he asserts, that a second sermon is superfluous and can only constitute an anti-climax. This practice has much to commend it as an occasional change from the regular sermon, but it certainly would not be recommended as a regular practice.

Another solution which has been proposed by those who object to the length of the cantata is the possibility of omitting selections or parts. This is already a common practice in the performance of

the passions. The solo arias, which frequently are most poorly suited for the liturgical music of formal worship, could be omitted. In the case of the *da capo* arias, the recapitulation might be omitted. Fr. de Fries warns, however, against excluding recitatives that are of special value. Among the resolutions which were passed at the 22nd *Deutsche evangelische Kirchengesangvereinstag* at Dessau in 1909, was the recommendation that attempts be made to incorporate Bach's chorale cantatas organically into the *Gottesdienst* in a shortened form. Depending upon conditions and circumstances, it was suggested that the arias might be shortened; the simpler choral numbers could be selected; the recitatives, however, were to be sung in their entirety.

This resolution was so objectionable to Arnold Schering that he wrote: "A serious criticism of these recommendations and their consequences is beneath our dignity; a criticism is also superfluous when we assume that those who read these words love their Bach." Schering was realistic enough, however, to recognize that the incorporation of the Bach cantata into the liturgy of today's divine worship service was a utopian dream. In his opinion either the order of worship would have to be changed or the Bach cantata would have to be altered. To the latter suggestion he would not agree for an instant. Practical considerations, rather than rules of art, alone could result in such a resolution as that passed in Dessau, he asserted. Here we plainly see the cleavage between the aims of the liturgist and the music aesthete. The latter is not so much concerned with bringing about an encounter of the congregation with the Triune God as he is in confronting the congregation with a musical masterwork.

Albert Schweitzer is much more accommodating to the purely liturgical needs when he even suggests that movements from various cantatas might be strung together when the lack of performance resources make the performance of a particular cantata difficult to realize. He readily concedes that this would have to be done with discretion, since there are cantatas from which parts cannot be readily incorporated into others because they constitute closed religious thought dramas (*Gedankendramen*). The last cantatas of Bach especially are textually heterogeneous, he writes, and show little inner unity.

One of the greatest impediments to the performance of a cantata is one which already confronted Bach in his day: the lack of adequately trained singers and instrumentalists. A Bach cantata generally calls for four solo voices, and so performances of Bach's cantatas for a church may frequently not be without financial considerations. Occasionally congregations would have no other recourse but to hire these musicians. Jannach considers this no tragedy since the pastor is also paid. The question as to whether performers should be paid or not paid, however, is not the crucial one. The question is whether performers of other confessions, or even atheists, should be hired to perform these works in the divine worship service. If a cantata is accorded a place in the liturgy, then this must be justified liturgically on the grounds that the performers act as the voice of the congregation. Whether performers who are of a different faith or confession can act as the voice of the congregation is theologically and liturgically very questionable.

Various suggestions have been made to facilitate the performance of the Bach cantatas in churches which are limited in the number and quality of singers and instrumentalists at their disposal. Small and medium-sized congregations would simply have to do without their performance. Since some of the cantatas have choral parts that are relatively easy, these choruses might be performed with organ accompaniment alone or with simple orchestral resources. Instructions on how to perform the Bach cantatas with limited resources have also been outlined by W. Voigt. B. F. Richter has also made various suggestions which would make it possible for smaller churches to perform individual parts of the cantatas. Richter has also compiled a list of individual selections from the cantatas, arranged according to the Church Year, to aid those who seek solo arias, duets, etc., with the simpler orchestral accompaniment, as well as *a cappella* selections. Experience has shown that a clear and clean performance of Bach's choral music is greatly facilitated by limiting the number of voices. The transparency of musical tex-ture of the polyphonic lines is much better achieved by limiting the number of singers and instrumentalists to a small ensemble.

Attempts to use recorded music in the divine worship service have met with almost universal disapproval. Dr. Franz Bachmann of Berlin, editor of *Kirchenmusik*, has written, "Its use is to be completely rejected where man as man is responsible for himself... Here we can recognize only the active participation of the congregation, and we completely reject the use of any artificial substitute." The choir, together with the other worshippers, must constitute a unity of purpose and will. Together they must form one fellowship and one body in bringing before the throne of the Triune God their prayers, their praise, and their thanksgiving.

The divine worship service is an encounter of the congregation with the Triune God. Everything that impedes this encounter, indeed, everything that does not directly further this encounter, has no rightful place in the liturgy. Although Bach's cantatas were written for the *Gottesdienst*, and while they are basically evangelical and oriented according to the pericopes of the Church Year, nevertheless they permit the music to usurp a position over and above its role as the servant of the Word. By their length they burst the bounds of today's liturgy. René Wallau is correct in declaring the Bach cantatas a manifestation of the deterioration which the liturgy of the divine worship service had already undergone in Bach's day.

All Christians need to learn and recognize that the church is no museum in which the great sacred art treasures of the past need to be preserved. Neither is the church a concert hall in which the great sacred music of the past needs to be performed. While the liturgy is deeply indebted to the rich heritage of church art, yet she should never be bound by it. The divine worship service constitutes a covenant act between the Lord and his congregation. Here his children listen to their Risen Lord; here they appropriate his grace in Word and Sacrament; and here, too, they respond in praise and thanksgiving. Whatever impedes or obstructs this conversation has no right to a place in the liturgy of the divine worship service.

Bibliography

The following books were invaluable in compiling this material:

Aland, Kurt, ed. *Synopsis of the Four Gospels: English Edition.* United Bible Societies, 1982.

Ambrose, Z. Philip, transl. *The Texts to Johann Sebastian Bach's Church Cantatas.* Neuhausen-Stuttgart: Hänssler-Verlag, 1984.

Dürr, Alfred. *The Cantatas of J. S. Bach*, revised and translated by Richard D. P. Jones. Oxford University Press, 2005.

Evangelical Lutheran Church in America. *Evangelical Lutheran Worship*, Leaders Desk Edition. Minneapolis: Augsburg Fortress, 2006.

Meyer, Ulrich. *Biblical Quotation and Allusion in the Cantata Libretti of Johann Sebastian Bach: Studies in Liturgical Musicology, No. 5.* Lanham, Md.: The Scarecrow Press, Inc., 1997.

Ramshaw: Gail. *Between Sundays: Daily Bible Readings Based on the Revised Common Lectionary.* Minneapolis: Augsburg Fortress, 1997.

Robertson, Alec. *The Church Cantatas of J. S. Bach.* London: Cassell & Company Ltd. 1972.

Stokes, Richard. *J. S. Bach: The Complete Cantatas.* Lanham, Md.: The Scarecrow Press, Inc., 1999.

Index of Bible verses

Numerical Index

The primary citation listed first

Alphabetical Index

The *BWV* number given in parentheses

✠

Supplement
Alternative Lectionaries

Lectionary
Lutheran Service Book

A, **B**, **C** indicate series of the three-year lectionary; where no letter is given, the reading may be used every year. § indicates the one-year lectionary.

✠

First Sunday in Advent (Nov. 27 – Dec. 3)
    A Matthew 21:1-11   *Himmelskönig, sei willkommen* (BWV 182)
       or Matthew 24:36-44 *Nun komm, der Heiden Heiland* (62)
    B Mark 11:1-10   *Sehet, wir gehn hinauf gen Jerusalem* (159)
       or Mark 13:24-37 *Nun komm, der Heiden Heiland* (61)
    C Luke 19:28-40   *Jesus nahm zu sich die Zwölfe* (22)
       or Luke 21:25-36 *Wachet! betet! betet! wachet!* (70)
    §   Matthew 21:1-11   *Nun komm, der Heiden Heiland* (61)

St. Andrew, Apostle (November 30)
        John 1:35-42   *Es ist das Heil uns kommen her* (9)

Second Sunday in Advent (December 4-10)
    A Matthew 3:1-12   *Es reißet euch ein schrecklich Ende* (90)
    B Mark 1:1-8   *Freue dich, erlöste Schar* (30) part 1
    C Luke 3:1-20   *Bereitet die Wege, bereitet die Bahn* (132)
    §   Luke 21:25-36   *Wachet! betet! betet! wachet!* (70)

Third Sunday in Advent (December 11-17)
    A Matthew 11:2-15   *Ärgre dich, o Seele, nicht* (186)
    B John 1:6-8, 19-28   *Freue dich, erlöste Schar* (30) part 2
    C Luke 7:18-35   *Tritt auf die Glaubensbahn* (152)
    §   Matthew 11:2-15   *Ärgre dich, o Seele, nicht* (186)

Fourth Sunday in Advent (December 18-24)
    A Matthew 1:18-25   *Schwingt freudig euch empor* (36)
    B Luke 1:26-38   *Wie schön leuchtet der Morgenstern* (1)
    C Luke 1:39-55   *Magnificat anima mea* (243)
    §   John 1:6-8, 19-28   *Bereitet die Wege, bereitet die Bahn* (132)
       or Luke 1:39-55   *Magnificat anima mea* (243)

St. Thomas, Apostle (December 21)
        John 20:24-29   *Ein Herz, das seinen Jesum lebend weiß* (134)

The Nativity of Our Lord
  CHRISTMAS EVE (December 24)
  A   Matthew 1:18-25   *Dazu ist erschienen der Sohn Gottes* (40)
  B   Matthew 1:18-25   *Schwingt freudig euch empor* (36)
  C   Matthew 1:18-25   *Christum wir sollen loben schon* (121)
  §   Matthew 1:18-25   *Schwingt freudig euch empor* (36)
  CHRISTMAS MIDNIGHT (December 25)
  A   Luke 2:1-14   *Unser Mund sei voll Lachens* (110)
  B   Luke 2:1-14   *Christum wir sollen loben schon* (121)
  C   Luke 2:1-14   Christmas Oratorio (248) part 1
  §   Luke 2:1-14   Christmas Oratorio (248) part 1
  CHRISTMAS DAWN (December 25)
  A   Luke 2:15-20   *Gelobet seist du, Jesu Christ* (91)
  B   Luke 2:15-20   *Süßer Trost, mein Jesus kommt* (151)
  C   Luke 2:15-20   Christmas Oratorio (248) part 2
  §   Luke 2:15-20   Christmas Oratorio (248) part 2
  CHRISTMAS DAY (December 25)
  A   John 1:1-18   *Ich freue mich in dir* (133)
  B   John 1:1-18   *Christen, ätzen diesen Tag* (63)
  C   John 1:1-18   Christmas Oratorio (248) part 3
  §   John 1:1-18   Christmas Oratorio (248) part 3

St. Stephen, Martyr (December 26)
        Acts 6:8 – 7:60   *Selig ist der Mann* (57)

St. John, Apostle and Evangelist (December 27)
        John 21:20-25   *Sehet, welch eine Liebe hat uns der Vater erzeiget* (64)

The Holy Innocents, Martyrs (December 28)
        Matthew 2:13-18   *Ach Gott, wie manches Herzeleid* (58)

First Sunday after Christmas (December 26-31)
  A   Matthew 2:13-23   *Schau, lieber Gott, wie meine Feind* (153)
  B   Luke 2:22-40   *Erfreute Zeit im neuen Bunde* (83)
  C   Luke 2:22-40   *Ich habe genug* (82)
  §   Luke 2:22-40   *Tritt auf die Glaubensbahn* (152)

New Year's Eve (December 31)
        Luke 12:35-42   *Gottlob! Nun geht das Jahr zu Ende* (28)

Circumcision and Name of Jesus (January 1)
  A   Luke 2:21   *Gott, wie dein Name, so ist auch dein Ruhm* (171)
  B   Luke 2:21   *Singet dem Herrn ein neues Lied* (190)
  C   Luke 2:21   Christmas Oratorio (248) part 4

Second Sunday after Christmas (January 2-5)
  A Luke 2:40-52   *Mein liebster Jesus ist verloren* (154)
  B Luke 2:40-52   *Lobe den Herrn, meine Seele* (143)
  C Luke 2:40-52   *Mein liebster Jesu, mein Verlangen* (32)
  § Matthew 2:13-23   *Schau, lieber Gott, wie meine Feind* (153)

The Epiphany of Our Lord (January 6)
  A Matthew 2:1-12   *Sie werden aus Saba alle kommen* (65)
  B Matthew 2:1-12   *Herr Gott, dich loben wir* (16)
  C Matthew 2:1-12   Christmas Oratorio (248) parts 5 and 6
  § Matthew 2:1-12   Christmas Oratorio (248) parts 5 and 6

The Baptism of Our Lord (January 7-13)
  A Matthew 3:13-17   *Christ unser Herr zum Jordan kam* (7)
  B Mark 1:4-11   *Wer da gläubet und getauft wird* (37)
  C Luke 3:15-22   *Liebster Immanuel, Herzog der Frommen* (123)

First Sunday after the Epiphany (January 7-13)
  § Matthew 3:13-17   *Christ unser Herr zum Jordan kam* (7)
     or Luke 2:41-52   *Mein liebster Jesus ist verloren* (154)

Second Sunday after the Epiphany (January 14-20)
  A John 1:29-42   *Es ist das Heil uns kommen her* (9)
  B John 1:43-51   *Gott der Herr ist Sonn und Schild* (79)
  C John 2:1-11   *Mein Gott, wie lang, ach lange* (155)
  § John 2:1-11   *Mein Gott, wie lang, ach lange* (155)

The Confession of St. Peter (January 18)
       Mark 8:27 – 9:1   *Ich hab in Gottes Herz und Sinn* (92)

Third Sunday after the Epiphany (January 21-27)
  A Matthew 4:12-23   *Lobet den Herrn, alle Heiden* (230)
  B Mark 1:14-20   *Tue Rechnung! Donnerwort* (168)
  C Luke 4:16-30   *Leichtgesinnte Flattergeister* (181)
  § Matthew 8:1-13   *Alles nur nach Gottes Willen* (72)

St. Timothy, Pastor and Confessor (January 24)
       Matthew 24:42-47   *Bleib bei uns, denn es will Abend werden* (6)

The Conversion of St. Paul (January 25)
       Matthew 19:27-30   *Sie werden euch in den Bann tun* (183)

St. Titus, Pastor and Confessor (January 26)
       Luke 10:1-9   *Sie werden euch in den Bann tun* (44)

Fourth Sunday after the Epiphany (Jan. 28 – Feb. 3)
- **A** Matthew 5:1-12   *Was willst du dich betrüben* (107)
- **B** Mark 1:21-28   *Jesu, der du meine Seele* (78)
- **C** Luke 4:31-44   *Liebster Gott, wann werd ich sterben* (8)
- §   Matthew 8:23-27   *Jesus schläft, was soll ich hoffen* (81)

The Purification of Mary and the Presentation of Our Lord (February 2)
   Luke 2:22-40   *Ich lasse dich nicht* (A159)

Fifth Sunday after the Epiphany (February 4-10)
- **A** Matthew 5:13-20   *Brich dem Hungrigen dein Brot* (39)
- **B** Mark 1:29-39   *Lobe den Herrn, meine Seele* (69a)
- **C** Luke 5:1-11   *Siehe, ich will viel Fischer aussenden* (88)
- §   Matthew 13:24-43   *Wär Gott nicht mit uns diese Zeit* (14)

Sixth Sunday after the Epiphany (February 11-17)
- **A** Matthew 5:21-37   *Allein zu dir, Herr Jesu Christ* (33)
- **B** Mark 1:40-45   *Alles nur nach Gottes Willen* (72)
- **C** Luke 6:17-26   *O Ewigkeit, du Donnerwort* (20)

Seventh Sunday after the Epiphany (February 18-24)
- **A** Matthew 5:38-48   *Warum betrübst du dich, mein Herz* (138)
- **B** Mark 2:1-12   *Ich elender Mensch, wer wird mich erlösen* (48)
- **C** Luke 6:27-38   *Ein ungefärbt Gemüte* (24)

St. Matthias, Apostle (February 24)
   Acts 1:15-26   *Ich ruf zu dir, Herr Jesu Christ* (177)

Eighth Sunday after the Epiphany (February 25-29)
- **A** Matthew 6:24-34   *Es wartet alles auf dich* (187)
- **B** Mark 2:13-22   *Ihr werdet weinen und heulen* (103)
- **C** Luke 6:39-49   *Barmherziges Herze der ewigen Liebe* (185)

The Transfiguration of Our Lord
- **A** Matthew 17:1-9   *Herr Gott, dich loben alle wir* (130)
- **B** Mark 9:2-9   *Singet dem Herrn ein neues Lied* (225)
- **C** Luke 9:28-36   *Nun ist das Heil und die Kraft* (50)
- §   Matthew 17:1-9   *Herr Gott, dich loben alle wir* (130)

Septuagesima
- §   Matthew 20:1-16   *Nimm, was dein ist, und gehe hin* (144)

Sexsgesiama
- §   Luke 8:4-15   *Gleichwie der Regen und Schnee vom Himmel fällt* (18)

Quinquagesima

   §   Luke 18:31-43   *Jesus nahm zu sich die Zwölfe* (22)

St. Joseph, Guardian of Jesus (March 19)

        Matt. 2:13-15, 19-23   *Schau, lieber Gott, wie meine Feind* (153)

The Annunciation of Our Lord (March 25)

        Luke 1:26-38   *Herz und Mund und Tat und Leben* (147)

Ash Wednesday

   A Matthew 6:1-6, 16-21 *Mein Herze schwimmt im Blut* (199)
   B Matthew 6:1-6, 16-21 *Ach Herr, mich armen Sünder* (135)
   C Matthew 6:1-6, 16-21 *Liebster Jesu, mein Verlangen* (32)
   §   Matthew 6:1-6, 16-21 *Ach Herr, mich armen Sünder* (135)

First Sunday in Lent

   A Matthew 4:1-11   *Dazu ist erschienen der Sohn Gottes* (40)
   B Mark 1:9-15   *Wo Gott, der Herr, nicht bei uns hält* (178)
   C Luke 4:1-13   *Widerstehe doch der Sünde* (54)
   §   Matthew 4:1-11   *Dazu ist erschienen der Sohn Gottes* (40)

Second Sunday in Lent

   A John 3:1-17   *Es ist ein trotzig und versagt Ding* (176)
   B Mark 8:27-38   *Ich will den Kreuzstab gerne tragen* (56)
   C Luke 13:31-35   *Schauet doch und sehet, ob irgend ein Schmerz sei* (46)
   §   Matthew 15:21-28 *Jauchzet Gott in allen Landen* (51)

Third Sunday in Lent

   A John 4:5-42   *Vergnügte Ruh, beliebte Seelenlust* (170)
   B John 2:13-25   *Herr, deine Augen sehen nach dem Glauben* (102)
   C Luke 13:1-9   *Meinen Jesum laß ich nicht* (124)
   §   Luke 11:14-28   *Widerstehe doch der Sünde* (54)

Fourth Sunday in Lent

   A John 9:1-41   *Aus tiefer Not schrei ich zu dir* (38)
   B John 3:14-21   *Also hat Gott die Welt geliebt* (68)
   C Luke 15:1-3, 11*b*-32 *Wo soll ich fliehen hin* (5)
   §   John 6:1-15   *Ich hatte viel Bekümmernis* (21)

Fifth Sunday in Lent

   A John 11:1-53   *Ich stehe mit einem Fuß im Grabe* (156)
   B Mark 10:32-45   *Was Gott tut das ist Wohlgetan* (98)
   C Luke 20:9-20   *Nimm von uns, Herr, du treuer Gott* (101)
   §   John 8:42-59   *Herr Jesu Christ, wahr' Mensch und Gott* (127)

Palm Sunday

	John 12:12-19	*Himmelskönig, sei willkommen* (182)
§	Matthew 21:10-19	*Himmelskönig, sei willkommen* (182)
	or John 12:12-19	*Himmelskönig, sei willkommen* (182)

Sunday of the Passion

A	Matthew 26:1 – 27:66	St. Matthew Passion (244)
	or John 12:20-43	*Jesus nahm zu sich die Zwölfe* (22)
B	Mark 14:1 – 15:47	St. Mark Passion (247)
C	Luke 22:1 – 23:56	*Gottes Zeit ist die allerbeste Zeit* (106)
§	Matthew 26:1 – 27:66	St. Matthew Passion (244)

Monday in Holy Week

	Matthew 26 – 27	St. Matthew Passion (244)
	or John 12:1-23	*Jesu, meine Freude* (227)
§	John 12:1-43	*Jesus nahm zu sich die Zwölfe* (22)

Tuesday in Holy Week

	Mark 14 – 15	St. Mark Passion (247)
	or John 12:23-50	*Jesus nahm zu sich die Zwölfe* (22)
§	Mark 14 – 15	St. Mark Passion (247)
	or John 12:23-50	*Jesus nahm zu sich die Zwölfe* (22)

Wednesday in Holy Week

	Luke 22 – 23	*Gottes Zeit ist die allerbeste Zeit* (106)
	or John 13:16-38	*Weinen, Klagen, Sorgen, Zagen* (12)
§	Luke 22 – 23	*Gottes Zeit ist die allerbeste Zeit* (106)
	or John 13:16-38	*Weinen, Klagen, Sorgen, Zagen* (12)

Holy (Maundy) Thursday

A	Matthew 26:17-30	*Ich bin ein guter Hirt* (85)
	or John 13:1-17, 31*b*-35	*Erwünschtes Freudenlicht* (184)
B	Mark 14:12-26	*Schmücke dich, o liebe Seele* (180)
	or John 13:1-17, 31*b*-35	*Ich bin ein guter Hirt* (85)
C	Luke 22:7-20	*Schmücke dich, o liebe Seele* (180)
	or John 13:1-17, 31*b*-35	*Erwünschtes Freudenlicht* (184)
§	John 13:1-17, 31*b*-35	*Schmücke dich, o liebe Seele* (180)

Good Friday

	John 18:1 – 19:42	St. John Passion (245)
§	John 18:1 – 19:42	St. John Passion (245)

Holy Saturday

	Matthew 27:57-66	*Ich stehe mit einem Fuß im Grabe* (156)
§	Matthew 27:57-66	*Ich stehe mit einem Fuß im Grabe* (156)

The Resurrection of Our Lord
EASTER SUNRISE
   A John 20:1-18   *Erfreut euch, ihr Herzen* (66)
   B John 20:1-18   *Auf, mein Herz, des Herren Tag* (145)†
   C John 20:1-18   Easter Oratorio (249)
   § John 20:1-18   Easter Oratorio (249)
EASTER DAY
   A Matthew 28:1-10   *Christ lag in Todesbanden* (4)
   B Mark 16:1-8   *Der Himmel lacht! die Erde jubiliert* (31)
   C Luke 24:1-12   *Lobe den Herren, den mächtigen König der Ehren* (137)
   § Mark 16:1-8   *Der Himmel lacht! die Erde jubiliert* (31)
EASTER EVENING *or* EASTER MONDAY
       Luke 24:13-35   *Der Friede sei mit dir* (158)
   § Luke 24:13-35   *Bleib bei uns, denn es will Abend werden* (6)
EASTER TUESDAY
       Luke 24:36-49   *Ein Herz, das seinen Jesum lebend weiß* (134)
   § Luke 24:36-49   *Der Friede sei mit dir* (158)
EASTER WEDNESDAY
       John 21:1-14   *Wer nur den lieben Gott läßt walten* (93)
   § John 21:1-14   *Ein Herz, das seinen Jesum lebend weiß* (134)

Second Sunday of Easter
   A John 20:19-31   *Halt im Gedächtnis Jesum Christ* (67)
   B John 20:19-31   *Am Abend aber desselbigen Sabbats* (42)
   C John 20:19-31   *Man singet mit Freuden vom Sieg* (149)
   § John 20:19-31   *Am Abend aber desselbigen Sabbats* (42)

Third Sunday of Easter
   A Luke 24:13-35   *Bleib bei uns, denn es will Abend werden* (6)
   B Luke 24:36*b*-48   *Ein Herz, das seinen Jesum lebend weiß* (134)
   C John 21:1-19   *Wer nur den lieben Gott läßt walten* (93)
   § John 10:11-16   *Ich bin ein guter Hirt* (85)

St. Mark, Evangelist (April 25)
       Mark 16:14-20   *Wer da gläubet und getauft wird* (37)

St. Philip and St. James, Apostles (May 1)
       John 14:1-14   *Wer mich liebet, der wird mein Wort halten* (74)

Fourth Sunday of Easter
   A John 10:1-10   *Er rufet seine Schafen mit Namen* (175)
   B John 10:11-18   *Ich bin ein guter Hirt* (85)
   C John 10:22-30   *Der Herr ist mein getreuer Hirt* (112)
   § John 16:16-22   *Wir müssen durch viel Trübsal* (146)

† = *So du mit deinem Munde bekennst* = *Ich lebe, mein Herze, zu deinem Ergötzen*

Fifth Sunday of Easter

A John 14:1-14   *Komm, Jesu, komm* (229)
B John 15:1-8   *Bringet dem Herrn Ehre seines Namens* (148)
C John 16:12-22   *Ach, lieben Christen, seid getrost* (114)
    or John 13:31-35   *Christus, der ist mein Leben* (95)
§ John 16:5-15   *Wo gehest du hin* (166)

Sixth Sunday of Easter

A John 14:15-21   *Es ist euch gut, daß ich hingehe* (108)
B John 15:9-17   *Erschallet, ihr Lieder* (172)
C John 14:23-29   *Wer mich liebet, der wird mein Wort halten* (59)
    or John 5:1-9   *Ich elender Mensch, wer wird mich erlösen* (48)
§ John 16:23-33   *Bisher habt ihr nichts gebeten in meinem Namen* (87)

The Ascension of Our Lord

A Luke 24:44-53   *Auf Christi Himmelfahrt allein* (128)
B Luke 24:44-53   Ascension Oratorio (11)
C Luke 24:44-53   *Gott fähret auf mit Jauchzen* (43)
§ Mark 16:14-20   Ascension Oratorio (11)

Seventh Sunday of Easter

A John 17:1-11   *Tritt auf die Glaubensbahn* (152)
B John 17:11*b*-19   *Was Gott tut, das ist wohlgetan* (100)
C John 17:20-26   *Mit Fried und Freud ich fahr dahin* (125)
§ John 15:26—16:4   *Sie werden euch in den Bann tun* (183)

Pentecost

PENTECOST EVE

John 14:8-21   *Auf, mein Herz, des Herren Tag* (145)†
§ John 14:15-21   *O ewiges Feuer, o Ursprung der Liebe* (34)

THE DAY OF PENTECOST

A John 7:37-39   *Erhötes Fleisch und Blut* (173)
B John 15:26-27; 16:4*b*-15   *Der Geist hilft unsrer Schwachheit* (226)
C John 14:23-31   *Wer mich liebet, der wird mein Wort halten* (74)
§ John 14:23-31   *Erschallet, ihr Lieder, erklinget, ihr Saiten* (172)

PENTECOST EVENING *or* PENTECOST MONDAY

John 3:16-24   *Ich liebe den Höchsten von ganzem Gemüte* (174)
§ John 3:16-24   *Also hat Gott die Welt geliebt* (68)

PENTECOST TUESDAY

John 10:1-10   *Er rufet seine Schafen mit Namen* (175)
§ John 10:1-10   *Er rufet seine Schafen mit Namen* (175)

---

† = *So du mit deinem Munde bekennst* = *Ich lebe, mein Herze, zu deinem Ergötzen*

The Holy Trinity
  A   Matthew 28:16-20   *Gelobet sei der Herr, mein Gott* (129)
  B   John 3:1-17   *Es ist ein trotzig und verzagt Ding* (176)
  C   John 16:12-15   *O heiliges Geist- und Wasserbad* (165)
  §   John 3:1-17   *Es ist ein trotzig und verzagt Ding* (176)

Proper 3 (Sunday, May 24-28) *
  A   Matthew 6:24-34   *Es wartet alles auf dich* (187)
  B   Mark 2:13-22   *Ihr werdet weinen und heulen* (103)
  C   Luke 6:39-49   *Barmherziges Herze der ewigen Liebe* (185)

First Sunday after Trinity
  §   Luke 16:19-31   *Die Elenden sollen essen* (75)

Proper 4 (Sunday, May 29 – June 4) *
  A   Matthew 7:15-29   *Es ist dir gesagt, Mensch, was gut ist* (45)
  B   Mark 2:23 – 3:6   *Die Himmel erzählen die Ehre Gottes* (76) part 1
  C   Luke 7:1-10   *Es ist nichts Gesundes an meinem Leibe* (25)

Second Sunday after Trinity
  §   Luke 14:15-24   *Der Himmel erzählen die Ehre Gottes* (76)

The Visitation (May 31 *or* July 2)
      Luke 1:39-56   *Meine Seele erhebt den Herren* (10)

Proper 5 (Sunday, June 5-11) *
  A   Matthew 9:9-13   *Ihr werdet weinen und heulen* (103)
  B   Mark 3:20-35   *Die Himmel erzählen die Ehre Gottes* (76) part 2
  C   Luke 7:11-17   *Komm, du süße Todesstunde* (161)

Third Sunday after Trinity
  §   Luke 15:1-10   *Ach Herr, mich armer Sünder* (135)
      or Luke 15:11-32   *Wo soll ich fliehen hin* (5)

St. Barnabas, Apostle (June 11)
      Mark 6:7-13   *Erhalt uns, Herr, bei deinem Wort* (126)

Proper 6 (Sunday, June 12-18) *
  A   Matthew 9:35 – 10:20 *Du Hirte Israel, höre* (104)
  B   Mark 4:26-34   *Ich habe meine Zuversicht* (188)
  C   Luke 7:36 – 8:3   *Nach dir, Herr, verlanget mich* (150)

---

* If this occurs *after* Holy Trinity Sunday

Fourth Sunday after Trinity
§ Luke 6:36-42 *Barmherziges Herze der ewigen Liebe* (185)

Proper 7 (Sunday, June 19-25) *
A Matthew 10:5a, 21-33 *Ach lieben Christen, seid getrost* (114)
B Mark 4:35-41 *Jesus schläft, was soll ich hoffen* (81)
C Luke 8:26-39 *Herr Jesu Christ, wahr' Mensch und Gott* (127)

Fifth Sunday after Trinity
§ Luke 5:1-11 *Siehe, ich will viel Fischer aussenden* (88)

The Nativity of St. John the Baptist (June 24)
Luke 1:57-80 *Ihr Menschen, rühmet Gottes Liebe* (167)

Proper 8 (Sunday, June 26 – July 2)
A Matthew 10:34-42 *Was mein Gott will, das g'scheh allzeit* (111)
B Mark 5:21-43 *Ich glaube, lieber Herr, hilf meinem Unglauben* (109)
C Luke 9:51-62 *Weinen, Klagen, Sorgen, Zagen* (12)

Sixth Sunday after Trinity
§ Matthew 5:17-26 *Vergnügte Ruh', beliebte Seelenlust* (170)

St. Peter and St. Paul, Apostles (June 29)
Matthew 16:13-19 *Wer nur den lieben Gott läßt walten* (93)

Proper 9 (Sunday, July 3-9)
A Matthew 11:25-30 *Herr Jesu Christ, du höchstes Gut* (113)
B Mark 6:1-13 *Erhalt uns, Herr, bei deinem Wort* (126)
C Luke 10:1-20 *Sie werden euch in den Bann tun* (44)

Seventh Sunday after Trinity
§ Mark 8:1-9 *Es wartet alles auf dich* (187)

Proper 10 (Sunday, July 10-16)
A Matthew 13:1-23 *Gleichwie der Regen und Schnee vom Himmel fällt* (18)
B Mark 6:14-29 *O Ewigkeit, du Donnerwort* (60)
C Luke 10:25-37 *Ihr, die ihr euch von Christo nennet* (164)

Eighth Sunday after Trinity
§ Mark 7:15-23 *Wo Gott, der Herr, nicht bei uns hält* (178)

---

*If this occurs *after* Holy Trinity Sunday

Proper 11 (Sunday, July 17-23)
- **A** Matt. 13:24-30, 36-43 *Was Gott tut, das ist wohlgetan* (98)
- **B** Mark 6:30-44 *Meine Seufzer, meine Tränen* (13)
- **C** Luke 10:38-42 *Ach Gott, wie manches Herzeleid* (3)

Ninth Sunday after Trinity
- § Luke 16:1-13 *Herr, gehe nicht ins Gericht* (105)

St. Mary Magdalene (July 22)
- John 20:1-2, 10-18 *Auf, mein Herz, des Herren Tag* (145)†

Proper 12 (Sunday, July 24-30)
- **A** Matthew 13:44-52 *Gott ist mein König* (71)
- **B** Mark 6:45-56 *Ich hatte viel Bekümmernis* (21) part 1
- **C** Luke 11:1-13 *Wahrlich, wahrlich, ich sage euch* (86)

Tenth Sunday after Trinity
- § Luke 19:41-48 *Schauet doch und sehet, ob irgend ein Schmerz* (46)

St. James the Elder, Apostle (July 25)
- Mark 10:35-45 *Was Gott tut, das ist wohlgetan* (98)

Proper 13 (Sunday, July 31 – Aug. 6)
- **A** Matthew 14:13-21 *Der Herr denkt an uns* (196)
- **B** John 6:22-35 *Ich hatte viel Bekümmernis* (21) part 2
- **C** Luke 12:13-21 *Was frag ich nach der Welt* (94)

Eleventh Sunday after Trinity
- § Luke 18:9-14 *Siehe zu, daß deine Gottesfurcht nicht Heuchelei sei* (179)

Proper 14 (Sunday, August 7-13)
- **A** Matthew 14:22-33 *Fürchte dich nicht, ich bin bei dir* (228)
- **B** John 6:35, 41-51 *Ich bin vergnügt mit meinem Glücke* (84)
- **C** Luke 12:22-40 *Mache dich, mein Geist, bereit* (115)

Twelfth Sunday after Trinity
- § Mark 7:31-37 *Geist und Seele wird verwirret* (35)

Proper 15 (Sunday, August 14-20)
- **A** Matthew 15:10-28 *Jauchzet Gott in allen Landen* (51)
- **B** John 6:51-69 *Wer weiß, wie nahe mir mein Ende* (27)
- **C** Luke 12:49-56 *Wir müssen durch viel Trübsal* (146)

---

† = *So du mit deinem Munde bekennst* = *Ich lebe, mein Herze, zu deinem Ergötzen*

Thirteenth Sunday after Trinity
§ Luke 10:23-37 *Ihr, die ihr euch von Christo nennet* (164)

St. Mary, Mother of Our Lord (August 15)
Luke 1:39-55 *Wie schön leuchtet der Morgenstern* (1)

Proper 16 (Sunday, August 21-27)
A Matthew 16:13-20 *Ich hab in Gottes Herz und Sinn* (92)
B Mark 7:1-13 *Siehe zu, daß deine Gottesfurcht nicht Heuchelei sei* (179)
C Luke 13:22-30 *Es ist dir gesagt, Mensch, was gut ist* (45)

Fourteenth Sunday after Trinity
§ Luke 17:11-19 *Wer Dank opfert, der preiset mich* (17)

St. Bartholomew, Apostle (August 24)
Luke 22:24-30 *Tue Rechnung! Donnerwort* (168)
or John 1:43-51 *Gott der Herr ist Sonn und Schild* (79)

The Martyrdom of St. John the Baptist (August 29)
Mark 6:14-29 *O Ewigkeit, du Donnerwort* (60)

Proper 17 (Sunday, Aug. 28 – Sept. 3)
A Matthew 16:21-28 *Jesus nahm zu sich die Zwölfe* (22)
B Mark 7:14-23 *Aus der Tiefen rufe ich, Herr, zu dir* (131)
C Luke 14:1, 7-14 *Wer sich selbst erhöhet, der soll erniedriget werden* (47)

Fifteenth Sunday after Trinity
§ Matthew 6:24-34 *Warum betrübst du dich, mein Herz* (138)

Proper 18 (Sunday, September 4-10)
A Matthew 18:1-20 *Ich ruf zu dir, Herr Jesu Christ* (177)
B Mark 7:24-37 *Geist und Seele wird verwirret* (35)
C Luke 14:25-33 *Liebster Gott, wann werd ich sterben* (8)

Sixteenth Sunday after Trinity
§ Luke 7:11-17 *Komm, du süße Todesstunde* (161)

Proper 19 (Sunday, September 11-17)
A Matthew 18:21-35 *Was soll ich aus dir machen, Ephraim* (89)
B Mark 9:14-29 *Ich glaube, lieber Herr, hilf meinem Unglaube* (109)
C Luke 15:1-10 *Erwünschtes Freudenlicht* (184)

Seventeenth Sunday after Trinity
§ Luke 14:1-11 *Wer sich selbst erhöhet, der soll erniedriget werden* (47)

Holy Cross Day (September 14)
> John 12:20-33   *Ach, lieben Christen, seid getrost* (114)

Proper 20 (Sunday, September 18-24)
- **A**   Matthew 20:1-16   *Nimm, was dein ist, und gehe hin* (144)
- **B**   Mark 9:30-37   *Wo gehest du hin* (166)
- **C**   Luke 16:1-13   *Herr, gehe nicht ins Gericht* (105)

Eighteenth Sunday after Trinity
> §   Matthew 22:34-46   *Herr Christ, der einge Gottessohn* (96)

St. Matthew, Apostle and Evangelist (September 21)
> Matthew 9:9-13   *Ihr werdet weinen und heulen* (103)

Proper 21 (Sunday, Sept. 25 – Oct. 1)
- **A**   Matthew 21:23-32   *Bisher habt ihr nichts gebeten in meinem Namen* (87)
- **B**   Mark 9:38-50   *Herr, wie du willt, so schick's mit mir* (73)
- **C**   Luke 16:19-31   *Die Elenden sollen essen* (75) part 1

Nineteenth Sunday after Trinity
> §   Matthew 9:1-8   *I will den Kreuzstab gerne tragen* (56)

St. Michael and All Angels (September 29)
> Revelation 12:7-12   *Es erhub sich ein Streit* (19)

Proper 22 (Sunday, October 2-8)
- **A**   Matthew 21:33-46   *Nimm von uns, Herr, du treuer Gott* (101)
- **B**   Mark 10:2-16   *Wohl dem, der sich auf seinen Gott* (139)
- **C**   Luke 17:5-10   *Die Elenden sollen essen* (75) part 2

Twentieth Sunday after Trinity
> §   Matthew 22:1-14   *Ach, ich sehe, jetzt da ich zur Hochzeit gehe* (162)
> *or* Matthew 21:34-44   *Nimm von uns, Herr, du treuer Gott* (101)

Proper 23 (Sunday, October 9-15)
- **A**   Matthew 22:1-14   *Ach, ich sehe, jetzt da ich zur Hochzeit gehe* (162)
- **B**   Mark 10:17-22   *Bisher habt ihr nichts gebeten in meinem Namen* (87)
- **C**   Luke 17:11-19   *Wer Dank opfert, der preiset mich* (17)

Twenty-first Sunday after Trinity
> §   John 4:46-54   *Ich glaube, lieber Herr, hilf meinem Unglauben* (109)

Proper 24 (Sunday, October 16-22)
  A Matthew 22:15-22   *Nur jedem das Seine* (163)
  B Mark 10:23-31   *In allen meinen Taten* (97)
  C Luke 18:1-8   *Ich lasse dich nicht, du segnest mich denn* (157)

Twenty-second Sunday after Trinity
  §   Matthew 18:21-35   *Was soll ich aus dir machen, Ephraim* (89)

St. Luke, Evangelist (October 18)
       Luke 10:1-9   *Selig ist der Mann* (57)

St. James of Jerusalem, Brother of Jesus and Martyr (October 23)
       Matthew 13:54-58   *Singet den Herrn ein neues Lied* (225)

Proper 25 (Sunday, October 23-29)
  A   Matthew 22:34-46   *Herr Christ, der einge Gottessohn* (96)
  B   Mark 10:46-52   *Du wahrer Gott und Davids Sohn* (23)
  C   Luke 18:9-14   *Siehe zu, daß deine Gottesfurcht nicht Heuchelei sei* (179)

Twenty-third Sunday after Trinity
  §   Matthew 22:15-22   *Nur jedem das Seine* (163)

St. Simon and St. Jude, Apostles (October 28)
       John 15:12-21   *Schmücke dich, O liebe Seele* (180)

Proper 26 (Sunday, Oct. 30 – Nov. 5)
  A Matthew 23:1-12   *Gott soll allein mein Herze haben* (169)
  B Mark 12:28-37   *Du sollt Gott, deinen Herren, lieben* (77)
  C Luke 19:1-10   *Ich armer Mensch, ich Sündenknecht* (55)

Twenty-fourth Sunday after Trinity
  §   Matthew 9:18-26   *O Ewigkeit, du Donnerwort* (60)

Reformation Day (October 31)
       Romans 3:19-28   *Ein feste Burg ist unser Gott* (80)

All Saints' Day (November 1)
       Matthew 5:1-12   *Was willst du dich betrüben* (107)

Proper 27 (Sunday, November 6-12)
  A Matthew 25:1-13   *Wachet auf, ruft uns die Stimme* (140)
  B Mark 12:38-44   *Falsche Welt, dir trau ich nicht* (52)
  C Luke 20:27-38   *O Jesu Christ, meins Lebens Licht* (118)

Twenty-fifth Sunday after Trinity
§　　Matthew 24:15-28　　*Du Friedefürst, Herr Jesu Christ*　(116)
　　or Luke 17:20-30　　*Er reifet euch ein schrecklich Ende*　(90)

Proper 28　(Sunday, November 13-19)
A　Matthew 25:14-30　　*Wär Gott nicht mit uns diese Zeit*　(14)
B　Mark 13:1-13　　*Ach wie flüchtig, ach wie nichtig*　(26)
C　Luke 21:5-36　　*Sie werden euch in den Bann tun*　(183)

Twenty-sixth Sunday after Trinity
§　　Matthew 25:31-46　　*Wachet, betet, seid bereit*　(70)

Proper 29　(Christ the King Sunday, November 20-26)
A　Matthew 25:31-46　　*Du Friedefürst, Herr Jesu Christ*　(116)
B　Mark 13:24-37　　*Nun komm, der Heiden Heiland*　(62)
　　or John 18:33-37　　*Sei Lob und Ehr dem höchsten Gut*　(117)
C　Luke 23:27-43　　*Himmelskönig, sei willkommen*　(182)

Last Sunday of the Church Year
§　　Matthew 25:1-13　　*Wachet auf, ruft uns die Stimme*　(140)

Anniversary of a Congregation
　　Luke 19:1-10　　*Höchsterwünschtes Freudenfest*　(194)

Mission Observance
　　Luke 24:44-53　　*Sie werden euch in den Bann tun*　(44)

Christian Education
　　Luke 18:15-17　　*Wohl dem, der sich auf seinen Gott*　(139)

Harvest Observance
　　Luke 12:13-21　　*Was frag ich nach der Welt*　(94)

Day of Thanksgiving
　　Luke 17:11-19　　*Nun danket alle Gott*　(192)

Day of Supplication and Prayer
　　Matthew 6:16-21　　*Mache dich, mein Geist, bereit*　(115)

Day of National or Local Tragedy
　　Luke 13:1-9　　*Schauet doch und sehet, ob irgend Schmerz sei*　(46)
　　or Matthew 24:32-35　　*Wachet! betet! betet! wachet!*　(70)

✠

Lectionary
Christian Worship

A, **B**, **C** indicate series of the three-year lectionary; where no letter is given, the reading may be used every year. § indicates the one-year lectionary.

✠

First Sunday in Advent (Nov. 27 – Dec. 3)
A	Matthew 24:37-44	*Nun komm, der Heiden Heiland* (BWV 62)
B	Mark 13:32-37	*Nun komm, der Heiden Heiland* (61)
C	Luke 21:25-36	*Wachet! betet! betet! wachet!* (70)
§	Matthew 21:1-11	*Nun komm, der Heiden Heiland* (61)

St. Andrew, Apostle (November 30)
	John 1:35-42	*Es ist das Heil uns kommen her* (9)

Second Sunday in Advent (December 4-10)
A	Matthew 3:1-12	*Es reißet euch ein schrecklich Ende* (90)
B	Mark 1:1-8	*Freue dich, erlöste Schar* (30) part 1
C	Luke 3:1-6	*Bereitet die Wege, bereitet die Bahn* (132)
§	Luke 21:25-36	*Wachet! betet! betet! wachet!* (70)

Third Sunday in Advent (December 11-17)
A	Matthew 11:2-15	*Ärgre dich, o Seele, nicht* (186)
B	John 1:6-8, 19-28	*Freue dich, erlöste Schar* (30) part 2
C	Luke 3:7-18	*Erforsche mich, Gott, und erfahre mein Herz* (136)
§	Matthew 11:2-15	*Ärgre dich, o Seele, nicht* (186)

Fourth Sunday in Advent (December 18-24)
A	Matthew 1:18-25	*Schwingt freudig euch empor* (36)
B	Luke 1:26-38	*Wie schön leuchtet der Morgenstern* (1)
C	Luke 1:39-55	*Magnificat anima mea* (243)
§	Luke 1:46-55	*Magnificat anima mea* (243)

St. Thomas, Apostle (December 21)
	John 20:24-29	*Ein Herz, das seinen Jesum lebend weiß* (134)

The Nativity of Our Lord
  CHRISTMAS EVE (December 24)
    A Luke 2:1-20   *Unser Mund sei voll Lachens* (110)
    B Luke 2:1-20   *Gelobet seist du, Jesu Christ* (91)
    C Luke 2:1-20   Christmas Oratorio (248) parts 1 and 2
    § Luke 2:1-20   *Unser Mund sei voll Lachens* (110)
  CHRISTMAS DAY (December 25)
    A John 1:1-18   *Ich freue mich in dir* (133)
    B John 1:1-18   *Christen, ätzen diesen Tag* (63)
    C John 1:1-18   Christmas Oratorio (248) part 3
    § John 1:1-18   *Ich freue mich in dir* (133)

St. Stephen, Deacon and Martyr (December 26)
        Acts 6:8 – 7:60   *Selig ist der Mann* (57)

St. John, Apostle and Evangelist (December 27)
        John 21:20-25   *Sehet, welch eine Liebe hat uns der Vater erzeiget* (64)

The Holy Innocents, Martyrs (December 28)
        Matthew 2:13-18   *Ach Gott, wie manches Herzeleid* (58)

First Sunday after Christmas (December 26-31)
    A Matthew 2:13-23   *Schau, lieber Gott, wie meine Feind* (153)
    B Luke 2:25-40   *Erfreute Zeit im neuen Bunde* (83)
    C Luke 2:41-52   *Mein liebster Jesus ist verloren* (154)
    § Luke 2:25-38   *Erfreute Zeit im neuen Bunde* (83)

New Year's Eve (December 31)
        Luke 13:6-9   *Gottlob! Nun geht das Jahr zu Ende* (28)

Name of Jesus: NEW YEAR'S DAY (January 1)
    A Luke 2:21   *Gott, wie dein Name, so ist auch dein Ruhm* (171)
    B Luke 2:21   *Singet dem Herrn ein neues Lied* (190)
    C Luke 2:21   Christmas Oratorio (248) part 4
    § Luke 2:21   *Das neugeborne Kindlein* (122)

Second Sunday after Christmas (January 2-5)
    A John 1:14-18   *Das neugeborne Kindlein* (122)
    B John 7:40-43   *Christen.ätzen diesen Tag* (63)
    C Luke 1:68-75   *Singet den Herrn ein neues Lied* (190)
    § Matthew 2:13-23   *Schau, lieber Gott, wie meine Feind* (153)

The Epiphany of Our Lord (January 6)
 A Matthew 2:1-12 *Sie werden aus Saba alle kommen* (65)
 B Matthew 2:1-12 *Herr Gott, dich loben wir* (16)
 C Matthew 2:1-12 Christmas Oratorio (248) parts 5 and 6
 § Matthew 2:1-12 *Sie werden aus Saba alle kommen* (65)

First Sunday after the Epiphany: THE BAPTISM OF OUR LORD (January 7-13)
 A Matthew 3:13-17 *Christ unser Herr zum Jordan kam* (7)
 B Mark 1:4-11 *Wer da gläubet und getauft wird* (37)
 C Luke 3:15-22 *Liebster Immanuel, Herzog der Frommen* (123)
 § Matthew 3:13-17 *Christ unser Herr zum Jordan kam* (7)

Second Sunday after the Epiphany (January 14-20)
 A John 1:29-41 *Es ist das Heil uns kommen her* (9)
 B John 1:43-51 *Gott der Herr ist Sonn und Schild* (79)
 C John 2:1-11 *Mein Gott, wie lang, ach lange* (155)
 § Luke 2:41-52 *Mein liebster Jesus ist verloren* (154)

The Confession of St. Peter (January 18)
  Matthew 16:13-19 *Ich hab in Gottes Herz und Sinn* (92)

Third Sunday after the Epiphany (January 21-27)
 A Matthew 4:12-23 *Lobet den Herrn, alle Heiden* (230)
 B Mark 1:14-20 *Tue Rechnung! Donnerwort* (168)
 C Luke 4:14-21 *Lobe den Herrn, meine Seele* (143)
 § John 2:1-11 *Mein Gott, wie lang, ach lange* (155)

St. Timothy, Pastor and Confessor (January 24)
  John 21:15-17 *Bleib bei uns, denn es will Abend werden* (6)

The Conversion of St. Paul (January 25)
  Luke 21:10-19 *Sie werden euch in den Bann tun* (183)

St. Titus, Pastor and Confessor (January 26)
  Matthew 24:42-47 *Sie werden euch in den Bann tun* (44)

Fourth Sunday after the Epiphany (Jan. 28 – Feb. 3)
 A Matthew 5:1-12 *Was willst du dich betrüben* (107)
 B Mark 1:21-28 *Jesu, der du meine Seele* (78)
 C Luke 4:20-32 *Liechtgesinnte Flattergeister* (181)
 § Matthew 8:1-13 *Herr, wie du willt, so schicks mit mir* (73)

The Presentation of Our Lord (February 2)
  Luke 2:22-40 *Ich lasse dich nicht* (A159)

Fifth Sunday after the Epiphany (February 4-10)
- **A** Matthew 5:13-20 *Brich dem Hungrigen dein Brot* (39)
- **B** Mark 1:29-39 *Lobe den Herrn, meine Seele* (69*a*)
- **C** Luke 5:1-11 *Siehe, ich will viel Fischer aussenden* (88)
- § Matthew 8:23-27 *Jesus schläft, was soll ich hoffen* (81)

Sixth Sunday after the Epiphany (February 11-17)
- **A** Matthew 5:21-37 *Allein zu dir, Herr Jesu Christ* (33)
- **B** Mark 1:40-45 *Alles nur nach Gottes Willen* (72)
- **C** Luke 6:17-26 *O Ewigkeit, du Donnerwort* (20)
- § Matthew 20:1-16 *Nimm, was dein ist, und gehe hin* (144)

Seventh Sunday after the Epiphany (February 18-24)
- **A** Matthew 5:38-48 *Warum betrübst du dich, mein Herz* (138)
- **B** Mark 2:1-12 *Ich elender Mensch, wer wird mich erlösen* (48)
- **C** Luke 6:27-38 *Ein ungefärbt Gemüte* (24)
- § Luke 8:4-15 *Gleichwie der Regen und Schnee vom Himmel fällt* (18)

St. Matthias, Apostle (February 24)
- Luke 6:12-16 *Ich ruf zu dir, Herr Jesu Christ* (177)

Eighth Sunday after the Epiphany (February 25-29)
- **A** Matthew 6:24-34 *Es wartet alles auf dich* (187)
- **B** Mark 2:18-22 *Ihr werdet weinen und heulen* (103)
- **C** Luke 6:39-49 *Barmherziges Herze der ewigen Liebe* (185)
- § Luke 18:31-43 *Jesus nahm zu sich die Zwölfe* (22)

Last Sunday after the Epiphany: THE TRANSFIGURATION OF OUR LORD
- **A** Matthew 17:1-9 *Herr Gott, dich loben alle wir* (130)
- **B** Mark 9:2-9 *Singet dem Herrn ein neues Lied* (225)
- **C** Luke 9:28-36 *Nun ist das Heil und die Kraft* (50)
- § Matthew 17:1-9 *Herr Gott, dich loben alle wir* (130)

St. Joseph (March 19)
- Matt. 2:13-15, 19-23 *Schau, lieber Gott, wie meine Feind* (153)

The Annunciation of Our Lord (March 25)
- Luke 1:26-38 *Herz und Mund und Tat und Leben* (147)

Ash Wednesday
- **A** Luke 18:9-14 *Mein Herze schwimmt im Blut* (199)
- **B** Luke 18:9-14 *Siehe zu, daß deine Gottesfurcht nicht Heuchelei sei* (179)
- **C** Luke 18:9-14 *Liebster Jesu, mein Verlangen* (32)
- § Luke 7:36-50 *Ach Herr, mich armen Sünder* (135)

First Sunday in Lent
- **A**   Matthew 4:1-11   *Dazu ist erschienen der Sohn Gottes* (40)
- **B**   Mark 1:12-15   *Wo Gott, der Herr, nicht bei uns hält* (178)
- **C**   Luke 4:1-13   *Widerstehe doch der Sünde* (54)
- **§**   Matthew 4:1-11   *Dazu ist erschienen der Sohn Gottes* (40)

Second Sunday in Lent
- **A**   John 4:5-26   *Vergnügte Ruh, beliebte Seelenlust* (170)
- **B**   Mark 8:31-38   *Ich will den Kreuzstab gerne tragen* (56)
- **C**   Luke 13:31-35   *Schauet doch und sehet, ob irgend ein Schmerz sei* (46)
- **§**   Matthew 15:21-28   *Jauchzet Gott in allen Landen* (51)

Third Sunday in Lent
- **A**   John 9:1-39   *Aus tiefer Not schrei ich zu dir* (38)
- **B**   John 2:13-22   *Herr, deine Augen sehen nach dem Glauben* (102)
- **C**   Luke 13:1-9   *Meinen Jesum laß ich nicht* (124)
- **§**   Luke 11:14-28   *Ein feste Burg ist unser Gott* (80)

Fourth Sunday in Lent
- **A**   Matthew 20:17-28   *Sehet, wir gehn hinauf gen Jerusalem* (159)
- **B**   John 3:14-21   *Also hat Gott die Welt geliebt* (68)
- **C**   Luke 15:1-3, 11-32   *Wo soll ich fliehen hin* (5)
- **§**   John 6:1-15   *Ich ruf zu dir, Herr Jesu Christ* (177)

Fifth Sunday in Lent
- **A**   John 11:17-45   *Ich stehe mit einem Fuß im Grabe* (156)
- **B**   John 12:20-33   *Tilge, Höchster, meine Sünden* (1083)
- **C**   Luke 20:9-19   *Nimm von uns, Herr, du treuer Gott* (101)
- **§**   John 8:46-59   *Herr Jesu Christ, wahr' Mensch und Gott* (127)

Sixth Sunday in Lent: PALM SUNDAY
- **A**   Matthew 21:1-11   *Himmelskönig, sei willkommen* (182)
- **B**   Mark 11:1-10   *Nun komm, der Heiden Heiland* (62)
- **C**   Luke 19:28-40   *Schwingt freudig euch empor* (36)
- **§**   Matthew 21:1-9   *Himmelskönig, sei willkommen* (182)

Maundy Thursday
- **A**   John 13:1-15, 34   *Erwünschtes Freudenlicht* (184)
- **B**   Mark 14:12-26   *Schmücke dich, o liebe Seele* (180)
- **C**   Luke 22:7-20   *Ich bin ein guter Hirt* (85)
- **§**   John 13:1-15   *Schmücke dich, o liebe Seele* (180)

Good Friday
    John 19:17-30   St. John Passion (245)
  § John 18:1 – 19:42   St. John Passion (245)

The Resurrection of Our Lord

  A John 20:1-18   *Erfreut euch, ihr Herzen* (66)
  B John 20:1-18   *Auf, mein Herz, des Herren Tag* (145)†
  C John 20:1-18   Easter Oratorio (249)
  § John 20:1-8   Easter Oratorio (249)
  A Matthew 28:1-10   *Christ lag in Todesbanden* (4)
  B Mark 16:1-8   *Der Himmel lacht! die Erde jubiliert* (31)
  C Luke 24:1-12   *Lobe den Herren, den mächtigen König der Ehren* (137)
  § Mark 16:1-8   *Der Himmel lacht! die Erde jubiliert* (31)

Second Sunday of Easter
  A John 20:19-31   *Halt im Gedächtnis Jesum Christ* (67)
  B John 20:19-31   *Am Abend aber desselbigen Sabbats* (42)
  C John 20:19-31   *Man singet mit Freuden vom Sieg* (149)
  § John 20:19-31   *Am Abend aber desselbigen Sabbats* (42)

Third Sunday of Easter
  A Luke 24:13-35   *Bleib bei uns, denn es will Abend werden* (6)
  B Luke 24:36-49   *Ein Herz, das seinen Jesum lebend weiß* (134)
  C John 21:1-14   *Wer nur den lieben Gott läßt walten* (93)
  § John 16:16-23*a*   *Ihr werdet weinen und heulen* (103)

St. Mark, Evangelist (April 25)
    Mark 1:1-15   *Freue dich, erlösste Schar* (30)

St. Philip and St. James, Apostles (May 1)
    John 14:8-14   *Wer mich liebet, der wird mein Wort halten* (74)

Fourth Sunday of Easter
  A John 10:1-10   *Er rufet seine Schafen mit Namen* (175)
  B John 10:11-18   *Ich bin ein guter Hirt* (85)
  C John 10:22-30   *Der Herr ist mein getreuer Hirt* (112)
  § John 10:11-16   *Ich bin ein guter Hirt* (85)

---

† = *So du mit deinem Munde bekennst* = *Ich lebe, mein Herze, zu deinem Ergötzen*

Fifth Sunday of Easter
  A John 14:1-12   *Komm, Jesu, komm* (229)
  B John 15:1-8   *Bringet dem Herrn Ehre seines Namens* (148)
  C John 13:31-35   *Christus, der ist mein Leben* (95)
  § John 16:5-15   *Wo gehest du hin* (166)

Sixth Sunday of Easter
  A John 14:15-21   *Es ist euch gut, daß ich hingehe* (108)
  B John 15:9-17   *Erschallet, ihr Lieder* (172)
  C John 14:23-29   *Wer mich liebet, der wird mein Wort halten* (59)
  § John 16:23*b*-30   *Bisher habt ihr nichts gebeten in meinem Namen* (87)

The Ascension of Our Lord
  A Luke 24:44-53   *Auf Christi Himmelfahrt allein* (128)
  B Luke 24:44-53   Ascension Oratorio (11)
  C Luke 24:44-53   *Gott fähret auf mit Jauchzen* (43)
  § Luke 24:36-53   Ascension Oratorio (11)

Seventh Sunday of Easter
  A John 17:1-11*a*   *Tritt auf die Glaubensbahn* (152)
  B John 17:11*b*-19   *Was Gott tut, das ist wohlgetan* (100)
  C John 17:20-26   *Mit Fried und Freud ich fahr dahin* (125)
  § John 15:26—16:4   *Sie werden euch in den Bann tun* (183)

The Coming of the Holy Spirit: THE DAY OF PENTECOST
  A John 16:5-11   *Erhötes Fleisch und Blut* (173)
  B John 14:25-27   *Der Geist hilft unsrer Schwachheit* (226)
  C John 15:26-27   *O ewiges Feuer, o Ursprung der Liebe* (34)
  § John 14:23-31   *Erschallet, ihr Lieder, erklinget, ihr Saiten* (172)

First Sunday after Pentecost: THE HOLY TRINITY
  A Matthew 28:16-20   *Gelobet sei der Herr, mein Gott* (129)
  B John 3:1-17   *Es ist ein trotzig und verzagt Ding* (176)
  C John 16:12-15   *O heiliges Geist- und Wasserbad* (165)
  § John 3:1-15   *Es ist ein trotzig und verzagt Ding* (176)

Second Sunday after Pentecost
  A Matthew 7:15-29   *Es ist dir gesagt, Mensch, was gut ist* (45)
  B Mark 2:23-28   *Die Himmel erzählen die Ehre Gottes* (76) part 1
  C Luke 7:1-10   *Es ist nichts Gesundes an meinem Leibe* (25)
  § Luke 16:19-31   *Die Elenden sollen essen* (75)

Third Sunday after Pentecost
- **A**   Matthew 9:9-13   *Ihr werdet weinen und heulen* (103)
- **B**   Mark 3:20-35   *Die Himmel erzählen die Ehre Gottes* (76) part 2
- **C**   Luke 7:11-17   *Komm, süße Todesstunde* (161)
- §   Luke 14:16-24   *Der Himmel erzählen die Ehre Gottes* (76)

The Visitation (May 31)
     Luke 1:39-47   *Meine Seele erhebt den Herren* (10)

St. Barnabas, Apostle (June 11)
     Matthew 11:25-30   *Herr Jesu Christ, du höchstes Gut* (113)

Fourth Sunday after Pentecost
- **A**   Matthew 9:35 – 10:8   *Du Hirte Israel, höre* (104)
- **B**   Mark 4:26-34   *Ich habe meine Zuversicht* (188)
- **C**   Luke 7:36-50   *Nach dir, Herr verlanget mich* (150)
- §   Luke 15:1-10   *Ach Herr, mich armer Sünder* (135)

Fifth Sunday after Pentecost
- **A**   Matthew 10:24-33   *Ach leiben Christen, seid getrost* (114)
- **B**   Mark 4:35-41   *Jesus schläft, was soll ich hoffen* (81)
- **C**   Luke 9:18-24   *Herr Jesu Christ, wahr' Mensch und Gott* (127)
- §   Luke 6:36-42   *Barmherziges Herze der ewigen Liebe* (185)

The Nativity of St. John the Baptist (June 24)
     Luke 1:57-67   *Ihr Menschen, rühmet Gottes Liebe* (167)

Presentation of the Augsburg Confession (June 25)
     Matthew 10:32-39   *Singet dem Herrn ein neues Lied* (190a)

Sixth Sunday after Pentecost
- **A**   Matthew 10:34-42   *Was mein Gott will, das g'scheh allzeit* (111)
- **B**   Mark 5:21-43   *Ich glaube, lieber Herr, hilf meinem Unglaube* (109)
- **C**   Luke 9:51-62   *Weinen, Klagen, Sorgen, Zagen* (12)
- §   Luke 5:1-11   *Siehe, ich will viel Fischer aussenden* (88)

St. Peter and St. Paul, Apostles (June 29)
     Mark 8:27-35   *Sehet, wir gehn hinauf gen Jerusalem* (159)

Seventh Sunday after Pentecost
- **A**   Matthew 11:25-30   *Herr Jesu Christ, du höchstes Gut* (113)
- **B**   Mark 6:1-6   *Erhalt uns, Herr, bei deinem Wort* (126)
- **C**   Luke 10:1-2, 16-20   *Sie werden euch in die Bann tun* (44)
- §   Matthew 5:20-26   *Allein zu dir, Herr Jesu Christ* (33)

Eighth Sunday after Pentecost
- **A** Matthew 13:1-23   *Gleichwie der Regen und Schnee vom Himmel fällt* (18)
- **B** Mark 6:7-13   *Ich ruf zu dir, Herr Jesu Christ* (177)
- **C** Luke 10:25-37   *Ihr, die ihr euch von Christo nennet* (164)
- § Mark 8:1-9   *Es wartet alles auf dich* (187)

Ninth Sunday after Pentecost
- **A** Matthew 13:24-30, 36-43   *Was Gott tut, das ist wohlgetan* (98)
- **B** Mark 6:30-34   *Meine Seufzer, meine Tränen* (13)
- **C** Luke 10:38-42   *Ach Gott, wie manches Herzeleid* (3)
- § Matthew 7:15-23   *Erforsche mich, Gott, und erfahre mein Herz* (136)

St. Mary Magdalene (July 22)
- John 20:1-2, 11-18   *Auf, mein Herz, des Herren Tag* (145)†

Tenth Sunday after Pentecost
- **A** Matthew 13:44-52   *Gott ist mein König* (71)
- **B** John 6:1-15   *Ich hatte viel Bekümmernis* (21) part 1
- **C** Luke 11:1-13   *Wahrlich, wahrlich, ich sage euch* (86)
- § Luke 16:1-9   *Herr, gehe nicht ins Gericht* (105)

St. James the Elder, Apostle (July 25)
- Mark 10:35-45   *Was Gott tut, das ist wohlgetan* (98)

Eleventh Sunday after Pentecost
- **A** Matthew 14:13-21   *Der Herr denkt an uns* (196)
- **B** John 6:24-35   *Ich hatte viel Bekümmernis* (21) part 2
- **C** Luke 12:13-21   *Was frag ich nach der Welt* (94)
- § Luke 19:41-48   *Nimm von uns, Herr, du treuer Gott* (101)

Twelfth Sunday after Pentecost
- **A** Matthew 14:22-33   *Fürchte dich nicht, ich bin bei dir* (228)
- **B** John 6:41-51   *Ich bin vergnügt mit meinem Glücke* (84)
- **C** Luke 12:32-40   *Mach dich, mein Geist, bereit* (115)
- § Luke 18:9-14   *Siehe zu, daß deine Gottesfurcht nicht Heuchelei sei* (179)

Thirteenth Sunday after Pentecost
- **A** Matthew 15:21-28   *Jauchzet Gott in allen Landen* (51)
- **B** John 6:51-58   *Wer weiß, wie nahe mir mein Ende* (27)
- **C** Luke 12:49-53   *Wir müssen durch viel Trübsal* (146)
- § Mark 7:31-37   *Geist und Seele wird verwirret* (35)

---

† = *So du mit deinem Munde bekennst* = *Ich lebe, mein Herze, zu deinem Ergötzen*

St. Mary, Mother of Our Lord (August 15)
      Luke 1:46-55   *Wie schön leuchtet der Morgenstern* (1)

Fourteenth Sunday after Pentecost
    A Matthew 16:13-20   *Ich hab in Gottes Herz und Sinn* (92)
    B John 6:60-69   *Ich geh und suche mit Verlangen* (49)
    C Luke 13:22-30   *Es ist dir gesagt, Mensch, was gut ist* (45)
    § Luke 10:23-37   *Ihr, die ihr euch von Christo nennet* (164)

St. Bartholomew, Apostle (August 24)
      John 1:43-51   *Gott der Herr ist Sonn und Schild* (79)

Fifteenth Sunday after Pentecost
    A Matthew 16:21-26   *Jesus nahm zu sich die Zwölfe* (22)
    B Mark 7:1-23   *Aus die Tiefen rufe ich, Herr, zu dir* (131)
    C Luke 14:1, 7-14   *Wer sich selbst erhöhet, der soll erniedriget werden* (47)
    § Luke 17:11-19   *Wer Dank opfert, der preiset mich* (17)

Sixteenth Sunday after Pentecost
    A Matthew 18:15-20   *Ich ruf zu dir, Herr Jesu Christ* (177)
    B Mark 7:31-37   *Geist und Seele wird verwirret* (35)
    C Luke 14:25-33   *Liebster Gott, wann werd ich sterben* (8)
    § Matthew 6:24-34   *Warum betrübst du dich, mein Herz* (138)

Seventeenth Sunday after Pentecost
    A Matthew 18:21-35   *Was soll ich aus dir machen, Ephraim* (89)
    B Mark 8:27-35   *Sehet, wir gehn hinauf gen Jerusalem* (159)
    C Luke 15:1-10   *Erwünschtes Freudenlicht* (184)
    § Luke 7:11-17   *Christus, der ist mein Leben* (95)

Eighteenth Sunday after Pentecost
    A Matthew 20:1-16   *Nimm, was dein ist, und gehe hin* (144)
    B Mark 9:30-37   *Wo gehest du hin* (166)
    C Luke 16:1-13   *Herr, gehe nicht ins Gericht* (105)
    § Luke 14:1-11   *Wer sich selbst erhöhet, der soll erniedriget werden* (47)

St. Matthew, Apostle (September 21)
      Matthew 9:9-13   *Ihr werdet weinen und heulen* (103)

Nineteenth Sunday after Pentecost
    A Matthew 21:28-32   *Herr Christ, der eine Gottessohn* (96)
    B Mark 9:38-50   *Herr, wie du willt, so schick's mit mir* (73)
    C Luke 16:19-31   *Die Elenden sollen essen* (75) part 1
    § Matthew 22:34-46   *Herr Christ, der eine Gottessohn* (96)

St. Michael and All Angels (September 29)

        Luke 10:17-20   *Man singet mit Freuden vom Sieg* (149)

Twentieth Sunday after Pentecost

    A Matthew 21:33-43   *Nimm von uns, Herr, du treuer Gott* (101)

    B Mark 10:2-16   *Wohl dem, der sich auf seinen Gott* (139)

    C Luke 17:1-10   *Die Elenden sollen essen* (75) part 2

    § Matthew 9:1-8   *Ich elender Mensch, wer wird mich erlösen* (48)

Twenty-first Sunday after Pentecost

    A Matthew 22:1-14   *Ach, ich sehe, jetzt da ich zu Hochzeit gehe* (162)

    B Mark 10:17-27   *In allen meinen Taten* (97)

    C Luke 17:11-19   *Wer Dank opfert, der preiset mich* (17)

    § Matthew 22:1-14   *Ach, ich sehe, jetzt da ich zu Hochzeit gehe* (162)

Twenty-second Sunday after Pentecost

    A Matthew 22:15-21   *Nur jedem das Seine* (163)

    B Mark 10:35-45   *Was Gott tut, das ist wohlgetan* (99)

    C Luke 18:1-8*a*   *Ich lasse dich nicht, du segnest mich denn* (157)

    § John 4:46-54   *Ich glaube, lieber Herr, hilf meinem Unglauben* (109)

St. Luke, Evangelist (October 18)

        Luke 1:1-4; 24:44-53   *Gott fähret auf mit Jauchzen* (43)

St. James of Jerusalem (October 23)

        Matthew 13:54-58   *Singet den Herrn ein neues Lied* (225)

Twenty-third Sunday after Pentecost

    A Matthew 22:34-46   *Herr Christ, der einige Gottessohn* (96)

    B Mark 10:46-52   *Du wahrer Gott und Davids Sohn* (23)

    C Luke 18:18-27   *In allen meinen Taten* (97)

    § Matthew 18:23-35   *Was soll ich aus dir machen, Ephraim* (89)

St. Simon and St. Jude, Apostles (October 28)

        John 14:21-27   *Erschallet, ihr Lieder, erklinget, ihr Saiten* (172)

Twenty-fourth Sunday after Pentecost

    A Matthew 25:14-30   *Wär Gott nicht mit uns diese Zeit* (14)

    B Mark 12:28-34   *Du sollt Gott, deinen Herren, lieben* (77)

    C Luke 19:1-10   *Ich armer Mensch, ich Sündenknecht* (55)

    § Matthew 22:15-22   *Nur jedem das Seine*

First Sunday of End Time: REFORMATION (Oct. 30 – Nov. 5)
  A Matthew 10:16-23   *Selig ist der Mann* (57)
  B Mark 13:5-11   *Ach wie flüchtig, ach wie nichtig* (26)
  C John 8:31-36   *Ich armer Mensch, ich Sündenknecht* (55)
  § John 17:6-19   *Erhalt uns, Herr, bei deinem Wort* (126)

Reformation Day (October 31)
      John 6:29-35   *Ein feste Burg ist unser Gott* (80)

All Saints' Day (November 1)
      Matthew 5:1-12   *Was willst du dich betrüben* (107)

Second Sunday of End Time: LAST JUDGMENT (November 6-12)
  A Matthew 25:31-46   *Du Friedefürst, Herr Jesu Christ* (116)
  B John 5:19-24   *Herr Jesu Christ, wahr Mensch und Gott* (127)
  C Luke 19:11-27   *Wär Gott nicht mit uns diese Zeit* (14)
  § Matthew 25:31-46   *Du Friedefürst, Herr Jesu Christ* (116)

Third Sunday of End Time: SAINTS TRIUMPHANT (November 13-19)
  A Matthew 25:1-13   *Wachet auf, ruft uns die Stimme* (140)
  B John 5:25-29   *O Ewigkeit, du Donnerwort* (60)
  C Luke 20:27-38   *O Jesu Christ, meins Lebens Licht* (118)
  § Matthew 25:1-13   *Wachet auf, ruft uns die Stimme* (140)

Last Sunday of End Time: CHRIST THE KING (November 20-26)
  A Matthew 27:27-31   *Ein Herz, das seinen Jesum lebend weiß* (134)
  B John 18:33-37   *Sei Lob und Ehr dem höchsten Gut* (117)
  C Luke 23:35-43   *Himmelskönig, sei willkommen* (182)
  § John 18:33-37   *Sei Lob und Ehr dem höchsten Gut* (117)

Christian Education
      Matthew 7:24-27   *Es ist dir gesagt, Mensch, was gut ist* (45)

Church Anniversary
      John 17:1, 13-26   *Was Gott tut, das ist wohlgetan* (100)

Church Dedication
      Matthew 16:13-19   *Hochsterwünschtes Freudenfest* (194)

Environment
      Matthew 6:24-35   *Es wartet alles auf dich* (187)

Evangelism
> John 1:35-42   *Es ist das Heil uns kommen her* (9)

Family
> Mark 3:31-35   *Die Himmel erzählen die Ehre Gottes* (76)

Installation/Ordination
> Matthew 9:35 – 10:4   *Du Hirte Israel, höre* (104)

Nation
> Matthew 22:15-22   *Nur jedem das Seine* (163)

Organ Dedication
> Luke 19:37-40   *Wir danken dir, Gott, wir danken dir* (29)

School Dedication
> Mark 10:13-16   *Wohl dem, der sich auf seinen Gott* (139)

Social Concern
> Luke 6:20-36   *Ein ungefärbt Gemüte* (24)

Stewardship
> Matthew 25:14-30   *Wär Gott nicht mit uns diese Zeit* (14)

Synod
> John 17:13-21   *Was Gott tut das ist wohlgetan* (98)

Thanksgiving Day
> Luke 17:11-19   *Nun danket alle Gott* (192)

Time of Crisis
> Luke 12:22-34   *Ein feste Burg ist unser Gott* (80)

Worker Training
> Matthew 20:1-16   *Ich bin vergnügt mit meinem Glücke* (84)

World Missions
> Matthew 28:18-20   *Gelobet sei dir, mein Gott* (129)

✠